HOUSING ON TRIAL

ELIZABETH BURNEY

Housing on Trial

A STUDY OF
IMMIGRANTS AND
LOCAL GOVERNMENT

Published for the
Institute of Race Relations, London

OXFORD UNIVERSITY PRESS

LONDON   NEW YORK   TORONTO

1967

Oxford University Press, Ely House, London W.1

GLASGOW NEW YORK TORONTO MELBOURNE WELLINGTON
CAPE TOWN SALISBURY IBADAN NAIROBI LUSAKA ADDIS ABABA
BOMBAY CALCUTTA MADRAS KARACHI LAHORE DACCA
KUALA LUMPUR HONG KONG TOKYO

The Survey of Race Relations in Britain

The Survey of Race Relations in Britain, a five-year project
which started in 1963 on a grant from the Nuffield Foundation,
is concerned with the implications for British society of the
presence of a substantial number of Commonwealth
immigrants. It has commissioned a number of full-scale
inquiries in cities with large immigrant settlements, within
the immigrant communities themselves and in industry.
From these studies and the basic information that is being
assembled the Survey will produce its own findings and will
advance proposals.

The Survey is being conducted under the auspices of the
Institute of Race Relations, an unofficial and non-political
body, founded in England in 1958 to encourage and facilitate
the study of the relations between races everywhere. The
Institute is precluded by the Memorandum and Articles of its
incorporation from expressing a corporate view. The opinions
expressed in this work are those of the authors.

Printed in Great Britain by
Billing & Sons Limited, Guildford and London

Foreword

By E. J. B. Rose,
Director, Survey of Race Relations in Britain

The next ten years will decide the course of race relations
in this country for several generations. By far the most
critical influence will be the nature of the housing available
to coloured families, for this will determine the future
pattern of settlement, the development of social relations,
the type of schooling offered to the children, and finally
the jobs for which they will be able to qualify. They have
come to the centres of our large industrial cities where
there is a growing shortage of rented property and where
they experience discrimination from landlords, building
societies, and estate agents, as the recent enquiry conducted
by Political and Economic Planning has shown. In this
situation the policies of the local authority can be decisive.

This is why Miss Burney's book—the first comprehensive study to be made of local authority housing policies in
areas of heavy immigrant settlement—is, we believe, so
important. The methods used in the P.E.P. enquiry, so
effective in revealing the extent of discrimination in the
private sector, were in the nature of the case less productive
in investigating local authority housing where the causes of
unequal treatment often lie too deep to be elucidated by
orthodox interview techniques.

Discrimination takes many forms and its victims are by
no means all coloured people; the British housing system
deals harshly with all newcomers to the city and especially
with families with young children. But, as Miss Burney
points out, it is the experience of the coloured immigrant
which shows up the weaknesses of the system. In some
boroughs their presence inhibits the authority from

tackling the housing that most urgently needs tackling; in others it is not colour but the very size of the problem that daunts the authority and delays action; in others housing policies are so framed that coloured people are confined and overcrowded and qualify with great difficulty for council housing; some other authorities which do rehouse immigrants scarcely ever place them on new estates but shift them out of sight to patched-up housing in an area which will later be condemned and which offers no better facilities or schools than before. One council may be generous with mortgages, thereby shifting its responsibility on to the private sector; another may wish to prevent coloured people buying houses and will lend only on very difficult terms.

In this and in other ways the author shows how public and private policy interact, for her book is not merely concerned with public housing but also examines the disabilities which the immigrant suffers in the open market and from the way municipal authorities operate the relevant legislation to prevent overcrowding.

While she thinks that legislation is needed to stop discrimination in the private sector, the central Government already has powers to ensure that local authorities deal fairly in allocating housing to the disadvantaged. It should use these powers more strongly. Miss Burney puts forward a number of proposals, and believes that, as a last resort, the central Government may need to play a direct part in the allocation of houses.

The Survey of Race Relations in Britain was fortunate to obtain the services of Miss Burney and we are grateful to the Editor of *The Economist* for giving her leave of absence to conduct the enquiry. We are also grateful to the Acton Society Trust which provided certain facilities for Miss Burney during the earlier stages of her research.

Contents

List of Maps and Charts

List of Tables

List of Illustrations

Photographs by John Brooke

Author's Preface and Acknowledgements

I should like to thank the Survey of Race Relations and its director, Mr. E. J. B. Rose, for asking me to write this book, and my employers on *The Economist* for giving me several months off to do so. I am also very grateful for my association with the Acton Society Trust during the main period of research.

Above all, thanks must go to those many local authority representatives and employees who so patiently answered questions, dug out facts, and allowed me to observe them at work. Nothing in the book should be taken to reflect personally on any of the individuals who helped in the inquiry. It must often have been obvious that my approach was a critical one, but it was rare to meet with anything but co-operation.

Inevitably the speed at which the research and writing had to be done (the entire project took under a year) ran certain risks. But at least I hope that when this is published it will be as up-to-date a picture as is physically possible. Of course, policies and administrative practices change all the time; no one will be more pleased than myself if by the time this is in print some of the causes for criticism have disappeared.

Many other people most generously helped by giving information or advice. The research was much strengthened by the intensive interviewing of immigrants in their homes carried out by Miss Margaret Etherington. Among the many valued advisers and critics to whom thanks are due I should like to mention Dr. Roy Parker of the London School of Economics, and especially Mr. Nicholas Deakin of the Survey of Race Relations.

Introduction | Strangers in the City

Cities are created and nourished by immigrants, yet never welcome them. The labour of the peasant turned proletarian serves the needs of urban society, but to his needs that society turns a blind eye. In extreme cases it may deliberately debar him from social equality through an enforced segregation of race, caste, or location (as in Johannesburg, Calcutta, or the ghettoes of Eastern Europe); more often, the mere fact of his poverty, and the poor services that go with a poor environment, depress his ambitions and attainments almost as effectively as if he were untouchable. This is one side of the picture. The other is what might be called the Dick Whittington syndrome. Poor boy arrives in big city and by dint of hard work and good luck makes the break to the top. Only cities provide the ladder to success. Only success makes the immigrant acceptable. Only success enables him to escape from the depressed environment of his fellow immigrants, breeding the vicious circle of low opportunities and low attainment to the third and fourth generation.[1]

Immigrants therefore set two contrasting tests to society. They test readiness to open the path of opportunity to

[1] Throughout, the word 'immigrant' can be taken to mean 'Commonwealth immigrant of the non-Anglo-Saxon Commonwealth'. Usually this definition is synonymous with the coloured races, but where there are locally significant numbers of Maltese or Cypriots this will be made clear. When the context embraces immigrants of Irish, Polish, or other European origin, this too will be made clear. The word 'foreigner' is used to describe anyone originating from overseas.

people whose background and ways of setting about things are not those generally accepted as normal. And they test the extent to which allowances are made, and redress attempted, towards those large numbers of the urban working class whose drive has been dissipated in the sheer struggle for survival. Both the most ambitious and the least ambitious among immigrants therefore make demands on the tolerance, adaptability, and efficiency of the community of which they become a part; this is indeed their most valuable contribution to that community. The demands are greatest when racial or religious characteristics ensure that the immigrant sticks out as a newcomer long after he has ceased in fact to be one; because he is distinct, the demands made by his presence can more easily be brushed aside as something unique to him, and therefore no one's responsibility except his own. The problem of child poverty in large families, with its obvious reference to Irish Catholics, is a case in point.

In housing, above all, immigrants expose the reluctance of Britain's social, economic, and political institutions to serve the demands of the weak, the unfortunate, and the unorthodox. This is far more than just a question of attitudes towards the immigrants themselves, for they are merely a handful among the millions of people affected by the ever-widening gap between the 'haves' and the 'have-nots' in housing. Nor is it a straightforward distinction between rich and poor; for only in the most expensive sector of the housing market does what you get depend directly on what you pay. For everybody else, although money obviously matters, it matters only as one of a complex of interacting circumstances which determine what sort of home, where, is available to whom. It matters far more what sort of person you are. It is, for instance, notorious—and, since the Milner Holland Report,[2] well documented—that the chief losers in the battle for a fair share of housing are working-class families with young children

[2] Report of the Committee on Housing in Greater London, H.M.S.O., London, 1965.

in big cities, especially if they are newcomers supplying essential labour. Among them are the overseas immigrants, whose plight is unique only in its particular combination of circumstances. Many of these circumstances are shared with, for example: young families, large families; low-paid workers, mobile workers, shift workers; unmarried mothers; and almost any non-English-looking, non-English-speaking, non-conforming people. Any of these features is equivalent to a minus mark in the competition for housing space. Racial discrimination is perhaps the biggest single minus; but even this can generally be overcome unless combined—as it nearly always is—with at least one, if not several, of the other factors listed.

The coloured population of Britain is probably today around the 900,000 mark, or under 2 per cent of the total population.[3] The most important single fact about these people is not their race but their age. At least one-third of the coloured population is under fifteen (including the children of mixed marriages) and a substantial proportion is under five. The adults are of fertile child-bearing age and most of their families are still growing (though some are artificially truncated by the absence of children, wife, or husband in the country of origin). These particular facts make the housing plight of these immigrants especially serious; it is not only this generation but the next which suffers—and who knows how many generations after that?

The bare facts of the 1961 Census demonstrate the problem. In the six main English conurbations,[4] where two-thirds of coloured Commonwealth immigrants live, there were 101,440 households whose head (or wife of the head) had been born in the Commonwealth countries of the Caribbean, India, Pakistan, Africa (not South Africa), and Cyprus. (Although not coloured, Cypriots and Maltese experience many of the disadvantages of other Commonwealth immigrants.) Near 80 per cent of these households

---

[3] Written before the results of the 1966 10 per cent Sample Census have been published.

[4] Ten per cent Sample Census, 1961.

4 Housing on Trial

were living in Greater London, where the worst housing
pressures exist. Of the whole, nearly a quarter lived above
the overcrowding standard of one-and-a-half persons per
room (the percentage for all households in the six conurbations was 3·9; for all households in England and Wales, 2·8
per cent). Over one-quarter of these Commonwealth households lived in shared dwellings without exclusive use of
their own stove or sink (conurbations: 3·5 per cent; England and Wales 2·1 per cent). Yet, despite these obvious
measures of need, only 4·5 per cent of the Commonwealth
households in the six conurbations were council tenants—
compared with 23 per cent of all households.

The trials faced by Commonwealth immigrants in the
housing contest are indeed formidable. But it is not only
they who are on trial. They are themselves, by their mere
presence, a test of the efficiency and humanity of the institutions which should be helping them. They are the barium
meal, which, processed through the digestive system of our
society, exposes to the X-ray eye the very points of weakness
in that system.

Unfair? Of course. All institutions are human and have
human imperfections in their physiology which make them,
working and in the flesh, very unlike any ideal model. The
criticisms in this book are mostly aimed at local government, which means in many instances conscientious, overworked individuals doing a difficult job. Nevertheless there
must be something wrong, wrong enough to matter, on the
occasions when the collective effort of such people has
results which are unjust, nonsensical, or a very long way off
the mark. When the effort is, on the other hand, successful,
and the success has a bearing on the housing of immigrants,
no chance will be missed to say so. This is not a mere
exercise in discrimination-spotting; it is an attempt, on a
small scale, to show up the weak places in the machine
where bias can creep in, where the easy solution is the one
which evades the issue, where legal duty is a cloak for social
irresponsibility. Sometimes the machine is asked to do
impossibly large tasks for which it is undermanned and
under-financed, and it therefore selects the attainable peri-

pheral tasks rather than the central ones. Political cowardice
and administrative myopia may permit this to happen.
Courage and vision alone can create both the will and the
way. This does not apply only to public institutions. Those
parts of the book which deal with the private sector indicate
how very far it is from supplying the sterling qualities
lacking in the public sector. But it does have more excuse
for its generally more outrageous behaviour: it does not
have to undertake social responsibility if it does not so
wish. Sometimes, in fact—for instance in the supply of
rented accommodation—it fills in, however inadequately,
where the social responsibility of the public sector has
fallen short.

An expected, but strongly confirmed, discovery in the
course of research was the enormous variation in problems
and policies from one local authority to another. This is
only another way of saying that the life of a Pakistani in
Bradford is a very different kettle of fish from that of a
West Indian in Birmingham or an Italian in Bedford. So
is life different for everybody in Bradford, Birmingham,
or Bedford. So are Pakistanis, West Indians, and Italians
different from each other. One can only hint at all the
possible permutations. In the housing context these include, for example: the social and industrial history of
the past hundred years—affecting the type and location of
the housing stock; the structure of industry today—affecting the demand for that stock; the skill and luck of success-
sive Borough Treasurers in arranging finance—affecting
the generosity of council-house provision today; the fact of
whether an immigrant comes first to this country as a
single man, and if and when he is joined by how many
members of his own family—affecting the intensity of his
housing need at any one time. The most one can hope in
a book of this size is to show how, in a few places, given a
particular set of circumstances, housing policies were such
as to aggravate or improve matters for immigrants and
other people in similar need.

In most places attention is directed to those parts of the
city which, in a convenient bit of jargon, are known as

B

'twilight areas'. These are the areas of old, decaying private housing which often contain the only available accommodation for newcomers of limited means near the city centre. Very often the accommodation is in large, once middle-class, houses now subdivided into ill-adapted furnished rooms and suffering from long-term neglect. Often these houses lie next to, or mingled with, neighbourhoods of smaller dwellings in the stage of passing from private unfurnished tenancies into owner-occupation, a process in which immigrants may take part. Depending on the town and the district, these smaller dwellings may be quite solid with some years of life ahead of them; or very dilapidated slums or near-slums. With or without the presence of coloured immigrants, the twilight areas present a challenge to central- and local-government policy. Are private landlords to be assisted or restrained? Are owner-occupiers to be actively encouraged to buy old houses with the help of council loans, and to improve them with the help of council grants? How do both these aspects fit in with policy towards the stock of older houses as a whole, in terms of redevelopment versus conversion and conservation? How far can the deficiencies in the housing stock and environment generally be offset by spending money on schools and other services designed to compensate for not only the poor living conditions but also the social disintegration which tends to be associated with them?

The association of coloured inhabitants with certain districts of this kind in British cities has given rise to a much worse and infinitely misleading bit of jargon: the description of these districts as 'ghettoes'. What began as mere metaphor is now taken seriously as sociological description, in a classic instance of the game of first deciding what you think a word ought to mean, and then describing a situation in terms which fit that meaning. It is perfectly possible, and correct, to discern a common range of characteristics of underprivilege and inadequacy in most of the locations connected with coloured immigrants. But the term 'ghetto' as applied to these locations is doubly misleading. In the first place, the coloured population is in the minority in all but the tiniest sections of a very few towns —one or two streets, here and there—and their under-privilege is shared with a very much larger population of white people. Secondly, and most important, there is not the same rigid system confining certain races to certain streets as there was for the Jews in Warsaw, and is for the Negroes in Chicago. The fact that there are many open and hidden pressures which *tend* to restrain the coloured man from moving far from existing areas of coloured settlement is by no means the same as a set of laws actually framed to ensure he does stay there.

The main responsibility for the rigid contrast between the 'black belts' and the white suburbs in American cities lies with restrictive property contracts enforced by the courts and upheld for generations by state and federal governments. For example, federally aided house purchase, the chief architect of American suburbia, was, right up to the Kennedy era, contingent on segregated housing, since integrated property was held to be a worse financial risk. In Britain, on the other hand, racially restrictive covenants have long been held void at common law, and they are par-tially (but not yet completely) banned by the Race Rela-tions Act of 1965. And public finance, in the form of local-authority loans, has in many places been the readiest means for a coloured house-purchaser to move, if not into, at least towards suburbia.

The absence of rigid racial barriers shows up statistically in the 1961 Census. Although the inadequacy of the Census as an accurate local count of coloured population is now widely recognized—birthplace, not race, is the criterion; landlords do not reveal the true numbers in a house, and so forth—the global picture cannot be so wildly inaccurate. This showed that in 1961, in London, over half (55.1 per cent) of coloured people were dispersed in districts where they formed under 8 per cent of the population, compared with only 10.5 per cent concentrated in districts where they formed over 16 per cent of the whole population. The biggest concentration recorded in any one enumeration district (the smallest census unit) of people born in the

Commonwealth countries of Asia, Africa, and the Caribbean was 37 per cent.[5]

These figures are for the former County of London, now known as Inner London, and if a wider suburban area were included it would probably be demonstrable that the proportion of coloured people in the outer rings diminishes sharply. Nevertheless, the important point is this: in big cities, where the great majority of coloured people live, there is scope for many or most of them to live in areas where they are so dispersed as to be scarcely significant as a phenomenon. There is, however, a tendency for a significant and very obvious minority to live in a relatively concentrated way in areas which, for other reasons, already experience social difficulties, especially in housing. In the words of the Centre for Urban Studies: 'It is not the immigrants who initiate the problems of these districts: they are received there because the problems already exist.' The chief housing problem of the most concentrated coloured areas is, usually, the shortage of private rented accommodation, which leads to the phenomenon known as multiple occupation. But even immigrants who buy houses for their own family use, often choose, or are forced, to do so close to the areas of concentration, within the twilight zones. They form new clusters, which enlarge themselves as white people move out, and, bingo, the process of 'natural' segregation has begun. It is our business to see that there is nothing 'natural' in this tendency; for if allowed to take hold, its grip becomes the vicious circle of depressed environment and depressed attainment described at the opening of this chapter. What must be avoided at all costs is the automatic association of racial characteristics with this vicious circle; because, once this happens, it becomes harder and harder for the racial minority to mingle freely with the majority.

Therefore there is no cause at all for complacency in the fact that we in Britain do not, on the whole, have laws

[5] R. Glass and J. Westergaard, *London's Housing Needs: Statement of Evidence to the Committee on Housing in Greater London*, London, Centre for Urban Studies, 1965.

which back our prejudices, our reluctance to treat dark-skinned people as true neighbours. Yet the habit of prejudice, or the equally insidious habit of expecting others to act prejudicially and taking evasive action accordingly, may be all that is necessary to maintain and reinforce the relationship between coloured minorities and socially underprivileged people. There is not much time to put things right, for a new generation is already entering the vicious circle. There are schools in some districts where, unless prompt action is taken, whole classes of young children will be coloured. These are the schools, and the districts, where mean physical provision is made worse by the impossibility of getting enough trained people to make the extra effort needed to lift children beyond the disadvantages of their background. The connection between housing and poor educational opportunity is not laboured in this book, but it should be implicit on every page; it is the most important single argument for crash programmes to improve the poorer urban areas at every level. So should the age and size of coloured families be the main argument for giving them not just equal treatment in housing, but something a bit better than that. The following chapters will show just how far even from equality they are at present.

I | Private Sickness and Public Health

Most coloured people live in the middle of large cities where the housing shortage obliges them to inhabit cramped, expensive, and poor-quality rented accommodation. The private rented sector is notoriously the most scare, least well equipped and (for unprotected tenants) the least secure of all types of tenure. The reasons for this are complex, and have been well defined in the Milner Holland Report and elsewhere, so they will not be repeated in detail here. Scarcity is aggravated by, among other things, redevelopment programmes which destroy old privately rented property; and by the many disincentives to landlordism which encourage the conversion of rented property into owner-occupation. A history of economic and political warfare on the private landlord lies behind this situation, in which the true victims are the would-be tenants, especially those whose income, family structure, or race handicap them at the very start of the housing contest. The archetypal victim is the young, mobile wage-earner with a growing family of young children—children being worse than the plague in the eyes of most landlords. Add to this the factor of race, and you have an apparently almost hopeless situation. The discriminatory attitudes of private landlords have many times been put to the test; it is beyond doubt that racial prejudice rules out to coloured immigrants (and some non-coloured) a substantial slice of whatever rented accommodation is going. For instance, the Milner Holland Survey[1] found that only 32 per cent of landlords said they would (in theory) consider a coloured tenant; only 11 per

[1] P. 346.

cent would both do this and advertise the vacancy. A survey of discrimination carried out for the Race Relations Board in 1966 included an experiment in which English, Hungarian, and West Indian actors applied for private rented accommodation (in person, by telephone, and through agents).[2] In nearly two-thirds of the applications the West Indian was either refused where the others were encouraged, or was offered stiffer terms.

For this reason, and through their own group network, immigrant landlords have become a major source of accommodation for immigrant tenants. Indeed it is hardly an exaggeration to say that they are the only people who see point at all in increasing their interest in cheaper rented property, and this is particularly true of certain ethnic groups—Sikhs and Maltese, for example—among the immigrants. In so doing, they provide not only for their fellow-countrymen, but for many other lame dogs in the housing race. This is not philanthropy: it is a market in which a living can be made, or at least a supplementary income, in a way which the immigrant can easily understand and in which he can become practised without reference to the world outside the twilight zone and the people in it. Yet having once adopted this role, the landlord at once inherits the mantle of stricture and restriction, of exploiting and being exploited, which is the unhappy character of the part. The most telling image thrown up in the study of a twilight area of Birmingham by Professor John Rex and Mr. Robert Moore was the 'scapegoat landlord'; the man who adopts a despised role, providing for despised people, and on whom society wreaks its vengeance by applying sanctions designed to limit that role.[3] While this is a melodramatic way of describing such mundane activities as the enforced installation of lavatories at the behest of the public health department, it has the ring of truth: for the

[2] *A P.E.P. Report on Racial Discrimination*, London, Political and Economic Planning, 1967. The P.E.P. survey found that over two-thirds of the Asian immigrants questioned had never sought rented accommodation from a landlord who was a stranger.

[3] *Race, Community and Conflict: A Study of Sparkbrook*, Oxford University Press, for the Institute of Race Relations, 1967.

landlord is blamed and punished for doing his job badly whilst denied the incentives to do it well.

Public health laws can, where strictly applied, result in considerably improved conditions for the occupants of rented rooms, but the usual corollary is a reduction in the number of occupants and in the permanent stock of permitted housing spaces. The fear of rendering families homeless, and therefore eligible for welfare accommodation provided by the local authority, is the chief reason why many authorities take care not to press the issue too hard. Others, on the other hand, believe that by pressing hard, they will displace bad landlords and unwanted tenants right outside their own jurisdiction, into some other local authority area. They are, however, sometimes thwarted in this purpose by the increased security of tenure available to tenants since December 1964.[4] Furnished tenants—and most immigrant lettings fall into this category—have up to six months' security which can be granted them through the furnished rent tribunal (and is sometimes renewable); no tenant can be evicted legally without a court order. As far as the landlord is concerned this cuts both ways—he may be prevented from getting rid of illicit tenants whom he has been ordered to evict; but he may also be unable to get rid of intransigent or cumbersome tenants.

A situation that often leads to trouble is when a landlord has taken lodgers to fill up his own house—either to help pay off the mortgage, or simply to raise a bit of extra money—and then wishes to get rid of them in order to accommodate his own friends or relatives. This is a characteristically immigrant situation. Not only do relatives frequently join a household from overseas, but a large proportion of immigrant landlords are also owner-occupiers. The Milner Holland committee did a survey in 1964 of private landlords, in London, and divided them into individual landlords, company landlords, and others (charities, etc.). The individual landlords comprised 51 per cent of all lettings, and were further subdivided as follows:

[4] The Protection from Eviction Act, whose provisions were later incorporated into the 1965 Rent Act.

TABLE 1

INDIVIDUAL LANDLORDS, BY NATIONALITY AND TENURE:
LONDON, 1964

Landlord's country of origin	Extra-mural landlords %	Owner-occupier landlords %	Tenant landlords %
Great Britain	91	49	96
W. Indies, Pakistan India, W. Africa	4	15	—
Other Commonwealth	—	5	—
Other (mainly European)	5	31	4
	100	100	100
TOTALS: 481	309	122	50

Thus over half the owner-occupiers who had tenants in their own homes were immigrant (in the broadest sense) but very few of the other non-corporate landlords were. Of the foreign-born extra-mural landlords shown in the table, half lived in the same building as their tenants, though in a different rateable unit. This survey backs up the impression that letting off part of one's own house is an immigrant characteristic, in which the coloured groups have followed in the footsteps of Poles, Jews, and others. There is no doubt that a lot of them are in it for the money; although two other reasons have rightly been emphasized. One is the fact that, because of the type of house concerned and the attitude of the conventional lending institutions, immigrant house-purchasers often have to borrow at phenomenally high rates of interest, or raise very large deposits, and therefore are obliged to take tenants to help pay off the debt. The other reason is that an immigrant house-owner may often have motives other than purely financial for taking tenants, especially when these are his own countrymen, perhaps kinsmen, who would otherwise have nowhere to go. There is a marked tendency for people of the same origin to stick together in one house with a landlord of their own nationality: thus the same street may contain a 'Ghanaian house', a 'Cypriot house', or a 'St. Lucian house' along with others of mixed nationality. In some cases—for instance among Pakistani shopkeepers and res- taurant-owners in Manchester—a more feudal situation exists: lettings may be virtually tied to employment in the shop or café of the landlord-proprietor, who may also have paid for the fare to England and to whom the tenant- employee is totally mortgaged.

Ill will flourishes among landlords and tenants of dif- ferent ethnic groups, as a visit to any furnished rent tribunal in any large city will reveal. In many places these tribunals are taken up most of the time with disputes where one or both parties is a coloured immigrant.[5] Uncomfortable relations always tend to breed when the landlord is land- lord within his own home: where people of strange origin are involved, the friction is compounded. In extreme cases behaviour is provoked which leads the local authority to use its powers of prosecution of landlords for 'harassment' of tenants, available under the 1965 Rent Act. Often an appeal to the rent tribunal is only a symptom of stress: a last-minute bid by the tenant to avert eviction, or simply a means of revenge against a landlord who will not, or cannot, do repairs. So often a straight reduction of rent simply compounds the problem; yet the tribunal has no powers to take a more conciliatory role, say to deduct so much from the rent until the repairs are done. To do so would require some means of technical inspection which could only be provided with the co-operation of the local authority public health inspectors; reluctance to involve them has prevented constructive use of the Rent Acts to secure the repair of old property. Yet if the Government

[5] The chairman of the North-west London Rent Tribunal told the Milner Holland committee (p. 191) that in the two years up to March 1964 90 per cent of applicants and landlords involved were Africans, West Indians, Indians, Pakistanis, Cypriots, Italians, citizens of Eire, and some Polish, German, or Austrian.

really heeds its own advisers on the need to encourage such repair, some creative role must surely be adopted by the tribunals and by the rent assessment officers and committees who deal with unfurnished property.

Very little of the rented accommodation available to immigrants is self-contained, or fully equipped with domestic necessities such as a bath, hot water, cooker, and lavatory to each family. This results from the subdivision of houses originally intended for middle-class single-family use into a series of separate units, without commensurate increase in the equipment of the buildings: a phenomenon which sanitary and housing laws have struggled over generations to control. It often originates in leasehold property where the original thread of control by the ground landlord has been lost in a sequence of subletting; as happened in parts of Victorian London (and even earlier) where the overflowing poor squeezed into large houses once occupied by the well-to-do.

The technical term embracing all shared dwellings, small or squalid, is 'multiple occupation': defined in the 1961 Housing Act as 'a house which, or part of which, is let in lodgings or which is occupied by members of more than one family'. A great variety of conditions is covered by this definition, and its meaning may be ambiguous when applied, for example, to a house full of kinsmen living communally—a not uncommon immigrant situation. 'Multiple occupation' is not generally held to apply to houses subdivided into self-contained units, whose occupants have their own front doors, and can remain within them to cook, bath or use the W.C. The term applies technically to some quite comfortable and smart accommodation, such as the well-equipped bed-sitters let to single professional people in South Kensington or Hampstead. It embraces housespace rented by floors, by rooms, and, in extreme cases, by beds. It includes conditions which may be tolerable for young, single workers but totally unsuitable for bringing up young children. It may cover facilities (such as one bath, one cooker, and one lavatory) which might be adequate for the use of seven members of the same family, but which create intolerable conditions if shared between seven people in two different families.

Yet the economic, social, and administrative mechanism is such that young families can often only find shelter in these conditions, at rents no cheaper, and often far higher, than those paid by other people for much more space and privacy. Rents, in London at least, appear to be fixed in a more or less arbitrary fashion depending on personal factors. To quote the Centre for Urban Studies' survey of North Kensington, cited in Milner Holland:

> Rents seemed to be far less determined by relevant objective criteria—such as the size and quality of accommodation pro- vided—than by fortuitous subjective ones, such as the date of the tenant's arrival on the landlord's doorstep, his origin and his colour. There was apparently a 'newcomers' tax, and on top of that a 'foreigners' levy, especially high in the case of coloured people.

In extreme instances, such as those exposed during the Rachman scandal, the young working-class family (especi- ally if coloured) becomes involved in a cycle of exploitation which runs as follows: landlord buys up cheap old property with sitting tenants; introduces new tenants into empty rooms at scarcity prices, if possible 'undesirable' or noisy people who will scare away the sitting tenants; evicts the new tenants and then converts the place into smart, ex- pensive bed-sitters. The cycle was encouraged by the 'creep- ing decontrol' of rents introduced by the 1957 Rent Act; and eviction has since been made much more difficult by the 1965 Rent Act. But there are still apparently many families who are too frightened or ignorant to use the machinery of the Act to apply for a reduced rent commen- surate with the low amenity standard of an unconverted house in multiple occupation. They are the victims, let it be repeated, not so much of a total shortage but of extreme maldistribution of housing space in cities. There is no economic incentive for anyone to create more private rented spaces other than at the two extremes: neglected old property on which as little money as possible is spent, but which may have a high capital value arising from the rents that can be charged; and expensively converted upper-class property where it pays the landlord to do the job properly.

The concentration of multiple occupation in certain parts of the city is the result of roomy, old property being available, and subject to no effective covenants or other hindrances to subdivision. In this type of house it is often easy for an immigrant to become a lessee, since it may have already degenerated into a state of repair which makes it a pretty unattractive proposition to the more wary or conventional purchaser; equally, it may well belong to an absentee lessee who has long since given up any attempt to maintain the place. What the steward to the Bedford estate, Bloomsbury, described in 1880 as 'the lodging-house dry rot',[6] may have entered into these houses generations ago; it may on the other hand be a new phenomenon, and as such likely to meet with much hostility from neighbours and local authorities. Because this is often the only type of accommodation available to immigrants, and because coloured immigrants—landlords as well as tenants—are easily seen to be associated with it, it is commonly assumed that coloured people are directly responsible for the squalid conditions inside and outside these houses. Peeling stucco, overflowing dustbins, dirty and broken windows hung with variegated curtains, often permanently drawn, mark the houses unmistakably to the passer-by, who is easily convinced that inside live dirty, degenerate people, up to no good. The fact that ordinary families do sometimes have to share premises with prostitutes and other deviants for whom this is also the only available housing, encourages this view.

Physically the problem of multiple occupation is one of maintenance and management. Where these are lacking, the inhabitants usually have a collective inability to do the superficial cleaning and tidying of shared yards, halls, stairways, and lavatories which in a properly run establish-

[6] D. J. Olsen, *Town Planning in London*, New Haven and London, Yale University Press, p. 175.

ment would be the duty of a caretaker. Sometimes a tenant
may do some communal cleaning, then give up in resentment that others are not doing their bit, Bickering over
dirty stoves and foul lavatories is just one of the stresses
arising from this disorganized hugger-mugger existence. In
the most neglected and ill-equipped buildings, any sem-
blance of civilized life is virtually impossible and the
problem is far beyond the powers of any individual tenant
to cope with. Here is a house in North Kensington as described by the borough Medical Office of Health in 1964:

A typical example of an individual house in bad multiple
occupation is a large five-storey and basement dwelling in this
area. In three storeys were eleven lettings with a weekly income
of £27 from the twenty-four occupants. For their use only two
waterclosets and two sinks were provided. No piped hot-water
supply existed and the communal bathroom and one of the
two common kitchens were quite unusable. In the former the
wash-basin had been removed and the remains of a broken
geyser, a large tin bath full of stagnant and offensive dirty
water, together with other rubbish, filled the bath. The floor
was littered with liquor bottles, paper cartons, and sundry
rubbish. The kitchen contained two filthy, unusable cookers
and an enormous collection of foul and dirty milk bottles
filling a large packing case. The entrance hall and staircase
were in a particularly dirty condition. Clearly no cleansing of
floors, walls or ceilings had been carried out for a very long
time. Two external balconies at the front of the house were
filled to parapet level with a long-standing accumulation of
offensive refuse, discarded cans and bottles. All the electric
light switches or ceiling fittings in the common parts were
inoperative—either wrenched out, damaged or dangling. In
many parts of the flats trailing flexes inexpertly fixed to heating, lighting or cooking appliances constituted a serious hazard.
Incidentally, two rooms were in part-time occupation as a day-
nursery, apparently in conjunction with the brothel which
operated on the premises.[7]

[7] J. H. Weir (Medical Officer of Health for the Royal Borough
of Kensington), 'The Problems of Multiple Occupation', *Public
Health*, May 1964. Report of a paper given to a symposium of
Medical Officers in February 1964.

In contrast, even in the worst-kept houses, individual rooms may display assertive decency, multicoloured wallpaper being stuck over damp cracks, different corners carefully screened for sleeping and washing, a running battle fought against mice and mildew. In many multi-occupied houses some families have lived for years, and put all their home-making instincts into one room. Their rooms have fitted carpets, fresh paint, and gleam with shiny furniture, vast television screens, and elaborate cocktail cabinets, decked about with starched runners and (if West Indian) a tide of sea-weed-like pink crochet. Yet one such room can never be adequate for a whole family, with very likely a new baby arriving every year. No wonder the statistics of respiratory diseases and psychological or psychosomatic disorders have a high correlation with this type of dwelling, where physical privation and the stresses of communal living continually take their toll.[8]

Coloured immigrants, because of their concentration in the child-bearing age-groups, and their tendency to have several children, are as a class least suited to this way of life—yet as a class they experience it with a far above average frequency.[9] The house described above was near a group of sixteen, containing about 300 people in 140 separate dwellings. Three-quarters of the inhabitants were coloured. Not far away, a survey undertaken by the Paddington Council for Social Service in 1963 of a Victorian estate (Walterton Estate) where the London County Council had taken over more than 600 houses in heavy multiple occupation, disclosed that an unusually high proportion —26 per cent—were children under 15 years. This was undoubtedly attributable to the large immigrant element. A separate survey conducted the following year in the same area of the people in a sample of sixty-seven coloured households found the following startling comparisons:

[8] J. H. Weir, paper referred to above.
[9] See, e.g., the Lambeth statistics on page 122.

TABLE 2

WALTERTON ESTATE SURVEY, 1964

Age Group	Coloured Households %	Whole Estate %	Whole of Paddington (1961)
0–4	22	13	7
4–14	15	13	9
15 plus	63	74	84
	100	100	100

Source: Paddington Council for Social Service, evidence to Milner Holland committee.

At least ten coloured mothers were expectant at the time of interview, and twenty-five of the families had a total of sixty-five other children left behind in their home country —accounting for the relatively fewer children over 5 years of age. These might at any time come to join the already growing households (although some Africans, unlike the West Indians, were sending children home rather than keep them in crowded rooms).

The life of a mother and small children in such congested circumstances must damage all but the most impervious or fortunate. Physical risks include not only the spread of disease, through close contact in stuffy rooms, dirty cooking conditions, and poor sanitation, but also the gruesome danger arising from the habit of heating rooms with movable oil stoves. This danger is compounded when several children are 'minded' in one room when the mother goes shopping, or out to work—yet with no play space other than the street or a yard full of broken glass what alternative is there? Fortunate indeed the mother who can obtain a space in one of the local authority's rare day nurseries (becoming rarer under the Government economy measure of 1966 which discouraged local authorities from spending on day nurseries).

The psychological risks to families are immeasurable. One room may contain a father on shift work who has to sleep during the day; a nursing mother with three children under five; and another child of 11 years who has just arrived from overseas having not seen his parents (only one of whom may be his natural parent) for six years. The only positive side to this mode of life is the *camaraderie* and spirit of mutual help which sometimes exist among the occupants of one house, especially if they are fellow-countrymen. Something of the community spirit of the old slum streets may sustain the inhabitants against their adversity.

A rather different problem is that of the intense sharing of rooms by single immigrant, or migrant, male workers, who usually, nowadays, are Pakistani—if they are not Irish. This is common, for example, among immigrant workers in the East London clothing trade, and in the Yorkshire textile towns. Multiple occupation by single Pakistanis, sleeping several to a room and sharing a communal kitchen-dining room, may be no bad solution as long as the men remain without their families and as long as the conditions in the house can be kept tolerable. Unfortunately neither can be guaranteed. Without their womenfolk the men may be incapable of keeping the house and their rooms in order. With their wives (or English girl-friends) present, the place becomes better kept, but all the problems relating to families and children in shared accommodation then arise. Young sons brought over by themselves to beat the labour ban[10] and to do the domestic chores, provide a far from ideal solution either in terms of the boys' lives or of housekeeping standards. When the men are chiefly bent on saving money as quickly as possible to send home, or to pay for fares, the idea of buying a bed-space at £1 a week per head may not seem intolerable to them, or at least it is something they put up with for want

[10] On the entry of over-16-year-olds without a work permit.

C

of anything better. From the health point of view, the worst risk is the spread of tuberculosis, as shown by statistics collected in Bradford and Rochdale.

Fortunately for the health authorities in the textile towns, none of whom foresaw the housing risks connected with the arrival of large quantities of imported labour, the worst overcrowding among Pakistanis has abated over the years, thanks to the large stock of cheap slum houses which in these towns can be bought for a few hundred pounds. In Bradford, which experienced the problem more intensely than anywhere else, the Corporation built a modern hostel for single Pakistani workers; but the price was too high to compete with the surrounding supply of sub-standard property, and the experiment failed. This has had the unfortunate effect of persuading other authorities, without the same cushion of cheap, easily obtainable, private housing, that hostels for immigrants are bound to flop; yet the idea has never been put to the test in places where the housing shortage is greatest.

In towns or neighbourhoods where the arrival of coloured immigrants has brought multiple occupation for the first time, much local hostility may arise, and exaggerated ideas about the numbers of the newcomers. There is a similarity about some of these which suggests apocryphal origin; for instance, from towns as far apart at Watford and Lancaster comes the tale of the poor old lady who heard rats in the roof which upon inspection turned out to be a row of slumbering Pakistanis who had forced their way through from the next-door attic. In response to public opinion local authorities may start to talk about multiple occupation as a 'disease' which they see as being spread by coloured immigrants. It is significant that the chief local government officer in charge of this aspect of housing is the Medical Officer of Health, whose historic duty it is to control epidemics. Medical Officers often talk about immigrants as though they were plague carriers: here is an extreme view: 'They produce a number of health and social problems which produce public disquiet. They show a preference for living in overcrowded houses in multiple occupation with few hygienic facilities and tend to bring deteriorating urban districts to the level of the worst slums.'[11]

In the early days of immigration some local authorities tried to get a grip in advance of where immigrants were intending to live by obtaining information about their destinations from the High Commissions or Embassies. This could be variously interpreted as a constructive wish to make sure the newcomers lived in adequate conditions; or an obstructive one designed to lend force to the argument that if no accommodation existed, immigrants should not be allowed to settle in a town. Certainly some local authorities argued that they should have the right to refuse entry to immigrants, and one (Bedford: see Chapter IX) actually obtained the co-operation of local industry in hiring immigrant employees only if they were known to have adequate lodgings. But over the years, as more and more immigrants have moved around outside their places of original settlement, this attitude has proved impossible to sustain.

The local authorities' use of the powers (mainly negative) which they possess to deal with bad conditions in multi-occupied houses, varies enormously, as subsequent chapters will show. Some of the big city authorities, Manchester for example, who have seen it all before, may shrug their shoulders and say they have not the staff to cope: others take pride in enforcing standards even where the net result is merely to push people from one crowded house to another. Some plead inadequate powers; others admit that their main concern is to avoid starting a sequence of events which may lead an evicted family eventually into council accommodation.

The legal powers available to local authorities to deal with multiple occupation are summarized in the Appendix (p. 250). Since 1954 it has ceased to be permissible for authorities to make their own by-laws controlling houses let in lodgings; many express regret at this. Various Acts

[11] Professor Andrew Semple, Medical Officer of Health for Liverpool, reported at the Royal Society of Health conference at The Hague (*The Times*, 9 September 1966).

of Parliament now convey uniform powers to all authorities; one or two very big authorities (see below) are regaining the initiative by means of local Acts. Briefly, the powers available to all authorities fall into three categories:

(1) Prevention of overcrowding on a room basis. The statutory definition of this sets a very low standard, geared to what was thought practicable in the 1930s when the rules were made. Statutory overcrowding concerns total numbers and the 'indecent' mixing of sexes: it is almost bound to occur where a family of over three people inhabits one room. Though far less common than it was thirty years ago, it is a not uncommon by-product of multiple occupation, particularly where several adults share rooms; in some places it is regarded as an almost exclusively immigrant phenomenon.

(2) Balancing the number of people against the domestic equipment of a house. This can take the form of requiring the landlord either to install more facilities or to get rid of some of his tenants. Since 1961 it has been possible for local authorities to reduce the risk of eviction by merely requiring the landlord not to take on new tenants when the existing ones leave. But this requires constant supervision to make sure numbers are not exceeded; therefore some boroughs still prefer to enforce old-fashioned eviction, particularly in the case of single men towards whom they have no responsibility as homeless people. The council can also, if the order to install facilities is disobeyed, carry out the work itself and recover the cost through the rent. Many authorities dislike spending money and labour in this way, and so avoid pursuing unco-operative landlords. One of the most expensive, and least often enforced, standards is the fire-proofing of houses in multiple occupation, although numerous catastrophes have proved the need.

(3) Seeing to a decent standard of maintenance and management. Once again authority can step in if the landlord fails to mend plaster, rewire, and so forth. Other powers exist to take emergency action on things like leaking roofs. In extreme cases of gross neglect and exploitation the

council has the power (since 1964) to take over the control and management of the house itself for up to five years, collecting the rent and paying only a small proportion to the landlord. This power has been used very sparingly indeed: most authorities say it is too much trouble and not worth while financially.

Cumbersome procedures enwrap the use of powers to limit the number of occupants or to enforce good management. A separate 'notice of intention to serve an order' has to be sent in each case, with a long time-lag and individual committee approval in each case before the full machinery can be brought to bear. It is true, however, that often the mere warning is sufficient; and that no procedure, short of direct intervention by the authority, is watertight to deal with the most recalcitrant or inefficient landlords. But most landlords do not mean badly: the best results have undoubtedly been achieved by public health departments who are willing to spend time persuading rather than threatening or prosecuting. Bradford for instance deals with Pakistani landlords entirely through Pakistani officials. Bedford public health inspectors (see Chapter IX) have learnt Italian in order to deal with immigrants.

'Parading immigrant landlords each week in court' was a practice for which Birmingham City Council was taken to task by the authors of the Sparkbrook study. By 1966 as much as 98 per cent of all legal action against landlords in Birmingham had been taken against Indian and Pakistani landlords. The authorities estimated that 83 per cent of the property owned by Indians and Pakistanis required action on overcrowding; 75 per cent on inadequate facilities; and 60 per cent on bad management. There is no doubt that many immigrant landlords do provide a low standard of property and maintenance; yet, as argued at the beginning of this chapter, this is primarily a consequence of the type of property they own, which again reflects the type of market to which they cater—and for which scarcely anyone else is willing to provide. These figures cannot be put in perspective without regard to the whole inadequacy of the private rented sector, of which the individual inadequacies of immigrant landlords are a symptom rather than a cause. There are many downright bad coloured landlords; on the other hand, because of their visibility and because they are mostly 'small men', living on or near the spot, they are easier to lean on than the man of straw, the well-defended company, or the hard-to-trace absentee owner.

Birmingham is the biggest authority in the country dealing with multiple occupation; it also has the largest coloured population of any single borough. Therefore its record is of particular interest and importance. From October 1961 to the end of 1966 it had inspected the bulk of the 4,800 houses in the city known to be in multiple occupation, and found that only 40 per cent were satisfactory. The rest had produced the following action:

TABLE 3

LOCAL AUTHORITY ACTION ON MULTIPLE OCCUPATION,
BIRMINGHAM, OCTOBER 1961–DECEMBER 1966

Direction to limit occupants	1,872
Management orders (concerning running and upkeep)	1,041
Notices requiring provision of facilities	1,485
Control orders (house taken over by local authority to protect the occupants)	4
Legal proceedings (under Public Health, Housing and Rent Acts)	2,143
Fines imposed	£15,639
Imprisonment (one case)	two months
Works carried out by local authority in multi-occupied houses (to end 1965)	£72,740

Source: Birmingham Health Department.

The Health Department and the Town Clerk's Department worked in the closest co-operation at all stages of the complex procedures, legal, technical, and clerical, which the system required. Unlike some local authorities (such as Lambeth), where the legal experts dislike taking action unless they have an absolutely watertight case, Birmingham sticks to the spirit of the law rather than peering at every letter: it sees it as its job to get at bad landlords.

The results, as described above, have been almost exclusively concentrated on Indian and Pakistani landlords. They must also have affected a very large number of coloured tenants. At the end of 1966 it was claimed that 'several areas are immeasurably better than they were five or six years ago'.[12] In so far as this represented a true improvement in living conditions for the inhabitants, Birmingham's policy could be said to be having a beneficial effect on immigrants—at least on those who had not been displaced by its 'clean-up' activities. But the rest, presumably, were left to crowd in elsewhere, as best they could.

Rather more disturbing were the indications that Birmingham was using town-planning powers, backed up by a special Birmingham Corporation Act passed in 1965, to limit the spread of multiple occupation outside the depressed areas where it—and therefore the coloured population—was already to be found. This has been referred to by the authors of the Sparkbrook study, but they wrote before the 1965 Act had taken effect. The vital point at issue was: was Birmingham reducing the numbers of people in the 'twilight areas' of multi-occupied housing, without allowing the displaced inhabitants to take up residence in similar property in other parts of the town? In other words, was it deliberately reinforcing the limits of the coloured zone? The methods which gave rise to this suspicion were twofold. The Corporation was using the Town and Country Planning Act of 1962 to define multiple occupation as a 'change of use' for which planning permission was necessary, and thus could refuse permission in areas from which (so the suspicion ran) it desired to exclude coloured people, on grounds such as that multiple occupation was 'detrimental to the amenities'.

[12] *Birmingham Post*, 6 December 1966.

In addition, the Birmingham Corporation Act 1965 created compulsory registration of houses let to more than two families or over four lodgers—including those to be let for the first time.[13] Permission could be refused if the Corporation considered that the house was unsuitable; that multi-occupation would spoil the neighbourhood; or that the person running the house was unsuitable. The last two provisions clearly could be interpreted in a racialist way. The scheme was welcomed by various residents' associations[14] who said they would report illicit multiple occupation; the Moseley area, where many immigrants live, was reported to have a particularly vigilant residents' group.

Under the Birmingham Act procedure is summary, and reasons for refusal need not be given; appeal is to the county court. Under the Town and Country Planning Act reasons have to be stated, and appeal is to the Ministry of Housing and Local Government—which in practice has nearly always upheld Birmingham's line. This Act continued to be used, during 1966, on houses which had been let before the registration scheme came into effect, though action could not be taken more than four years after the alleged 'change of use'. During the first year of the Birmingham Act, 3,000 of the 4,800 houses known to be already multi-occupied were registered; so were fifteen newly let ones. Permission was refused sixteen times—three houses were judged to be unsuitable, and in thirteen it was thought that multi-occupation would spoil the neighbourhood. No appeals were made against these decisions.

The city Health Department felt that landlords were

[13] All local authorities can, under the 1961 Housing Act, introduce registration schemes. But they cannot refuse registration, so very few bother at all.

[14] Residents' associations tend to spring from opposition to local events of almost any kind; that they occasionally become the focus for anti-immigrant activity is beyond doubt, although the border between 'keeping up the amenities' and 'keeping out the blacks' is hard to define (see below, p. 213). Paul Foot, in *Immigration and Race in British Politics* (London, Penguin Books, 1965), describes some residents' associations which definitely have, or had, a racial motivation.

being effectively discouraged from intensive multiple occupation—indeed from the small numbers applying to let for the first time it looked as though they were being discouraged altogether. There was, however, the possibility that non-registrable houses—containing only two families or up to four lodgers—were increasing. There was said to be a growing tendency for smaller houses to be used in this way (possibly reflecting the spread of immigrant owner-occupation). But certainly no attempt was made by the Corporation to encourage sub-letting under suitable conditions, although the demand for private rented accommodation was still unquenched. While it is difficult to prove or disprove any 'racialist' tendency in Birmingham's use of its new powers, they do seem to be regarded as entirely preventive, rather than as a means of spreading more rented spaces, more thinly. Immigrants were not the only ones to suffer—for example, a man letting rooms to university students was reported as having been told he must cease to do so.

Despite the dangers of the misuse of this machinery (and the dangers could be partly offset by requiring that the reasons for banning multi-occupation must always be given) it would be a good thing if every city had powers equivalent to Birmingham's. Leeds does already have them—used sparingly so far—and Manchester has applied for a similar Act. By this machinery, combined with a positive attitude, much better use could be made of the stock of old, large houses, too big for single family use. It could be decided from the start how many people there should be room for, given the proper adaptation of the house and installation of sufficient amenities. If this were combined with a more realistic and generous policy on improvement grants, especially as they affect landlords, multiple occupation could be turned into a positive asset rather than seen merely as a 'disease' to be stamped upon.

At present, opportunities to use the powers to control multiple occupation in a constructive way are rare: shortage of staff, or an overall shortage of available housing, may prevent it (although not perhaps as much as some authorities make out). Possibly the only hope is for the local authority itself to take a much more active part in the purchase of large old houses suitable for conversion, or at least put more pressure on their owners to convert them properly. Leeds is frequently held up as an example; it is perhaps fortunate in having an unusually large number of comparatively inexpensive houses suitable for this treatment. But even in some London boroughs—for example, Lambeth, as described in Chapter VI—there are still many houses not yet in multiple-family occupation which would be perfectly suitable for the purpose given the right treatment. Other houses now ill-adapted to the use of more than one family, could be decently habitable by conversion to proper self-contained units; in others, a little face-lifting might be all that would be required to make acceptable lodgings for the many single people who need them (and who are least likely to qualify for council house accommodation). All these things must be part of the total approach to the recovery of the 'twilight areas'.

Scapegoats or no, immigrant landlords would have to play a part in this process. There is no reason to suppose they would not, on the whole, do so willingly and well, given the right approach by the authorities. Individual public health inspectors are frequently on decent personal terms with individual coloured landlords, whom they often find docile and anxious to co-operate, and whose difficulties they come to appreciate. More tact and imagination in dealing with the immigrant occupants of houses is, however, much to be desired; the elephantine knock on the door and unbidden entry into rooms with the call 'Health Department!' do not help to endear the authorities to the rooms' occupants. These officials are overworked and have to get their job done quickly; nevertheless there is a noticeable 'colonial style' in many inspectors' approach to immigrant landlords and tenants which is markedly different from their manner to English people—who respond to them quite differently. These men see far more of the immigrants' housing plight than do most members of the host community; and their genuine sympathy is often aroused. Nevertheless sympathy could be better expressed than in the words with which one official turned to the author in front of a West Indian woman: 'You should see this lady's husband. Caught his trousers in the oil stove and you've never seen such a mess—a great big black burn on a great big black leg! Sorry you missed it.'

II | A House for Mr. Biswas

Readers of V. S. Naipaul's Trinidadian masterpiece from which the title of this chapter is taken, will remember the passion with which the central character pursues his ideal —a house of his own. There is something of Mr. Biswas in many an immigrant, be he from east or west, who reaches these shores. The mere fact of emigration is a break with tradition and a gesture of individuality. Considerable determination may be required. The ability to save for a purpose—the fare to Britain—has already been demonstrated before the immigrant even arrives. Once here, more saving and long-term planning may be needed to support relatives at home and to provide yet more fares in order to bring the rest of the family over or to return home to visit them. These objects alone may be an overwhelming burden on a modest wage. But through them the immigrant is conditioned to the bold outlay, to the financial commitment on a scale which may be still unfamiliar to his English workmates. The goal of owner-occupation is to many immigrants (as indeed to growing numbers of Englishmen) the ultimate symbol of self-sufficiency and success, for which it is worth making still further sacrifices and risks.

It would be absurd to write a book about housing policies as they affect Commonwealth immigrants without taking this into account. Yet much criticism in this field (for example, the recent study of Sparkbrook, Birmingham),[1] ignores what must be one of the very strongest desires among the immigrants whom the authorities are accused of failing to help. Of course, it is also true that owner-

[1] *Race, Community and Conflict: A Study of Sparkbrook.*

TABLE 4

NATIONALITY AND HOUSEHOLD TENURE: LONDON, 1961

	English*	Jamaican	Caribbean, excluding Jamaican	Indian	Pakistani	Polish	Irish	Cypriot
Owner-occupiers	13	25	9	16	18	33	8	34
Renting furnished	7	61	75	48	58	18	34	28
Renting unfurnished	53	12	14	26	16	35	40	30
Renting from Council	24	1	1	7	5	13	15	6
Other	3	1	1	3	3	1	3	2
	100	100	100	100	100	100	100	100
Number of households	9,604	7,597	5,211	2,190	269	3,793	13,914	1,891

* English households 1 in 25 sample

Source: 1961 Census (analysed by R. B. Davison, *Black British*, London, Oxford University Press for the Institute of Race Relations, 1966, p. 52).

occupation is for many a mere expedient, undertaken
because private rented accommodation is scarce and expensive, because council housing is denied them, or (in some
parts of the country) just because old terrace housing is
cheap and plentiful. There is still no excuse for policies
which deny priority in the public sector to the people who
need it most or which grant council mortgages as a
conscience-salver for not welcoming immigrants to public
housing estates. But it ought to go on record that, barring
perhaps the National Health Service, the mortgage finance
available from the majority of local authorities has probably
been the public service from which immigrants have gained
most benefit.

An analysis of the 1961 Census in the London boroughs,
corresponding to what is now known as inner London,
demonstrated dramatic variations from the English pattern
of household tenure among various immigrant groups,
shown in Table 4. The variations must partly reflect different tastes as well as the different parts of London in which
the separate groups have concentrated. But one of the most
striking things is the extent to which owner-occupation
features compared with the English pattern, especially
among Cypriots and Poles (mostly longer established than
the coloured groups) and Jamaicans. It is hard to separate
cause and effect when comparing the numbers in owner-
occupation with the very small proportions of immigrants
in council housing. But buying your own house is not easy
in central London. Desire as well as expediency must surely
be reflected in these figures.

Outside the London region, where houses are cheaper,
the census shows an even higher proportion of house-
ownership among immigrants. Whereas a second-hand,
three-bedroomed terrace house in London and the south-
east averaged a price of £4,514 in 1966, in the Midlands the
average price was little more than half (£2,306) and in the
north-west, with a huge stock of sub-standard terrace housing, it was only £1,889.[2] In Bradford, for instance, a slum

[2] Co-operative Permanent Building Society Occasional Bulletin,
December 1966.

house with several years' 'life' can be bought for £200–
£600. As a result there is very little demand by Pakistanis
for council houses, although these are going begging.

A survey of Pakistani-owned houses in Halifax carried
out in the winter of 1964–5, found that over half the houses
were due for slum clearance within the next six years.[3] A
back-to-back house with a 'life' of five to ten years could
cost as little as £100–£200, so that where single Pakistanis
were earning up to £20 a week house purchase presented
few problems. The ninety-nine houses only contained eight
tenants between them, so easy was it to acquire a house of
your own. Thirty-eight per cent of the owners had bought
their houses mainly or entirely from their own savings;
34 per cent did so with loans from the city Corporation—
only 5 per cent had a building society loan as their main
method of purchase. But conditions in Halifax are exceptional, applying only to outworn industrial areas with
declining populations—as far as coloured immigrants are
concerned, this means mainly the Yorkshire and Lancashire
textile towns.

To the extent that old sub-standard housing supplies the
wants of immigrants, it also reinforces the tendency for
them to live in the dim old industrial districts, associated
with underprivilege and social need. The purchase of a
smaller terrace house is often the next step on from the
lodging-house. But the larger house of the type associated
with multiple occupation may itself be in demand by
immigrant families, at least in places (such as Nottingham;
see Chapter VIII) where price does not necessarily enforce
sub-letting on a room by room basis. Built for the large
Victorian family, with its servants, governesses, and poor
relations, such a house may be ideally suited to the immigrant 'extended family'—for example the families of two
brothers—which is by no means the same thing as sharing
your house with a series of strange lodgers. What may seem
makeshift by English standards, may not always be unacceptable to the immigrant. Clearly, too, tastes vary

[3] The author is grateful to Mr. Eric Butterworth and Mr. Brian
Hartley for permission to use this material.

among different immigrant groups as greatly as some of
them vary from the English norm; what suits an East
Pakistani peasant may be anathema to a man from King-
ston, Jamaica. Very much study is required in this field.
But it would be wrong to assume that every time a Commonwealth immigrant lives in conditions which do not
conform to English ideals, it has nothing to do with his
own choice.

Some of the most bitter prejudice against immigrants
arises from differences, real as well as imaginary, in matters
of sanitation, cooking and eating habits, waste disposal,
and so forth. Exaggerated as these matters so often are,
uneducated immigrants, particularly those of rural origin,
genuinely may not know how to live in an English house
in an English city. Engels remarked how Irish peasants in
Manchester in the 1840s kept pigs inside their homes and
allowed them to wander all over the street; the modern
equivalent may be chicken-slaughtering in the back bedroom or running a motor-repairing business from the front
pavement—there are many activities, normally unacceptable in an English residential district, which the immigrant
may regard as quite reasonable. The facile generalizations
which are so often the excuse for not offering better housing
to immigrants—such as 'They don't mind crowding in
together'—inevitably have their share of relative truth. It
has all been heard before in the 'coals in the bath' days of
pre-war slum clearance; yet apparently there are still those
in positions of responsibility who do not understand that
people cannot learn to use a better environment if they are
not offered it in the first place.

It is supremely important that when an immigrant does
wish to identify himself with English ideals, he should not
be thwarted by the prejudice of others. There are plenty of
coloured people who either arrive in this country wanting
to identify themselves with the host community, or who
acquire English ambitions about housing as about other
things. What happens when they wish to achieve the suburban 'semi', the modern house on the new 'spec-built' estate?
If prejudice thrusts them back into the old terraced neigh-

bourhoods and lodging-houses, much bitterness is in store.

The immigrant therefore sets two contrasting tests to the institutions controlling the market in house purchase. If (out of choice or necessity) he wishes to buy one of the older unfashionable houses on the market, or to use it in some not quite orthodox way, what sort of help can he get? If, on the other hand, he wishes to conform to English conventions of social status by buying an 'ordinary' family house which would appeal equally well to a skilled working-class or lower-middle-class Englishman, what sort of encouragement does he meet with? How far, in fact, are immigrant house-purchasers controlled by what other people think they ought to have? What are the attitudes of estate agents and building societies towards what they regard as 'unconventional' property or 'unconventional' people? How far is the immigrant penalized for 'unconventionality' by being forced into the arms of high-interest moneylenders? And how far does public finance for house purchase and house improvement compensate for the deficiencies of private institutions? The rest of this chapter will try to give some answers to these questions, without which the more detailed surveys of local authority housing policies in later chapters cannot be seen in focus.

There is absolutely no question but that racial prejudice plays an influential role in the property market. While its importance has yet to receive adequate statistical assessment the evidence is unmistakable. Before examining the effect on the immigrant house-buyer, it is perhaps necessary to recall that the whole market is, as it always has been, subject to judgements of class, fashion, and status by those who build, sell, and finance housing. Personal tastes and income limits are not the only factors which determine where and how different people live, as anyone will know who has tried to buy a cheap house in an unfashionable district from an agent who thinks he can sell him something better. Sometimes developers try to impose a more permanent censorship. Leases and covenants are a historic method of seeking to perpetuate the 'class' of a neighbour-

D

hood, and one which meets with approval from town-planners—for instance by stipulating that gardens must be maintained. But even these rules cannot succeed for long in preventing a neighbourhood from going downhill if there is too great a demand from the poor and too little from the well-to-do—hence the rapid decline in the later nineteenth century of areas like North Kensington and parts of Bloomsbury.

It is no longer legal to enforce a colour bar through covenants controlling the sale of leaseholds or sub-letting.[4] There is, however, still a gap in the law in the case of free-hold covenants. Territorial *apartheid* does not have the force of law and, therefore, can exist only by the limited and inefficient means of social sanctions. These can never-theless be strong, and carry economic force. In many ways coloured people are at much the same sort of disadvantage in the housing market as the Victorian working man—they are thought to lower the tone, and hence the value, of property. Even the language used is strikingly similar: 'low standards', 'barely literate', 'it'll take generations for them to catch up', are phrases heard time and again from people anxious to explain why they do not want to live near coloured people and would never do their neighbours the disservice of selling to anyone with a dark skin. These prejudices are shared, fostered, or simply steered through by the various business and professional people who attend to housing—rarely actively discouraged. But the presence of coloured people in the housing market is of much con-cern and fascination to them. In talks with estate agents, building society managers, builders, and solicitors up and down the country, mention of the subject seemed to scratch a secret itch: nearly always they were eager to talk (once assured of anonymity) and some were even anxious for enlightenment themselves. To the more sensitive among them ethical problems have been raised, at least to the extent of soft-pedalling discriminatory instructions; to others, prejudice is simply a market force to be exploited.

It goes without saying that the immigrant's individual

[4] Race Relations Act 1965, Section 5.

experience in the housing market and the satisfaction of his housing aspirations can be greatly influenced by the attitudes, as by the skill, experience, or other attributes, of the man with whom he deals. To illustrate the point, here are just three contrasting views from the same Midland town. A partner in an estate agency, director of a local building society:

I would do my best to head off coloured buyers from a good suburban area or a new estate. In fact it would be my duty to do so in the interests of the community and for the sake of people who have bought houses in good faith. If a house comes up in a neighbourhood likely to interest coloured people I always ask the vendor if they have any objection to selling to a coloured man and it's rare for them to say no—they'd have to be very broad-minded. In the better-class older areas people are extremely concerned. I don't blame them. There's difficulty in selling owing to infiltration. Our building society often turns down coloured applicants on status grounds. This isn't a colour bar—it's a question of education. I've heard they're not very well behaved, which doesn't help either. I wouldn't like to sell my own house to a coloured person or to live next door to one. Well, if he was a doctor or something I suppose it might be all right.

A solicitor with an active conveyancing practice:

I took on a great many Indian clients in the early 1950s and I used to do the majority of Indian business in the town. But I found my practice was being swamped by them and all my time was taken up with people who had no idea of business, no idea of how to keep an appointment. . . . I was younger then and had ideals. I had a positive desire to demonstrate that these people could live better but in the end I was forced to modify my views. They have totally different concepts of comfort and convenience and invariably pack their houses to the roof. They use every bit of space and they don't mind letting off every square inch . . . and the sort of property they choose always leads to difficulties. I got fed up and I've now shooed away all but the reliable ones.

The manager of the local branch of a national building society:

We deal with coloured applicants rather carefully. They are conscious of their colour when they walk into this office. If we give them 'no' for an answer we try to explain the reasons so that they won't think its just because of their skin. . . . As long as we keep them controlled in twilight areas we are storing up trouble. It's wrong to think that's where they belong. It only keeps down their standards . . . those who have integrated have already raised theirs. Like all foreigners they know it's in their interests to toe the line. . . . I live among them and I know. I've just moved into [an area of medium-sized inter-war houses] where about one in ten of the faces in the street is dark. Soon it will be more. The first day I met the milkman and he said, 'Everyone's very glad you've come and not one of the blacks', so I said, 'But you haven't met my wife yet have you?' Poor man, he nearly sank through the floor.

How capable or desirous of a 'normal' English way of life immigrants are believed to be depends on the experience as well as the basic outlook of the commentator. Of these three men, the estate agent appeared to have least personal knowledge of coloured immigrants and his views were of a fairly stereotyped kind often met among men of his trade. In fairness to the disillusioned solicitor, he probably had encountered a much greater social range among his Indian clients (many of whom had the most unsophisticated peasant origins) than had the sympathetic building society manager whose immigrant neighbours may have been more middle-class and anglicized from the start. When an immigrant shares the Englishman's ideal of a single family surburban 'semi', the battle is half won—his half. Those with other ideals pose much subtler problems to society. Meanwhile the most unsubtle distinctions ('If he was a doctor it might be all right') are commonly drawn by those who manipulate the clumsy social strings of the housing market. With only partial success, they frequently seek to frustrate the ambitions of the suburban-minded immigrant, on the well-worn grounds of 'status' or 'standards'. This may only strengthen the determination of the would-be integrated coloured man to dissociate himself from his 'low-class' compatriots. It is bound to discourage those who already find it hard to break away from the society of the twilight zone.

There are strong economic reasons why estate agents, in particular, are inclined to categorize the majority of immigrants as 'unsuited' to suburbia. Their bread-and-butter lies in the easy sale of conventional family houses—'conventional' meaning something not too big, not too old, (i.e. not more than about forty-five years old), and no more, or less, than commuter distance from the city centre. They do not want to upset this market. Moreover, some agents have made a killing out of the demand from immigrants for 'unconventional' houses—that is, the older and/or larger houses nearer the city centre—which but for this demand would in many places be virtually unsaleable. If, in these places, coloured people were able to buy houses freely in suburbia, the market for old houses could collapse.

How active a role do the agents themselves play in perpetuating these distinctions? Here again much depends on individual practice. It is supposed to be part of the skill of the business to know what sort of property appeals to what type of person, and coloured people are commonly typed as a single group. An agent will normally claim to know at once the districts which have already 'gone' and where nobody except a coloured person is expected to buy; and also the 'posh' areas where price alone is likely to deter coloured buyers—though the occasional anecdote is told of the Indian business man or West African diplomat who has successfully established himself in such a neighbourhood. The test comes between these two extremes. In neighbourhoods where coloured infiltration is a live issue—that is, where coloured people are buying houses in the middle-income range which might also appeal to English buyers—the agent almost invariably 'protects himself' by asking his client whether there would be any objection to a coloured purchaser.

Although the effect may be to save himself and other people time, this practice may often introduce the idea of discrimination into the minds of clients who would otherwise not have thought of the colour question. Someone who

might accept a coloured buyer who simply turned up on the
doorstep, might not accept the idea in the abstract. This
practice does create yet another barrier to be penetrated by
the immigrant. Not one agent—out of a selection statistically insignificant but reasonably representative of their
respective areas—told the author that he would refuse to
accept discriminatory instructions, although one or two
said they would like to but feared to lose business. There is
said to be a risk that if an agent is known to have sold a
house in a suburban neighbourhood to a coloured person,
he will lose his potential clients. On the other hand,
although the author has come across no first-hand proof of
this, there are said to be some agents in London who operate the technique known in America as 'block-busting'—
putting in one coloured family, then scooping other houses
in the street as they come on the market at 'panic' prices.

There are plenty of first-hand stories about angry neighbours ringing up the agent if they have seen a coloured
person looking at a house that is up for sale. Almost invariably, a vendor gives as his reason for not wanting to sell
to a coloured person consideration for his neighbours. Some
people are apparently prepared to lose quite a lot of money
or incur considerable inconvenience in the process, like the
Manchester couple who postponed their own emigration
plans for months on end rather than sell to a coloured
buyer ('We did persuade them in the end to take a *very*
quiet Indian,' said the agent). This attitude can cut both
ways: a West Indian in Nottingham said he had been told
by the lady who sold him her house that she was doing it
'to spite the neighbours'.

It makes a good deal of difference to the immigrant house-
buyer in what manner, and at what stage, he is refused.
Some agents will state at the outset if a colour bar applies
to a particular house; some immigrants have learnt from
bitter experience to ask outright, rather than risk an
oblique snub. Most coloured people would probably prefer
that vendors should have the courage of their convictions,
however unpalatable. Agents who openly admit to a colour
bar may do less of a disservice than those who merely try to

invent some excuse, such as that the house is already under offer, so that the coloured buyer is still in doubt about its availability. Worst of all are those agents, or vendors, who simply hope that the deal will fall through in some way—perhaps that the building societies will operate the colour bar for them—and then have to retract shamefacedly at the last minute. This has put many a coloured buyer to enormous frustration and unnecessary expense, and it is little comfort that this sort of prevarication may in fact be caused by a local climate of opinion which is more favourable to him, to the extent that hypocritical subterfuges take the place of open discrimination.

A point glossed over by agents is that immigrants do quite often pay over the odds for a house which suits their ambitions—obviously, this modifies the agents' willingness to operate a colour bar. How often the immigrant's desire to 'buy respectability' or his mere ignorance of bargaining conventions are deliberately exploited by agents and vendors it is impossible to say. Certainly the widespread belief among coloured people is that 'the price goes up to us' and there are many authenticated examples where this is known to have happened. Sometimes a coloured person is known to have deliberately offered a higher price in the hope of overcoming a colour bar. Exploitation is seldom so blatant as that of the estate agent who sent out a touting circular to house-owners in Leyton reminding them that 'we usually obtain a much higher price than the market value from our Commonwealth friends'.[5] Scope for the grosser forms of exploitation exists mainly in old dilapidated property and coloured people are not the only victims.

Because of the possibility of exploitation, and because of the impossibility of defining the precise market price of an individual second-hand house, no reliable estimate of the effect of a coloured population on house prices can be given without far more extensive study. It is sometimes suggested that, roughly parallel with American experience, the presence of the first few coloured people in a street has a depressing effect on prices but that thereafter, as more

[5] *Focus*, Vol. I, No. 2, March 1966, p. 12.

coloured people buy, the prices rise slightly above what might normally have been expected. This was borne out by the writer's information from several estate agents who believed that prices were relatively high for the type of house and locality which was recognizably the 'coloured market', but that a few coloured residents in an otherwise conventional suburban street were likely to depress the prices of neighbouring houses or at least make them harder to sell. But their view may have been influenced by the fact that 1966 was a sticky year for house sales generally. Until some more systematic research has been done it will be impossible to say whether the colour factor has any uniform influence on the housing market. Fear of depressed prices must to a certain extent be a self-fulfilling prophecy; this is one of those things which cannot be disentangled from the common assumption that most English people are hostile to colour and will react adversely to it given the chance.

In the housing market this assumption is most damaging in the rented sector, and in the sale of new houses. Many landlords profess to believe that 'black and white don't mix' and that any coloured tenants in a house or block will eventually make the rest unlettable to white people, or at any rate aggravate management problems. The persistent shortage of rented accommodation makes discrimination easier to operate than in house purchase. Agents who manage property on a large scale often refuse coloured tenants on principle, while at the same time being far more flexible in the matter of house purchase.

The most interesting situation of all arises over new houses. Most new houses are built in estates. When builders and their selling agents believe, as they almost always do, that the presence of coloured people will make the remaining houses on the estate harder to sell, they are forced into a policy decision which they do not have to face on individual houses. Their record is not impressive. Salesmen are almost always instructed either to refuse coloured buyers or to 'go slow' with them. They may do so, anyway, uninstructed, if worried about the indirect effect on their commissions. In places like Wolverhampton, where there is a shortage of decent second-hand accommodation, this can lead to great bitterness. Even a liberal policy decision may become narrowed in the course of implementation. The sales director of one large Midland building firm put it like this:

We built some cheap houses and our agent reported an influx of inquiries from blacks—what should he do? I thought we should refuse them and said so to the Board, but they did not want to go on record as racialists. So the policy is 'sell to blacks'. I say to our agents 'You're supposed to refuse blacks but use your discretion . . .' They say to the site salesman 'Be careful how many blacks you sell to'. We certainly didn't broadcast the official policy or we'd never have sold to any English people at all.

Also in the Midlands, the regional sales director of one of the biggest national house builders described how the problem of coloured buyers was a perpetual worry to him. He constantly has to deal with protests from purchasers who consider they have been cheated if another house in the same development has been sold to a coloured person— by some obscure logic this even happens sometimes over resales. Once he had to go so far as to promise a woman who refused to be pacified that if after six months she failed to get on with her coloured neighbours the firm would re-house her elsewhere. He told of his embarrassment over a Jamaican who bought one of their houses and, being a keen gardener, was always out with the roses, unconsciously acting as scarecrow to prospective buyers of the remaining few houses. One this principle the sales director does sometimes advise his staff not to let in coloured buyers at the very beginning of an estate, and apparently allows them a good deal of discretion in the matter: however, he encourages them to ring him if in doubt and he has sometimes had to exercise what he calls 'the judgement of Solomon' in individual instances. Once again, this is hardly a description of a non-discriminatory policy in action.

To the ordinary building society, the immigrant is

doubly suspect as someone whose 'status' is questionable, and whose choice of a house (often because a conventional one is denied him) is even more dubious. Moreover, the society may avoid lending to too many coloured people for fear of scaring off investors. From the rather limited inquiries made by the author to individual building society managers, there did appear to be local differences of emphasis which may be explained by the fact that managers of different societies in the same town tend to consult each other informally over problems that puzzle them. Chiefly, however, practice is dictated by head office and in most societies the manager does not have much individual scope, except in the exercise of his own veto in the early stages of an application. This, of course, is where his personal prejudice, or lack of it, is most important.

Some 75 per cent of mortgages are arranged with building societies and the great bulk of this business is with firms whose ideas of income and property status are conventional in the extreme. They are often criticized for taking such very small risks and not playing sufficient part in extending house purchase to different classes of people. The immigrant is certainly not the only one who suffers. The Government's mortgage guarantee incorporated in the 1967 Housing Act is likely to only marginally improve the situation. According to the records of one large society, over half of mortgages are already made to people earning not more than £25 a week.[6] Few building societies would refuse a 90 per cent loan on a modern house to a young Englishman earning £20 a week (subject to variations in the economic climate). But as soon as 'older' property— usually interpreted as anything over forty years old—is involved, then the situation changes and loans, if made at all, are not on such a generous basis (varying of course with the condition of the house). Many societies on principle refuse anything pre-1919 or offer only a 60 per cent mortgage on a conservative valuation, with second mortgages forbidden. Expensive modernization may often be a con-

* Co-operative Permanent Building Society, Occasional Bulletin, No. 76, December 1966.

dition of the loan—the society, after all, has to consider the marketability of mortgaged property throughout the period of the loan. Here for a start is a serious obstacle to the coloured man whom prejudice often thwarts from buying the sort of house approved by the lending institutions.

What special, personal difficulties may the immigrant meet? Nationality is nearly always required on mortgage application forms and aliens may be asked to state how long they have lived and worked in Britain. Since Commonwealth immigrants can state 'British', where their application is not made in person, and where an Asian or an African name does not give the game away, this obstacle may not occur. However, some societies have deliberately changed the form to 'place of birth', and if this is outside the British Isles they may stipulate as much as ten years' residence before they will lend. Is colour regarded as creating a special risk to the mortgagee? In answer to this question one branch manager of a leading national society replied with unconscious irony, 'Not on the terms we take them', and this sums up the attitude of perhaps the majority of societies. The coloured man may be accepted—but he tends to be treated cagily and probably not given as large a loan as an Englishman would be, even for the equivalent house, or charged a higher rate of interest. Of course this is not true of all societies everywhere. Some genuinely try to lend to coloured people on absolutely equal terms and say they find them good, steady payers. Some managers, according to their experience, draw distinctions between different immigrant groups, perhaps classifying West Indians as more reliable, or Indians as more businesslike. Some make openly discriminatory rules, such as insisting that a coloured buyer must have saved with them for a year before getting a loan, without making the same stipulation to white people.

Building societies are sometimes influenced by fear that coloured occupation reduces the value of a house—and of other houses in the neighbourhood on which they may have lent—although others consciously discount this factor. Some, like the man quoted on page 39, certainly do steer immigrant buyers away from 'respectable' areas and even the benevolent ones may see it as their duty not to lend to a coloured man in a neighbourhood which will be unfriendly to him. All of the conventional building societies avoid any loan which risks multiple occupation and take particular care with immigrants to limit occupation to the 'immediate family'—a concept which conflicts at once with many immigrant ideas of kinship. They may automatically rule out anything but small houses in the belief that any coloured man buying a large house, even if he has a large family, intends to sublet. Joint ownership—for example between bothers—is also unacceptable.

The more 'liberal' societies are sometimes embarrassed by the fact that, if they are more ready than others to lend on older property, they may find themselves in certain areas with an almost exclusively coloured clientèle which, they feel, is bad for their image if it becomes known. Their usual answer is to impose some sort of unofficial quota. This may also happen to local societies in areas with many coloured house-buyers. The manager of a London society which includes in its district the Brixton area said:

Because this is a black area we used to get telephone calls from as far away as Luton asking us to lend to coloureds. We've had to restrict our service to our own offices and agents. We don't accept applications from mortgage brokers. The maximum loan we give to coloureds is 70 per cent of valuation, and to whites 80 per cent. Why? Because coloured property depreciates faster.

The point is often made that coloured buyers seem to be able to raise larger deposits than English people. This often reflects generosity within the group: if a West Indian or Pakistani needs money, his friends will lend liberally. Much was heard, in the early days of immigrant house-buying, of group pooling arrangements by which several people contributed funds which would be used by one to buy a house. This practice seems to have died down—it may never have been widespread. The most important thing for the immigrant purchaser of a house which is not easily mortgageable, is that his estate agent or solicitor should have access to loan sources of one kind or another. This is the most important function of the agent of 'coloured' property and his success depends on his skill as mortgage broker. The loans may come sometimes from 'respectable' societies, sometimes from the ones who charge an extra percentage or two for the extra risk, sometimes from private sources. The service may be expensive in itself, involving higher than the usual agency cut, or extras such as 'introduction fees'. Second mortgages, or first mortgages on really sticky property, may come from the politely named 'merchant banks'—moneylenders who charge high interest on a hire-purchase basis, expressed in terms of so much per month or week, and amounting to as much as 15 or 18 per cent interest. Some of these money-lenders specialize all over the country in loans to coloured buyers. Some localities have their own Indian financiers serving other Indians, for example. A typical transaction was that which took place in July 1964 between a Pakistani, who was buying a terrace house in Nottingham, and the General Housing Finance Company of Streatham, London (a name which crops up frequently). A loan of £500 was to be repaid in eighty-four monthly payments of £9 14s. over seven years, so that the total interest charge was £314 16s. and the interest rate 'in accordance with the Moneylenders Act 1927' was 17·79 per cent per year. Steep enough, but then £9 14s. a month for a whole house does not seem much if you have been paying £2 a week for one room.

While some of the agents in this end of the market are sharks, and worse—several have been sent to prison for embezzling deposits and other illegal practices—many nevertheless perform a useful public function. It is better to have an overpriced slum house than no house at all. The agent may not be too scrupulous about telling you if the property is due to be pulled down by the council, but at least he spares no pains to obtain finance of a sort. He steps in where others disdain to tread, and without him the immigrant owner-occupier would be a far rarer bird.

All the legal snags connected with this kind of property —short leaseholds, dilapidation, sitting tenants, and so on— are things of which immigrant house buyers are still far too ignorant (as are many working-class English buyers). This is all part of the ignorance and lack of proper advice which beset the immigrant in the housing field and seem only to have been overcome where efficient local leadership within the immigrant group (as among the Indians in Nottingham) protects its own members from expensive follies.

How far can the immigrant turn to the local authority as a source of finance between the extreme conservatism of the building societies, and the 'ask no questions' money-lender? The answer to this may spell the difference between a tolerable and intolerable housing situation, and, like everything else, the answer entirely depends on where you are. Subject to periodic 'squeeze' limits set by the central Government, borough finance committees can be as generous as they like with mortgages. Some dispense 100 per cent loans freely, uninhibited by the borrower's income; others are almost as cautious as the building societies in the type of house they lend on and the terms of the loan and its relation to income. Some raise no objection to second mortgages, to joint ownership, or even to lodgers to help pay off the debt; others sent round public health inspectors in the middle of the night to make sure the house contains no more than the mortgagee's immediate family. There was a typical variety of response to the ministerial circular of April 1966 which recommended that lending be confined to people in housing need and to 'supplementing other sources of finance'.[7] Local authorities were encouraged to lend to their own tenants who wanted to move out, or those high on the waiting list or in redevelopment areas; to people who were homeless or living in unhealthy or even crowded conditions; to those who wanted to buy a pre-1919 house on which a building society was unlikely to lend. The circular even recommended loans to owner-occupiers buying large houses for partial sub-

[7] Ministry of Housing and Local Government Circular 24/66.

letting. Some authorities accepted this circular completely
—others put their own gloss on these priorities (very few,
for example, accepted the idea of lending for multiple
occupation, and this recommendation became virtually a
dead letter).

On the whole, local authorities have regarded the granting of mortgages as a social service, and many take the view
that it is a useful way of preventing deterioration of older
houses. With the emphasis on older, cheaper houses many
of these schemes have been of immense help to immigrants.
(For instance, one Yorkshire borough, in 1966, gave 30 per
cent of its mortgages to immigrants, mainly Pakistanis
buying old terraced houses.) If one had to name one thing
which more than anything else has helped the housing of
coloured people in Britain it would be the G.L.C. mortgage
scheme, the largest and most generous of all. This is worth
looking at in some detail.

Between March 1963, when the (former) London County
Council's 100 per cent mortgage scheme started, and July
1965 (when government sanction for corporation mortgages
was suspended) the L.C.C. and (after April 1965) the G.L.C.
lent nearly £150 million to over 31,000 borrowers—
although only two-thirds of the loans were actually at 100
per cent of valuation. Anyone living or working in London
and buying a house within a fifty-mile radius was eligible,
regardless of income (though the G.L.C., when it took over
the scheme, did start to be a little more careful: in the
terms of one critic 'they were giving loans to beggars').
The philosophy behind this was, and still is, that the
Council is more interested in the value of the property than
in the status of the applicant, and it realizes that, because
many of its loans are to working-class people whose jobs
may be precarious, there may be difficulties from time to
time. Nevertheless, in the autumn of 1966 it was thought
to be quite a good record that all but 4.5 per cent of borrowers were up to date on payments. Immigrants, on the
whole, were regarded as good payers anxious to establish
complete ownership.

When the G.L.C. started a new scheme in June 1966,

with a total limit imposed by the Government of £40 million until April 1967 (later increased to £50 million) and under the general priorities set out in the government circular, it also introduced modifications of its own. Lending was related more closely to income. The territorial limits were narrowed to, in most cases, Greater London or New (or 'expanded') Towns. A condition of a loan was that the applicant should have been unable to obtain one from a building society or a local authority other than the G.L.C.—which has certainly resulted in the London boroughs sending along their 'riskier' applicants to the G.L.C. This can mean all immigrants, or virtually all. It was significant that one-third of all the lending done by the G.L.C. in the early months of their new scheme was in three London boroughs only—Harrow, Ealing, and Wandsworth, The last two of these both have substantial immigrant populations (Ealing contains the Sikh community of Southall) and both decided to restrict lending to people who had been resident for two years in the borough. The G.L.C. has had protests from a residents' association in Southall at its lending to Indians, and this is by no means the only suburban area from which irate letters come to the G.L.C. Treasurer when he has given a mortgage to a coloured applicant (although usually the protesters are people who have been turned down themselves). But the administrators who run the scheme seem, as far as one can judge, to be rather proud of helping the under-dog—perhaps because this is almost the only chance their department has to dispense bounty in person. They see a great many coloured applicants and believe that immigrants may prefer personal interviews, rather than inquiring by post or telephone; but there is no reliable means of telling what proportion of all applicants are immigrant. They tried at one time to ask for nationality on the form but learnt little, as the immigrants were mainly British citizens; and to be more specific would have been politically unacceptable. But it is generally agreed that coloured people benefit from the scheme out of all proportion to their total numbers.

However willing it may be to help the coloured house-

buyers, the G.L.C. has to become cautious on two matters
which affect them more than most people. The first is the
'valuation gap'—the difference between the market price
and the value given by the mortgagee's surveyor, on which
the mortgage is calculated. This is often large, especially
on older properties and especially—the Council found—in
the case of ignorant coloured buyers. The 1966 printed
form warned of differences of '£300 or more' between price
and valuation and said a loan would be refused unless there
were adequate means of meeting the difference. In practice
this has provided buyers with a good bargaining counter
(and may give some immigrants their first idea of haggling),
so that it has helped hold down some prices—agents
grumble that the G.L.C. does this deliberately. But they
also agree that without council mortgages old house prices
would not be as high as they are. The G.L.C. has, since
June 1966, tried to ensure that the gap is not met by means
of a second mortgage; although agents frequently find ways
round this. The same caution is now attempted where a
house needs a large repair bill before it is fit to lend on.

The second cause of greater strictness is the vexed question of taking lodgers in a mortgaged house. Normal
building-society loans are always restricted to houses for
single-family use only, and local authorities generally take
the same line—even when there is little means of checking
whether the rules are being kept. Nottingham (see Chapter
IX) goes further and refuses loans to immigrants in areas
where it believes multi-occupation might spread, so that
this acts as a containing influence.

A more liberal policy does run risks. During the eleven
months' gap between the end of one G.L.C. scheme and the
beginning of the next, the G.L.C. valuers' department—
aided and abetted by some public health inspectors (see
Chapter V)—started to check on breaches of agreement and
found, amongst other things, that out of a sample of 9,630
borrowers, 977 were sub-letting without permission, and
that 138 borrowers were not even living in their houses,
mostly because they were letting them at rack-rents.[8]

[8] *Guardian*, 14 October 1966.

Illegal sub-letting, and the even more common failure to do repairs, seemed, however, to have been reduced when 100 per cent mortgages cut down the buyer's financial burden.

The G.L.C. has had some bitter experience in the past with immigrant buyers who say they want a house for their own family and then only fill it with tenants—the Council now demands sworn proof that the family really is coming. This cannot be very satisfactory from anyone's point of view—those bent on so doing could still ignore the rule at the cost of breaking an oath, and those who really did want to bring their family over might still have the problem of synchronizing two large expenditures—house purchase and fares—without any interim way of bridging the gap.

All these things make the G.L.C., and many other local authorities, take special care in explaining the risks and obligations of house purchase and borrowing to coloured immigrants. Just how they do it must vary with the individual responsible. One London borough official, asked if he felt obliged to treat coloured applicants any differently from others, said: 'It's not how you treat them, it's how you speak to them. Between ourselves if you bring these coloured people up here and put the fear of God into them it pays off. This could be unfavourably criticized, but the Council has more than once said that it's not going to lend money to pack a house to the roof.' Maybe the coloured people concerned feel this is just another of the things you have to put up with in order to get a house.

The encouragement given by local authorities to immigrants and others who want to buy old- or middle-aged houses depends on each authority's attitude to the conservation and improvement of the existing housing stock. A corporation mortgage may be conditional on repairs and modernization being done; some councils give generous loans for this purpose. Repairs are not, as they should be, included in the work for which improvement grants may be given. Again, there is a great deal of difference in the encouragement that different councils give to the use of grants; for, though the bulk of the cost is borne by the exchequer, grants are partly paid for by the Council itself, and some take the line that 'it isn't worth spending rate-payers' money on something which may have to be pulled down in a few years anyway'. If a slum clearance area is loosely designated for clearance in 'ten to fifteen years' time', grants can be refused. The standard grant, statutorily available for half the price of installing that five standard amenities (bath, inside lavatory, hot water supply, wash-hand basin, and ventilated food cupboard) is limited to dwellings with a 'life' of over fifteen years; the 'discretion-are grant', which a council may give up to a sum of £500 per dwelling is available only for houses which after conversion will have a 'life' of over thirty years. Many people would like to see these rules made more flexible, and the anomaly of the ventilated food cupboard (expensive, and unnecessary in the days of the refrigerator) removed. At present there are too many ways in which councils can discourage improvements if they are so inclined. Moreover, the advantages to landlords are limited. Grants are not available, for example, for increasing tenants' facilities in houses in multiple occupation. When they are used the subsequent rent increase is limited to $12\frac{1}{2}$ per cent of the landlord's share of the approved cost.

Strong advice has been given to the Government on making the whole approach to renovating and condemning old houses more positive and realistic.[9] Much depends on the willingness of local authorities. The example of the city of Leeds, which has used persuasion and coercion to improve large areas of privately owned housing, is held up for emulation. At the same time, some economists point out that even the short-term renovation of old houses can be worth while, given a subsidy system that gives proper due to the gains made.[10]

Now the point of all this, in this context, is that immigrants have shown themselves at least as receptive as other

[9] *Our Older Homes: A Call for Action*, Report of the Ministry of Housing's Sub-Committee on Standards of Housing Fitness, 1966.
[10] Cf. L. Needleman, *The Economics of Housing*, London, Staples Press, 1965.

owner-occupiers to the idea of improving and modernizing
their houses. And they are more than likely to live in houses
which qualify for the treatment. Externally, their attitude
shows up in brilliant paintwork and gaudy colourwashes
which would endear them to Civic Trust 'face-lift' propa-
gandists. Internally (contrary to common belief), a higher
standard of hygiene may prevail than in 'traditional' English homes which have never known a bath, a modern sink,
or an inside lavatory. Muslim laws, for example, place
washing next to godliness, and it is interesting that, in the
Halifax survey mentioned earlier, nearly 20 per cent of the
Pakistani owners had installed their own baths.[11]

The rampant respectability that bristles from glossy
brickwork, dazzling pointing, and starched curtains denotes
a pride in all things pertaining to the home which is in
various degrees a characteristic of many immigrant families,
be they from the Caribbean, the Mediterranean, or the
Indian Ocean. Education in the virtues of less visible assets,
such as damp courses and drainage, may still be necessary
—but so it is to many English house-owners. The contrast
with the tattay houses tenanted room by room is positively
painful; pride of ownership works miracles. There is a
phrase often heard from people who are familiar with
homes in the old working-class neighbourhoods: 'Inside,
you know, they're little palaces.' Pride in one's surroundings is an instinct in common to many of the old and many
of the new inhabitants of the old urban neighbourhoods.
It is not fanciful to see in this a very positive source of
physical and social improvement in many areas now written
off as 'decayed', or 'twilight zones', or any of the other
clichés which mean that nobody is going to bother about
the houses except, eventually, to pull them down. Aware-
ness is dawning that millions of old houses will, somehow,
have to be rejuvenated, to last at least another generation.
The spread of owner-occupation into cheap old houses is
already beginning to do this. This is something in which

[11] A 'bath' may have sometimes meant a 'shower': because of the
Muslim rule about washing in running water, these are often
preferred.

the Mr. Biswas's of Halifax, Hackney, and Handsworth could play a far more important role than their small total numbers would suggest—if anyone has the will and imagination to turn their homemaking inclinations to the good of the whole community. If all local authorities were as positive as Leeds in their use of improvement grants, and as generous as the G.L.C. in granting of mortgages, three important and interlinked aims could be realized: rescue of the worthwhile old housing stock; help to would-be house-owners who can expect limited help from the private sector; and a new lease of life for the old dying residential sectors of cities.

III | How to Keep Clean and Win a Council House

Acute difficulties are experienced by most immigrants, especially coloured immigrants, in obtaining a decent home in a private rented or purchased house. This is where the public sector might be expected to step in, fulfilling its obligation to provide homes for people in 'housing need'.[1] Or so it might be supposed by one unacquainted with the thorny political and administrative barriers which surround the allocation of council houses.

Housing is the greatest source of power and controversy in local government. Its favours are jealously guarded. It is up to the 1,400 individual housing authorities in England and Wales to decide their own priorities of housing need; and it is by now a cliché that these in no way guarantee that the most obviously needy cases are in fact first served. Sometimes the rules are devised to keep out certain categories of people altogether. Preference is, in many cases, given to people of local origin as opposed to newcomers (even people from the next-door town) whose housing plight may be worse and whose presence in the area is in response to essential economic demands. Flagrant cooking of the rules —as, for instance, in the case of the London metropolitan borough which told the Milner Holland committee that it gave more points for being native British than living in damp insanitary conditions—is no longer as common as it

[1] In the Housing Act 1949, Part I, Section I, local authorities are required to take into account 'the housing conditions and housing needs of all members of the community'. Previously their obligation had been solely to 'the working classes'.

used to be; and in London things have improved since the
new local government structure of 1965. But such are the
obstacles, deliberate and unconscious, that lie across the
road to the council estate for the family of the immigrant,
mobile worker, that the presence of immigrants, especially
coloured immigrants, on these estates, is still exceedingly
rare.

That this sometimes reflects the true wishes of the
immigrant there is no doubt. But it also unquestionably
represents the fact that coloured council tenants are frequently regarded as a political liability and an administrative risk. They embody, in the eyes of the authorities, the
'awkward case' which they would rather not handle. If the
rules happen to keep them out anyway, so much the better.
In 1961 only 4.5 per cent of Commonwealth immigrant
households were found by the Census to be council tenants
in the big conurbations where the vast majority of them
lived. Six years later, while some progress has been made,
the situation has not visibly improved.

Later chapters will describe how immigrants are affected
by the council housing policies of individual boroughs. But
it is necessary first to have an understanding of how the
system works, and of the logic it obeys. Local authorities
are not in the same position as private landlords. They are
supposed to give houses to all kinds of people who could
not make their way in the private market. And they operate
a system which is heavily subsidized, although the subsidy
is not geared to the intensity of local demand. Some councils can barely afford to build houses cheap enough for the
people who most need them, even with heavy rate subsidies;
others are virtually in a position of building only in order
to use up the subsidy on older houses long since paid for.
Even when immigrants do live in towns (like Bradford)
where council houses are going begging, there is in these
places an equal surplus on the private market which absorbs
most immigrant demands. In London, the Midlands, and
the north-west, where most Commonwealth immigrants
live, council houses are much sought after as the only
accommodation, other than slum houses, where a working-

class family can have the space it needs at a price it can afford.

In these circumstances, some method of priority in allocation is essential. There is even a justification for some form of residential rule. What absolute rules can there be between, say, a large, poor overcrowded family; a better-off family with a handicapped child; and a young couple with two babies living with their in-laws? There are still places where such things depend on the patronage of individual councillors; but the bigger and better-run authorities usually rely on some sort of mathematical weighting for different types of need. This may still result in too many 'top scores' for too few houses, and therefore it is common to rely on some sort of residential qualification, and/or time spent on the housing list, to pick out residual winners.

Yet when the largest housing authority in the country, the G.L.C., still gives preference to the countless sons and daughters of its quarter of a million tenants, it cannot be said that the balance between old-established residents and newcomers has yet been anything like redressed. Successive governments have for years been pressing the housing authorities to make a twofold reform of their allocation priorities. First, to give more consideration to young couples with growing families whose need is greatest, rather than allocating houses to middle-aged couples whose need is no longer so great but who may have been on the housing list for twenty years. Second, to give at least equal consideration to the families of workers newly arrived in the area to take up employment. The White Paper on housing of November 1965 made this point fairly strongly. An amendment to the Housing Subsidies Bill of 1966 made special provision for building for the purposes of 'industrial relocation'. A circular sent out from the Ministry of Housing and Local Government in January 1967 reminded local authorities once again that they were not required to give newcomers precedence over people already on the waiting list, but did ask them 'to accept those who have no past associations with their areas, and second to make housing need the main consideration in allocating tenancies'.

Few, if any, housing authorities of any importance refuse altogether to accept applicants who are not native sons within the sacred boundary born and bred. But they do often look at them askance, and either apply general residential rules which are by their nature weighted against newcomers, or apply a different set of rules which deliberately handicap strangers or, sometimes specifically, immigrants from abroad. For instance (see the chapter on Wolverhampton in this book) the system may be especially devised to put a brake on Irish and other overseas immigrants whose crowded housing circumstances would otherwise give them swift priority. This often carries the implication that immigrants have 'lower standards' and therefore lesser deserts; or that they even deliberately take advantage of the system, as expressed in one popular opinion: 'They breed children on purpose to get high on the list.'

The balance can be shifted by the weighting given to various factors, for example: a period of residence before the applicant can be accepted on the list at all; a period spent on the list before he can start to earn 'points'; the number of 'points' awarded for time spent on the list, or in the borough. Even the London boroughs—most of which have agreed to a residential qualification of five years spent in Greater London, including one in the housing authority, before anyone can be rehoused—can still, if they wish, gear their systems internally in a way which still takes too little account of the manner in which, in a large conurbation, people do not pause to think whether they are crossing a local authority boundary whenever they move house.

At present, however, in most big cities, these distinctions are more apparent than real. This is because priority has to be given to people displaced from large slum-clearance and redevelopment programmes. Most people on the lists of inner London boroughs, for example, have so little hope of being rehoused within the foreseeable future that residential distinctions have ceased to count for much. Of course some waiting-list candidates will be rehoused in the course of clearance: but if they live in an area scheduled for clearance within anything up to ten years, they are unlikely to get any consideration as waiting-list cases even if they reach the top of the list. Boroughs which are densely built up within their own boundaries, and without adequate overspill facilities, find that the more houses they build, the greater share of these houses goes to people displaced to make space for the house-building sites. Apart from special allocations made on medical or welfare grounds (rationed in a fairly arbitrary fashion) clearance cases are in many boroughs absorbing all but the least desirable council houses. Mere overcrowding, or sharing of baths and lavatories, may earn high points but still means nothing unless there is a really shattering accumulation of disabilities. Indeed slum programmes, burdensome as they are, secretly provide some official relief from having to pay attention to other bad forms of housing.

The selection of areas for slum clearance or redevelopment, and the order in which they are dealt with, therefore become supremely important. A great many variables come into play, of which the most important are town-planning considerations: which sites, when cleared, will provide most room for new houses? Neither the worst slums, nor those most densely inhabited, therefore necessarily receive the first treatment; indeed, density of occupation is regarded as a valid reason for postponing redevelopment of such sites until leeway has been obtained by first rebuilding the less populated sites. It may be necessary to pull down houses which are not slums at all in order to gain space for housing appreciably more people than inhabit the site already. As the chapters on Tower Hamlets and Manchester in the present book will show, there are numerous other factors which determine the point at which any particular house or street is picked for demolition: some of these reasons are positive, sometimes neutral; some can be held to be an avoidance of responsibility by the authorities.

Too much has been made by prejudice-spotters of the notion that local authorities avoid clearing areas containing coloured people because they do not want to rehouse them. While this does sometimes appear to be true of individual houses, the whole process of slum clearance[2] is so long-drawn-out, cumbersome, and interrelated to so many other factors that it is scarcely conceivable that an authority would allow, or even be able, to carry out such a policy over a whole area. It would require very much more co-ordination between the different departments involved than most authorities are capable of even in worthy causes. The basis of this suspicion seems to be one remark by an Opposition councillor about one area in Birmingham.[3] Birmingham Corporation put forward the quite normal explanation that the area in question was too densely occupied for them to redevelop it at that stage. Maybe they were relieved that this let them off rehousing the immigrant occupants for the time being; but there is no conclusive evidence in this or any other case known to the author that the presence of immigrants has been the *deciding* factor in postponing clearance.

Nevertheless this is politically explosive material. Frustrated people on the waiting list already express resentment at the housing priority given to slum-clearance families. When some of these families are coloured, they may well become the focus for resentment.[4] This is recognized apprehensively by councils who are on the verge of clearing immigrant areas—by which time it is nearly always too late for them to turn back.

This is not to say that immigrants do not find themselves handicapped in slum clearance, as in other housing processes. The density factor mentioned above is one such handicap, for it does mean that houses in multiple occupa-

[2] Summarized in the Appendix.

[3] *Race, Community and Conflict*, p. 265. The councillor was reported to have said that an area of Sparkbrook could not be redeveloped because '600 immigrant families would have to be rehoused'.

[4] In Smethwick the Labour Council, in 1961, successfully defied a rent strike called against the rehousing of a Pakistani whose house had been demolished by slum clearance. *Immigration and Race in British Politics*, p. 38.

tion tend to be deferred in favour of clearing smaller houses in single-family occupation which may, anyway, come nearer to the narrow physical definition of a 'slum'. The Government has been strongly advised to revise this definition, in favour of something more flexible, and which takes environmental factors more into account.[5] On the whole, slum-clearance programmes concentrate on houses which were built to a low standard in the first place—the small, dark industrial cottages, without baths or inside lavatories, without damp courses, often badly built with cheap materials. The programmes are less likely to include houses which were originally spacious and sound, which on paper at least have baths and lavatories, and which become slums only through long-term neglect or misuse. The typical decayed house in multiple occupation may be as damp and unhealthy as any in Coronation Street; but it may stand among other reasonably sound houses and qualify for treatment only on an individual basis. Individual clearance is something many authorities dislike doing; it is tiresome, and unless the house is actually demolished it may still be broken into and used, so it may be feared, by families who then again require rehousing. If it is demolished, expensive shoring-up of adjacent buildings may be necessary. These are not very good arguments, and they do sometimes mean that individually shocking houses remain in use.

Yet it is wrong to say categorically that local authorities do not clear houses in multiple occupation. Those with the most active slum-clearance records—such as Manchester and Liverpool—are already doing so. Multiple occupation is anyway not always limited to the so-called twilight zones —it is often found in the archetypal working-class slum neighbourhoods, where these happen to contain slightly larger houses, sometimes of earlier construction than the Victorian 'industrial dwellings' which surround them. Whether houses in multiple occupation are included in clearance programmes therefore depends on town planning

[5] *Our Older Homes: A Call for Action*, Report of the Sub-Committee on Housing Fitness Standards, Ministry of Housing and Local Government, 1966.

and social history as well as on the vigour of present
policies.

An alternative procedure to the straightforward clearance
of areas declared as slums is available to local authorities.
Known as 'deferred demolition', this permits local councils
to buy up slum houses well in advance of planned clearance,
patch them up to the minimum habitable standard, and use
them as a temporary addition to their own housing stock,
so that any vacancies which occur can be used for people
who otherwise would have to be housed on permanent
council estates. Once again Birmingham has come in for
criticism. It uses its 'patched houses' to rehouse coloured
people, who are thereby retained within the decayed city
core, rather than dispersed to council estates in the suburbs.
Similar policies, on a smaller scale, are used in Nottingham (see Chapter VII) and Lambeth (see Chapter V): the
other local authorities studied by the author did not use
sub-standard housing for their own tenants on any significant scale. The correlation of coloured tenants and sub-
standard council property is no accident; the authorities
admit that they regard this type of housing as being particularly suitable for immigrants, even if this is genuinely
intended only as a temporary arrangement. The test comes
when the patched houses are themselves demolished: do
the tenants then get the offer of a council estate house, or
are they merely moved to another house due for demolition in a few years? There are few places, outside Birmingham, where this is yet demonstrable. But what can be
shown is how all through the normal machinery of housing
allocation the coloured family tends, for a number of
reasons, to be classed as one of second- or third-class citizens.
And it can also be shown how easy it is for an immigrant
family (and many others) to slip through the public housing
net altogether, even when residence in a clearance area
might be presumed to qualify them for a council tenancy.

Take first the question of who is eligible for rehousing
under slum clearance. The law is ambiguous. Authorities
have a duty to house, or obtain housing for, people living
in clearance areas for whom 'suitable accommodation . . .

does not already exist'. Yet before a council obtains permission from the Government to undertake compulsory
purchase for slum clearance, it has to submit a list of all
those living in the area at the time of its declaration as a
clearance area, and show that it is able to supply the necessary quantity of housing. In practice many authorities
simply make a rule-of-thumb calculation in their programmes, on the basis of 'one family housed for every house
pulled down—or 'one-and-a-half families' as the case may
be—and then devise and enforce rules with whatever
strictness is thought necessary to keep the problem to
manageable proportions. An outcry from the waiting list
may result in a tightening-up of the rules; on the other
hand, some councils have taken the point that the fewer
people you rehouse from slum clearance now, the more
crowd into the remaining old houses and create a problem
later.

Stringency is thought necessary because the authorities
live in terror of being taken advantage of by people who
recognize a condemned house as a short cut to a council
tenancy. Some councils go to absurd lengths to circumvent
the circumventers, taking the earliest possible point in the
clearance process,[6] the health inspector's survey, as the
ultimate day for residents to qualify for rehousing. As
subsequent chapters will show, this can be several years
before actual demolition. More reasonably, others take the
first day of official 'publication' of the scheme, or the date
of approval of the Compulsory Purchase Order, though
even this presupposes either close reading of the local Press
or a very efficient local grape-vine. Merely informing landlords is notoriously unreliable, for they will always be
anxious to let, up to the lost possible moment, and may
even (as has happened in some London tenement blocks)
charge a premium for the privilege of having one's home
demolished. Plenty of immigrants, both landlords and
tenants, are as familiar with the game as anybody. But as a
group they are more likely to be unfamiliar with its often
obscure rules and rent or buy a slum house in genuine

[6] See Appendix on procedure.

ignorance of the consequences. To authority, they may simply be 'taking advantage'—in this as in many other ways housing management claims almost occult powers of sorting innocent and guilty which can go badly awry when faced with the unfamiliar speech and manner of the immigrant.

A convenient obscurity surrounds those people who, though eligible for rehousing, 'voluntarily' find their own accommodation from a clearance area. These too seem to contain a comparatively large number of immigrants, and one cannot but suspect that their apparent preference for private accommodation may sometimes stem from the fact that the alternative of council housing was not sufficiently explained to them—or may even have been presented in a deliberately discouraging way. The Milner Holland Committee found that in London 5 per cent was the average for this 'voluntary' rehousing with the percentage varying very much from area to area. In one part of Kensington 37 per cent of those eligible for council housing rehoused themselves.

Deliberate inflexibility towards the many human circumstances which may exist in clearance areas often seems built into the rules adopted. The tenure often appears to count for more than the man: the only householder almost always sure of a place is the working-class archetype, the long-standing tenant of an unfurnished self-contained house. Sub-tenants, lodgers, tenants of furnished accommodation, owner-occupiers—any of these may be in the category which the local authority does not count it its responsibility to rehouse. Single people are frequently omitted. All these things can and do frequently deprive immigrants and others of the chance of a council tenancy through slum clearance, with the result that they have to crowd more closely into other old neighbourhoods. This was often accepted as a matter of course by officials when asked about rehousing coloured people from clearance areas. 'They often aren't eligible and when they are they often don't want a council house', was a stock answer which left much unsaid.

A great deal of heart-burning is caused by the meagre provision for compensation of those whose homes are condemned. The only criterion is site value, with a few exceptions. Special Acts of Parliament give market value to owner-occupiers of slum property who bought during the period of post-war shortage. Immigrants will rarely qualify for this. They may, however, qualify for the 'well-maintained payment' which is just what it says and which may be claimed or shared by a tenant if he can show he has done decoration or repairs. Some authorities dislike using compulsory purchase because of the hardship caused to owner occupiers—Bristol, for example, negotiates all slum properties at market price.[7]

At most clearance area inquiries, the bulk of objections come from shopkeepers whose premises are included in the order. The law says that if a building contains living accommodation it can be judged by slum standards and bought at site value, whether or not there is a business in the premises which could have a commercial value. The authorities can, entirely at their own discretion, make a small payment for loss of trade, usually related to the annual turnover. If the shopkeeper is only a tenant, this is all he receives, if that. 'Living over the shop' is such a common way of life, and so many buildings originally designed as terraced dwellings have been adapted over the years into the cafés, workshops, and other activities which are woven through and through the old working-class districts, that this often causes considerable hardship. Not nearly enough new shops are built to go round and these are anyway too expensive for most of the displaced tradesmen. This too has considerable bearing on immigrants, since shop-keeping in a poor district is a familiar way of making good in a British city.

Slum programmes are not the only occasion when housing policies are played very close to the chest in order to prevent the wily public devising sufficient discomforts for itself to circumvent the rules. (Sometimes, too, it looks

    [7] J. B. Cullingworth, *Housing and Local Government*, London, Allen and Unwin, 1966.

suspiciously as though it is in order that Councillor Joe Bloggs can say that *he* was the man who fixed up Mrs. Brown.) Whatever the reason, much obscurity and suspicion often surrounds the working of things like the housing list. Immigrants may find this particularly baffling, and take it as proof that they are being unfairly treated. It is surprising how rare it is, for instance, for a housing department to publish its points scheme.

In no context is this suspicion carried to greater lengths than in dealing with homeless families. This is one aspect of housing which has been well publicized and (except in parts of London) only affects coloured immigrants to a very limited extent, so it will not be dealt with in detail here. But the overriding principle is that the homeless must in no way be 'encouraged' to throw themselves into the streets; above all they must not by this means jump the queue to the council estate. Obviously certain precautions are reasonable, but as this is an emergency service usually run not by the housing but by the welfare department it is hard to see why such caginess is necessary. Sometimes, the same sort of caginess is displayed by housing departments towards those who are thought to have 'deliberately' put themselves to acute discomfort in order to earn housing points.

The *reductio ad absurdam* of this attitude is contained in the following extract from a letter received by Mr. A. Thomas of 47 Walsall Road, Willenhall, Staffordshire, in April 1963, from the housing manager of Willenhall Urban District Council, Mr. J. E. Pearson: 'As there was insufficient room for your family when you went to live at No. 47 Walsall Road, it appears that you have created the conditions under which you are living and I regret to inform you that while you remain at No. 47 Walsall Road your application cannot be dealt with.'

The identical answer was received a year later by Mr. Thomas in response to his renewed application. He obediently moved from Walsall Road but could only find even more cramped accommodation in an attic, whence he and his family were evicted by the landlord in August

F

1965. By 1966 his friends had lost track of him—he has perhaps returned to Jamaica, where he came from.

If Mr. Thomas had not been coloured, would he have met with the same response? Either way little credit is reflected on the erstwhile Urban District Council of Willenhall, now absorbed into the enlarged borough of Walsall. But a higher standard of government is after all the purpose of creating larger units better suited to the job. If this incident was an example of straight discrimination, it is of a kind unlikely to be found in a large housing department. This is not to say that prejudice never distorts the workings of larger machines. But it may occur in more tortuous, or even accidental, ways. In this sense it may be harder to deal with.

This is primarily a question of administration, which can never be perfect. It is very rare for a local council to produce any declared policy on dealing with coloured tenants. One or two, like Wolverhampton and West Bromwich, have announced that they favour dispersal. But this would be left to the housing manager to implement as he saw fit. It is therefore important to understand the methods used in allotting certain houses to certain people, in order to see where human bias can creep in.

The biggest bias of all is in the basic philosophy of public housing in Britain, still rooted in its nineteenth-century origins. An American critic of the British system has written: 'Housing policy is informed by the Victorian conviction that cleanliness and sanitation will in themselves produce satisfaction, if not saintliness.'[8] Even where policy may recognize that housing must be provided for incorrigible sinners as well as potential saints, practice still separates sheep from goats, clean from dirty.[9] It is as though, in order to prove that nice new houses make nice people, only nice people are permitted to live in them. There is some fact behind the fantasy. Local authorities cannot refuse to house people simply on the suspicion that they

---

[8]   A. L. Schorr, *Slums and Social Insecurity*, London, Nelson, 1964.

[9]   For a racy and by no means inaccurate account of this process, see J. Tucker, *Honourable Estates*, London, Gollancz, 1966.

will make bad tenants, as a private landlord can; but they have, all the same, to balance their books and keep their property in a reasonable state of repair. So they like to know what sort of people they are taking on. They can, and do, evict tenants for persistent arrears even when by so doing they may have to bear the more expensive charge of taking the children into care. To lessen the risk of this their main concern when taking on a new tenant is to make sure, first, that he is given a house he can afford and, second, that the family has a standard of domestic cleanliness which does justice to the council's property.

The principle is simple: a clean person gets a clean house and a dirty person gets a dirty house. In between are all kinds of subtle gradings which are the everyday material of housing management. Quiet, clean, steady-earning families with not more than three children are highly prized because they make life easy for management and their neighbours. They are usually repaid by being put near other 'good' families in better houses. The most unsatisfactory tenants may only get old terraced property awaiting demolition, or rehabilitated as part of the council's permanent stock; or simply one of the shabbier inter-war houses. These are also the cheaper as well as larger properties, so the worse-off tenants, and big families, for instance unskilled workers with several young children, may also be housed there. Those of a lower standard both economically and socially are therefore segregated in public-sector housing in much the same way as they would be on the private market. It is in this context that practices like Birmingham's use of 'patched houses' must be seen.

This tendency is reinforced by the fact that most new council building in the big cities is now in the form of flats with only one or two bedrooms, to make up for the over-supply of three-bedroomed houses in the past. But there is also a shortage of houses for families who need more than three bedrooms—not after all an uncommon requirement—quite apart from the fact that things like spare bedrooms simply do not enter into the local authorities' scheme of things. There is very little building to make up the shortage of four- and five-bedroomed houses, because councils are scared of having to subsidize the occupants too heavily; like so many other faults in housing, only bigger family allowances and/or a system of subsidies paid to people in need rather than housing authorities can put this right. It is easy to see that for many Commonwealth immigrants, with young, growing families and not very large incomes, the chance of a tenancy in one of the newer council estates is not very great, before any question of prejudice comes in.

Where prejudice can and does come in, is at the point of personal contact of the immigrant with the key figure in this process, the 'housing visitor', or 'investigator' (slight variations in title sometimes indicate whether this official is expected to play a mainly passive part, recording facts, or a more active role in assessing and advising the future tenant). Either way, an important element of personal assessment comes into it. The investigator is rarely a trained social worker and the job is generally a low-grade one. Apart from the tenant's own application form, the investigator's report is in most cases the sole raw material from which more senior officials decide placings—unless the applicant is also the subject of a medical or welfare report from another department. Where social workers are employed by housing departments it is generally at a later stage, as support to 'problem' families or others who may have difficulties settling in as a council tenant. But even these workers are rare, and rarely trained. In a very big authority the actual selection of tenants for particular houses may be very far removed from any personal knowledge of them. In very small authorities, the whole process may be done almost single-handed, which also has its disadvantages.

There are great differences in the details required on the form the housing investigator has to complete, but the aim usually seems to be to fill it in as quickly as possible, without allowing much time to bring out special needs or correct misapprehensions. All authorities need to know family size and income, but their bias is reflected in many other facts which may or may not be required. Some are constructive—place of work, baby expected; some cagey—place of birth, date of marriage; or pointed—state of rent book, state of furniture and bedding, any sign of bugs? The more sensitive matters which are supposed to reveal whether this will be a good or bad tenant, such as the rent record, and cleanliness of house and person, are filled in on the spot by observation and judgement. The investigator always asks to see the rent book (if there is one) and those up in the game may respond with something like 'the landlord hasn't been round for a month but I've got the money put away'. Lack of a rent book is sometimes the excuse for a low grading, 'to be on the safe side'; immigrants as a group are less likely to have rent books than tenants as a whole.[10] When it comes to placing an applicant in a category (such as 'good', 'fair', 'poor', or 'undesirable') the scope for bias is wide. Yet on this snap judgement may depend a whole family's future home.

There is, for example, the woman investigator who plainly gives higher marks for new highly polished furniture than for a well-cared-for baby in a shabby cot. There are others who are quite obviously biased, or baffled, or both, in dealing with coloured people, and therefore play safe by giving low marks. As a result it is rare for a coloured family to be placed in a category which qualifies them for a new house. When all the evidence showed a bright, spotless room—and some investigators remark on the efficiency with which West Indian housewives, in particular, cope with the most adverse circumstances—a good mark was sometimes justified with the comment 'Although she's coloured she does seem very clean'. Another favourite comment is: 'The coloured ones are cleaner than the Irish, mind you.' Usually immigrants are not as wise to this status game as English housing applicants. But some have learned, like the Jamaican lady in Brixton who apologized for the crumbs the children had left on the floor, saying:

[10] Landlords are legally obliged to provide tenants with a book stating the rent and recording payments. But not all do so. See Chapter V, p. 123, n. 12.

'You don't get a house if you're dirty, do you?' and then went on to explain her respectable status: 'Lots of my aunties are sisters and teachers.'

Another reason given for the placing of coloured tenants in older property, especially when it is non-purpose-built terraced property in some twilight district far from the housing estate, is that the person concerned has expressed a preference for this. There are many reasons why this 'choice' may be a genuine one. But one has one's doubts after hearing several interviews which go something like this:

Housing Investigator: Now, if we offer you a house where would you like to go?

Mrs. Macaulay Brown: Oh, almost any place, we're mad to move from here.

H.I.: But I've got to put your preference on the form. Would you like somewhere central?

Mrs. M. P.: Yes, but——

H.I.: Somewhere near here?

Mrs. M. B.: Yes, I suppose so.

H.I.: It may be a house like this one, only all to yourself, your own front and back door. Is that all right?

Mrs. M. B.: Yes, please, all right.

A local person invariably responds quite differently, knowing the various estates by name and reputation, wanting specifically to be near a mother or sister, or on the bus route to work. Local knowledge as much as anything else may explain why when coloured families are found on conventional estates the wife is often English—she knew the answers.

As with other social services, the immigrant is often handicapped not only by ignorance and linguistic difficulties, but by the very insecurity of his present situation. Families in furnished rooms may move every few months, and unless they inform the housing department each time they will miss the call (sometimes deliberately unannounced) of the housing investigator—an essential preliminary to the offer of a tenancy.

Personal preferences are only one factor in the allocation of tenancies. The choice at any one time is limited, and is further narrowed by what is thought suitable for that tenant. In the case of coloured tenants another factor may be introduced—how tolerant are the neighbours? Housing management is frequently unwilling to risk trouble on the more 'respectable' estates, or in new blocks of high flats, even if racial tolerance there has never been put to the test. One housing manager in the West Midlands justified it like this: 'I wouldn't put coloured people on a new estate mixed up with all the young couples. It's got to go slowly. Better to start them off among the older people who are more tolerant.'

Exceptions are sometimes made for coloured candidates of dazzling respectability. In London, a G.L.C. housing visitor of many years' experience recollected that in her area:

We did once put a coloured couple from a slum clearance scheme straight into a new estate, but they were exceptional— he was *very* well educated, training to be a lawyer. There was a fuss at first, people wrote on their door and so on. But now he's the one who does nothing but complain about his neighbours, saying they break the rules of the estate.

The further one goes into suburbia, the more do council estates adopt suburban attitudes of self-conscious respectability—with the exception of certain overspill estates which have rather defiantly gone to seed. A complex history of uneasy decanting of population from city to suburb helps to explain why the council estate does not appear to be of much service so far in dispersing immigrants into suburbia. A central London housing official put it this way:

I ring up my opposite number in [an outer London district] and say 'I've got a very nice family for you, the Ks.' He says 'That sounds Cypriot and we've had two Cypriot families from you already.' *Two*, for Christ's sake, when we've got hundreds! But they don't like anything that doesn't sound true British.

Because of this difficulty, real and imaginary, in placing coloured families and (evidently) other 'foreigners' these families tend to get pigeon-holed into the 'problem' category, although they may have nothing at all in common with 'problem families' in the social sense—the unstable or ne'er-do-wells who may need special handling. It is significant that when the G.L.C. first started taking housing 'quotas' from the London boroughs, some boroughs saw this as a fine opportunity to get their coloured families housed for them in exactly the same way as they were also trying to include what the G.L.C. regarded as an unfair share of difficult and unreliable white families in the quota. A familiar issue in housing management is how far to segregate the social problems into old property where they disturb mainly each other. No authority does not practice such segregation to some degree, whether deliberately or not. Any housing visitor can show you the 'problem corner' —and there, like as not, will also be seen coloured faces. This is sometimes openly justified on grounds that people who are themselves of low status will not object to coloured neighbours as much as will 'normal' people.

Unmarried mothers, who are not uncommon among West Indian immigrants or among English girls with coloured babies, may also be judged suitable only for the company of others who do not conform to accepted standards. Another factor linking colour with a 'low-grade' housing classification is that English girls who marry or cohabit with coloured men may, in a chain of social reaction, be unstable or of low intelligence. They may themselves be the cause of 'problem' families in the normal sense, if that is not a contradiction in terms. Without having any statistics on the subject, one can only record that where housing departments mentioned a coloured family that had found it hard to cope with life in a council house, this nearly always turned out to be a mixed marriage. Because the wife's origin may make it easier for a mixed family to qualify for a house than if both partners were immigrants, it is possible that difficult 'mixed' families are over-represented among coloured council tenants.

This would bolster up the determination to treat coloured tenants very gingerly.

Council houses have so far been of much less use than council mortgages in helping the dispersal of coloured people from the decayed city core in a suburban direction. At a guess, however, on the rare occasions when coloured families are found right outside any town of original immigrant settlement, it will be because they have moved on to an overspill estate or even—more rarely still because of the skills involved—through an industrial selection scheme into a new or expanded town. Nevertheless, the general rule is that the further a council estate is from the city centre (unless it is a brand new estate on a cleared site) the less likely it will be to contain a coloured family. And of all types of housing, council estates are the most likely to contain no immigrants at all—for the reasons outlined above.

There remains the question, which unfortunately cannot be answered very thoroughly here, of how far the various ethnic groups among Commonwealth and other immigrants feel any desire to inhabit council estates. Like so many other things, this can more or less be summed up in relation to their desire to adopt English working-class habits. It must to some extent be modified by their apparently very strong desire to own their own houses, discussed in Chapter II, and in this their feelings are echoed by growing numbers of English workers. Some further guesses about this are made in Chapter VIII, in the light of observations made in Nottingham and Wolverhampton. Sheer ignorance of the council house system is still perhaps the biggest deterrent to immigrants to trying to take advantage of the system; local contrasts are enormous in this respect.

It is reasonable to discern a contrast in attitude between West Indian and other coloured immigrants, since West Indians are already more anglicized when they arrive. Research carried out by Mr. Michael Lyon in Bristol shows, as might be expected, that the West Indians who choose to go to council estates and say they are happy there, are the ones who were keenest to be assimilated in the first place.[11]

It still remains supremely important that council houses should be readily available for immigrants who otherwise would continue to live and raise families in the worst possible surroundings; and that those who have the right to a council tenancy on equal terms with their white neighbours should not automatically be thrust into low-grade accommodation. What scrappy evidence there is suggests that the absorption of ordinary coloured families into ordinary council estates is a less prickly process than nervous authorities fear. It is depressing and alarming that both councillors and administrators seem agreed to put the least possible strain on tolerance—rather than going ahead impartially, and dealing with trouble-makers firmly.

[11] Under the auspices of the Institute of Race Relation's Survey of Race Relations in Britain.

IV | Abroad Begins at Aldgate

East London is one of the world's great entrepôts; its bones are the docks, canals, railways, trunk roads and goods yards on which the flesh of social capital lies thin. It is also a workshop to the huge consumer market of the metropolis, a function which today has dwindling import-ance in that market as a whole but which is still the essence of life in the oldest and most congested parts of the East End. Both these functions depend, as they have always done, on the life and labour of the poor. And of these poor, a substantial minority have always been foreign-born. Indigence and immigration have long been co-terminous in the East End and have remained so because, on the whole, anyone who can get on gets out. In spite of its huge post-war rebuilding programme, if one had to name one London borough which displays the marked character of an under-privileged urban community, it would be Tower Hamlets, formed in 1965 out of the three metropolitan boroughs of Stepney, Poplar, and Bethnal Green.

Much history and sociology has been writted about the East End—indeed among its immigrant population might be numbered a floating army of chroniclers and case-workers. The story is familiar enough to be kept brief here. The worst problems of the borough are concentrated in its western end, right next door to the nine-to-five white-collar world of the City of London. This area is above, below and between the confluence of the Mile End and Commercial Roads. It is not only the traditional home of successive waves of immigrants; much of it was originally created by them. The Jews who came to England from

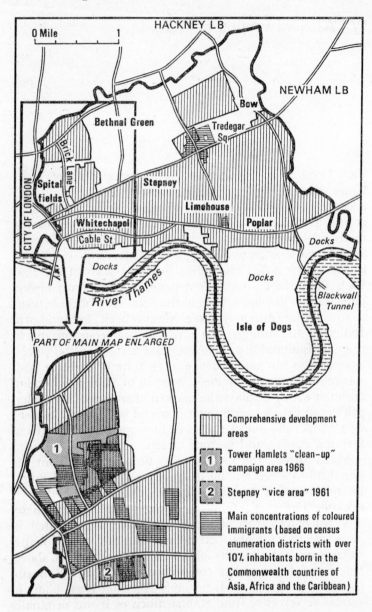

HACKNEY LB

0 Mile   1

NEWHAM LB

Bow

Tredegar Sq.

Bethnal Green

Brick Lane

Spital fields

CITY OF LONDON

Stepney

Limehouse

Poplar

Whitechapel

Cable St

Docks

Docks

Docks

River Thames

Blackwall Tunnel

Isle of Dogs

PART OF MAIN MAP ENLARGED

1

2

Comprehensive development areas

Tower Hamlets "clean-up" campaign area 1966

Stepney "vice area" 1961

Main concentrations of coloured immigrants (based on census enumeration districts with over 10% inhabitants born in the Commonwealth countries of Asia, Africa and the Caribbean)

I. London Borough of Tower Hamlets

1655 onwards settled outside the walls of the City of London and set up their businesses to avoid apprenticeship to Christians.[1] Also in the late seventeenth century came the Huguenot silk weavers who settled in newly developed Spitalfields.[2] In the eighteenth century, while some of the houses were still almost new, the area degenerated into poverty, where it has remained ever since. By 1749 houses were divided into lodgings. In 1797 a soup kitchen was opened in Brick Lane and ran for nearly a century.[3] It was Spitalfields, Whitechapel, and the contiguous parish of St. George's in the East which in the nineteenth century housed refugees from the Irish famine and the Central and East European pogroms, as well as Germans, Scandinavians, Chinese, and a host of other foreigners.

They were only a minority, however, among the many who flocked from the English provinces seeking work in the capital—work which was intermittent, casual, and miserably paid. By the time Charles Booth conducted his famous survey[4] in the 1880s, the East End was a byword for sweated industries of the most appalling kind, run on the poorest immigrant and female labour, often working for immigrant masters. The clothing and furniture trades, both component industries fragmented into many separate operations, wove themselves into the life of Stepney and Bethnal Green. Here they still remain—and to root them up is like rooting up ground ivy. The many small factories and slummy workshops, together with the wholesale and street markets, and the shops, pubs, and cafés that go with them, are so meshed in with living quarters in the western part of the borough that redevelopment is a planner's nightmare, postponed as long as can be.

It is in this area that today's immigrants, like those of

[1] P. G. Hall, *The Industries of London since 1861*, London, Hutchinson University Library, 1962.

[2] F. H. W. Sheppard (ed.), *The Survey of London*, Vol. XXVII, London 1961, Athlone Press for London County Council, p. 4.

[3] *Survey of London*, Vol. XXVII, p. 126.

[4] Charles Booth and others, *Life and Labour of the People in London*, London, Macmillan, first published 1889 and 1891; references to 1902 edition.

the past, are mainly concentrated. Indeed it has been demonstrated[5] that the most self-contained group of immigrants today—the Pakistanis—are living precisely in those streets where Jewish immigrants concentrated in the late nineteenth century, and where Huguenots had lived before them. But it is important to realize that, in sheer numbers, immigrants in the East End in the 1960s are nothing like so significant as those of sixty to eighty years previously, although they appear more clearly in the shrunken population. And even the streets with the largest proportions of immigrants do not match up to the concentrations of some other parts of London today. Although the influence of past immigration is strongly apparent—in the synagogues and kosher shops, in the strong Catholic faction in local politics —the more recent arrivals are merely the top of a complex ethnic pyramid which already exists, which is indeed the essence of the East End.

The census of 1881 revealed 21,500 or 5 per cent of the inhabitants of Tower Hamlets born outside the British Isles, as compared with 12,900 and 6 per cent in 1961. The peak population was reached in 1901, when Stepney alone had a population of 298,600 of whom 18 per cent were born overseas. In the twentieth century the population of Tower Hamlets has steadily declined, drastically accelerated by the blitz and the evacuation of the Second World War. The population in 1961 was 205,682, compared with 488,521 in 1931.

In 1961 the three boroughs which now make up Tower Hamlets contained a wide range of people born outside Great Britain (see Table 5).

Of these boroughs, Stepney had by far the biggest proportion of foreign-born population, although this was less than half the proportion of the 'bed-sitter' boroughs of Paddington, Kensington and Hampstead.[6] It will be seen that the identifiable coloured population was very small—under 3·5 per cent of the total. Allowances must be made for under-

---

[5] Kenneth Leech, in Institute of Race Relations *Newsletter*, July 1965.
[6] *London's Housing Needs*, p. 67.

TABLE 5

ORIGIN OF MAIN IMMIGRANT GROUPS: TOWER HAMLETS, 1961

Living in Metropolitan Borough of	Population born in:										Total Population
	Ireland	Cyprus	Malta	India	Paki-stan	Other Asian Coun-tries	Africa not S. Africa	West Indies	Poland	Russia	
Bethnal Green	515	282	137	173	86	25	52	356	249	347	47,078
Poplar	6,039	164	128	236	799	185	23	1,171	109	66	66,604
Stepney	2,362	698	770	905	885	296	443	1,599	1,742	2,247	92,000
TOTALS:	8,916	1,144	1,035	1,314	1,770	506	518	3,126	2,000	1,660	205,682

Source: 1961 Census

enumeration, especially of Pakistanis. It was noted in 1881
that foreigners in Stepney were under-enumerated owing
to their living conditions, and this has remained true.
Stepney contained only seventeen census enumeration districts, with an identifiable 'coloured commonwealth' population of over 10 per cent, compared with forty-seven such
districts in nearby Hackney and fifty-six in Lambeth.[7]
Poplar and Bethnal Green had no such districts. Bethnal
Green has always been a much more settled, self-contained
community. Much of Poplar (10 per cent Irish-born population) is literally isolated. Charles Booth in the 1880s
heard of inhabitants of 'the Island' who had never seen St.
Paul's. Remoteness is often the fate of dockside communities, and similar characteristics until recently prevailed in
Wapping, in south Stepney. The Poplar–Stepney border,
around Limehouse, has traditionally been London's 'China-
town', although redevelopment has much affected this
community. West Indians, the biggest single coloured
group, numbered little over 3,000 in 1961, and are to be
found not only in the traditional, western, 'immigrant
quarter' but also off the Mile End Road around Tredegar
Square and in Bow—demonstrating the eastward drift that
takes so many Cockneys out to the Essex side of London.
The West Indians are not all that thick on the ground. In
January 1967 the greatest number of West Indian children
in any one school was sixty—at a Secondary school in
Poplar.[8]

The most concentrated and least integrated group of
immigrants in Tower Hamlets are the Pakistanis. They
are the modern heirs, economically as well as residentially,
of the nineteenth-century East European Jews; they too
find work in the rag trade and other low-grade occupations;
they too have their own language, their own shops, eating
habits and religion. They even echo the Jewish passion for
gambling noted by Beatrice Webb. Just to illustrate the
way one ethnic group slots neatly into the hole left by the

previous one, it is worth recording that the headquarters
of the Pakistani Friends League in Fournier Street, Spitalfields, is in an eighteenth-century house originally associated with a French Huguenot church and school and later
with the synagogue and strict Jewish school which succeeded the church.[9] The census of Pakistanis was certainly
an undercount, but in spite of its rapid increase stimulated
by fear of the Commonwealth Immigrants Act of 1963, the
community is still notable more for its concentration than
its numbers.

A more recent count showed that on the voters' roll in
1964—soon after Pakistani leaders had encouraged registration—there were four polling districts in Stepney where
Muslim and Sikh names accounted for over 10 per cent of
the totals.[10] In one polling district the figure was nearly
20 per cent—438 Asian names out of 2,192 on the roll. In
this area (centring on Brick Lane, although Brick Lane
itself has more Irish than coloured inhabitants) the two
most 'Asian' streets were Princelet Street, with 61 per cent
Sikh and Muslim names, and Old Montague Street, with
44 per cent. The Pakistanis are mainly single men from a
few Bengal villages and live closely controlled by their own
village elders. Recently some of them have been bringing
over their young sons, presumably to avoid the immigration
ban at the age of 16—the life which some of these boys
live, often doing chores for a houseful of men rather than
going to school, has given concern to social workers. This
is closely connected with the actual housing conditions of
this group, of which more will be said later.

Other immigrant groups which have received unflatter-
ing attention from time to time include the Maltese and
the Somalis—the latter being one among several small but
distinct groups of African immigrants in Stepney. The
attitude towards the Maltese and the various coloured
groups in Stepney is inseparable from the attitude towards

[9] *Survey of London*, Vol. XXVII, p. 222.
[10] Kenneth Leech, 'The Role of Immigration in Recent East London History', article in *Cosmos* (published by the Royal Foundation
of St. Catherine, London, E.14), Summer 1966.

G

the squalid environment in which they live, which is no more and no less than the centuries-old character of the neighbourhood. The post-war notoriety of parts of Stepney as neighbourhoods of vice and violence echo the background to the Gordon Riots and Jack the Ripper. Some immigrants have been, and are, closely associated with the profits of vice; many more are not. The significance of this will be discussed later. In the context of this book, and because these things are the product of an environment which encourages social disintegration, it is important to look closer at the environment of the borough of Tower Hamlets and the steps being taken to improve it or to remove people from its worst spots.

Very poor physical conditions and a gross shortage of sanitation are the keynote of private housing in Tower Hamlets (and some of the older public housing is not much better). The faults reflect the fact that most of the borough was developed to Victorian standards of working-class requirements. Except in the parts of Spitalfields, Mile End, and Bow, built at an earlier period when the East End was still respectable for sea captains and merchants, there are few houses conceived on a spacious scale; these few are mostly hopelessly decayed or used for purposes other than housing, although there are rare spots of recent rehabilitation. The mid-nineteenth-century 'working man's cottage' was superseded by dense, grim, tenement flats built by charitable and not-so-charitable private enterprise. Although intended as model dwellings, even at the time the low space standards and communal facilities of most of these aroused misgivings; so did the effect of redevelopment on this scale without heed to the people displaced. Booth's survey noted:

The model blocks do not necessarily . . . provide for the *actual* displaced population, so much as for an equivalent number of others, sometimes of a different class . . . the 'reclamation' of part of Flower and Dean Street and Thrawl Street, in Spitalfields, by the erection of the Lolesworth and Rothschild Buildings, has had the result of causing part of the semi-criminal class who haunt those streets to transfer their haunts, and with them the supremacy in evil repute, across Commercial Street to Dorset Street and its surrounding alleys.[11]

Not, somehow, such an old-fashioned theme. Will the same thing be said when this very site is redeveloped, according to current plans, in 1972?

More private tenements, and local authority blocks of equally utilitarian design, formed the bulk of building in this part of London between the wars. In the post-war era, stimulated by the devastation of the blitz which reduced the inhabited houses in Stepney alone by one-third,[12] public house-building has been active. In 1966, the publicly owned housing stock of the borough, about 60 per cent of all dwellings, was as follows:

TABLE 6

PUBLIC HOUSING STOCK: TOWER HAMLETS, 1966

G.L.C. figures as at 31 December 1966,
Tower Hamlets Borough Council figures as at 1 May 1966

Pre-1945 purpose-built council estates:

G.L.C.	4,292
T.H.B.C.	3,193

Post-1945 purpose-built:

G.L.C.	15,115
T.H.B.C.	7,098

Acquired (including conversions):

G.L.C.	3,853*
T.H.B.C.	2,485

Temporary (prefabs., mobile homes):

G.L.C.	969
T.H.B.C.	approx. 300

TOTAL:	37,305

* Including dwellings acquired for clearance.

---

[11] *Life and Labour*, Vol. III, pp. 79–80.
[12] D. L. Munby, *Industry and Planning in Stepney*, London, Oxford University Press, 1951, p. 85.

By 1967, there were 13,854 old terraced houses acknowledged by the authorities as slums, and on top of that 8,166 tenement dwellings unfit or in need of modernization (the proportion in each category being subject to dispute). The low amenity standard is recorded by the 1961 Census. Over half the households in Stepney and Poplar had no access to a bath; over 60 per cent of the households in Stepney and Bethnal Green lacked or shared at least one of the four basic amenities (hot and cold water, bath and W.C.). Eight per cent of households in Stepney lived in shared dwellings without exclusive use of either stove or sink. Overcrowding was a still more serious problem; 16.2 per cent of Stepney's population lived at over $1\frac{1}{2}$ persons per room, and these were concentrated in certain areas. The worst overcrowding was concentrated in the extreme west of the borough, and only partially coincided with the main areas of comprehensive redevelopment.

The horror stories which lie behind these statistics paint a picture of rottenness, filth, and unhealthiness which can scarcely be exaggerated. (A man who had been chief city-planner for Chicago, who was shown Spitalfields by the author, could not believe his eyes.) It goes without saying that the immigrant is likely to suffer as much as anybody. Two examples must serve here. In 1966 a social worker made the following report on an Indian family in Burselm Street, Stepney (due for redevelopment in about 1970):

The A.s live in the basement of a dilapidated shop with their four children aged fourteen, four, two, and six months, where they have been since 1963. Down a narrow dark flight of stairs they have two small rooms; one, the kitchen, has a small window and contains the only running water and cooking facilities for the house, which is shared by about ten other Indians, mostly single men. The fourteen-year-old sleeps in this room. The other room has no window or ventilation, the ceiling is slatted, stuffed with dust and part of it falling down, the plaster on the walls has come away, leaving holes, and there are several holes in the lino in the floor which Mrs. A. fears to be verminous. The two middle children and their parents share a double bed, the baby sleeps in a home-made wooden cot. There is an inadequate toilet in the back yard, which is also shared by the rest of the house . . . None of them have very much sleep . . . Mr. A. is unable to keep a job . . . the eldest boy was in hospital at the beginning of the year and recently Mrs. A. took an overdose . . .

Six months later no appeal to any public department had succeeded in closing this basement or rehousing the occupants. The most that could be hoped was that the G.L.C. would accept responsibility once their compulsory purchase order had been confirmed (not before mid-1967).

The second description (dated October 1966) is admittedly that of a pressure group, the tenants' association of an old tenement block, Blackwall Buildings, Whitechapel. But it is not an exaggeration of the conditions in many of these blocks. The tenants complained of excessive damp, dry rot, vermin, falling plaster, broken windows, and bad wiring in the majority of flats. Twenty unlit wash-houses were the sole source of water for 156 flats. There were two families to each W.C. Most cisterns and bowls were broken, and most doors without locks so that tramps slept and drunks vomited freely in them. Stair-rails and roof-rails were broken. Rubbish spilled from the chute on to the stairs. There was allegedly no fire security. This block stands on a site zoned for open space and loosely programmed '1972-2005'. It is unlikely to get any priority for clearance. The G.L.C. did not in 1966 even classify it as a slum, since despite the conditions it comes up to certain standards of space and light. Yet it is hardly an environment in which to bring up not just this generation but the next.

Conditions in west Stepney are part and parcel of an environment whose worst features vie for publicity with each other: where yesterday the campaign was waged on 'vice and prostitution', today it is 'drugs and meths. drinkers'. Blackwall Buildings is only a block away from the area covered by the 'Tower Hamlets Clean Up Association' (see map on p. 80) which centres on Brick Lane, and is also the centre of Pakistani settlement. This area in 1967 bore something of the notoriety of the Cable Street 'vice area' of a few years previously (see the same map), for much the same reasons. The 'clean-up' campaigners, at a meeting with the Mayor on 18 October 1966, complained of late-night cafés; soliciting; debris and chaotic street parking from the 'Club Row' market which invades the narrow streets every Sunday; and the perennial meths. drinkers. The meths. men live in derelict sites and by day sit in a small public garden consequently known as 'itchy park'. A local church which opened its crypt to sleep and disinfest the meths. drinkers was refused help by the borough council; it is presumed because of the fear that to offer any such facility would attract more derelicts into the area.

This is just one example of a recurring attitude which has an important bearing on housing policy: the belief that people in wretched circumstances will simply disappear if you do not take any notice of them; and whatever you do you must not 'encourage' them. The homeless are a case in point. Since April 1965, when Tower Hamlets, along with the other London boroughs, took responsibility for the first time for the homeless within its boundaries, its main desire has been to administer a 'tough' policy of recognizing as few homeless people as possible and therefore cutting down the number to be provided for and the places available for them. By devising stringent rules this policy was successful, and homelessness artificially 'reduced' to under half the rate of early 1965.

This was hard on any homeless family that could not prove at least a month's residence in the borough and pass various other tests. What about the effect on 'immigrants' in the sense of this book? In late 1966, out of the seventy-odd places still provided for homeless families in the borough, it was roughly estimated that about a quarter were occupied by coloured families. They frequently became homeless through eviction as illegal sub-tenants. Because of their notorious fondness for risky oil-stoves (often the only way to heat a rented room), coloured people were more likely than other groups to come into the 'catastrophe' category of homelessness which must be treated as genuine and is not regarded with the same degree of suspicion as other kinds. A recently burnt-out house had, for example, contained five coloured families and one Irish. Given the general policy of providing the minimum for the homeless, there seems to be no particular reluctance to deal with coloured homeless as such; indeed some officials and social workers regard them as more reliable prospects than other groups.

'Jumping the housing queue' is a crime of which homeless people tend to be suspected, and this applies to other types of misfortune too. Tower Hamlets Council seem to see this villainy lurking behind every basement door. For years the former Stepney Borough Council virtually ceased to enforce closing orders on unfit basements of the kind described on page 88 and the policy is being perpetuated in the new borough. In 1965 there were 1,500 underground rooms used for sleeping or living in the borough, of which fifteen had been closed in the year. Most of these had been recognized as unfit since the 1930s. Any rehousing commitment is avoided as far as possible, and there is the additional fear that once a basement is emptied and officially 'closed' there is still no certainty that another family will not be allowed in by the landlord and again expect to be rehoused.

The same attitude governs action on other public health aspects of housing, such as multiple occupation. This is all the more so since the borough assumed responsibility for the homeless and therefore does nothing to cause homelessness by its own action. Thus the health inspectors have instructions to go very easy with Section 19 of the 1961 Housing Act (which forbids a landlord to take new tenants above an approved number for the house) but, in the case of houses full of single men for whom there is no housing or welfare responsibility, to be quite strict with Section 90 of the 1957 Act—which forces the landlord to get rid of excess numbers by eviction. For fear that the Council will be forced to do work in default, there is no attempt to make landlords install extra amenities instead of getting rid of tenants. The Pakistani houses in Spitalfields are frequently the scene of 'pyjama raids'—midnight swoops by the in-

spectors to count illegitimate heads.[13] In fact this activity
is entirely limited to Asian houses, just as prosecutions of
landlords for offences under the Housing Acts have so far
always been of coloured and Maltese landlords—mainly
Pakistanis.

TABLE 7

TOWER HAMLETS HOUSING ACT PROSECUTIONS:
APRIL 1965–NOVEMBER 1966

	Pak.	W. In-dian	Maltese	Chinese	Total
Offence committed under:					
1961 Act: breach of management regulations	12	4	1	–	17
1961 Act: Sect. 19	1	1	1	–	3
1957 Act: Sect. 90	17	1	–	1	19
TOTAL:	30	6	2	1	39

Source: Tower Hamlets Health Department.

One can admit that many bad landlords are coloured
immigrants whilst still finding it hard not to smell discrimination here, comparable (on a much smaller scale)
with that recorded in Birmingham.

The West Indian landlord who offends is often in the
familiar position of being forced into buying a house too
big for his own needs—one of those in the Bow Road, or

[13] The health inspectors have less fine feelings than their predeces-
sors a hundred years ago. The Medical Officer to the Vestry of St.
George in the East, Stepney, reported in 1867–8: 'Great difficulty has
been found in endeavouring to frame regulations for houses let in
lodgings or occupied by more than one family under the 35th Section
of the Sanitary Act 1866, which whilst enabling the Officers of the
Vestry to bestow the necessary supervision, would not allow unnecessary interference or undue trespassing upon the privacy of the inhabitants.'

Tredegar Square, for example—and then having to take
tenants to pay off a heavy mortgage or rental. For instance,
one West Indian fined £120 in November 1966 for failing
to do repairs required by the health department had the
following budget: cost of lease, £500; rent of house, £550
p.a.; rates, £247 p.a.; weekly wage, £13; weekly rent from
twenty people in five tenancies, £15. Assuming cash had
been paid for the lease, this left only £659 p.a. gross for
the owner to keep his own family and maintain the house.

Such expedients are forced on immigrants by the acute
shortage of private rented accommodation of any kind in
east London, and by the extra handicap of colour prejudice
in many of the slightly more desirable areas. A typical issue
of the local paper in late 1966 had 397 inches of classified
advertisements of jobs vacant and only twenty-three inches
of accommodation to let: of these, a third specified 'no
coloured' (counting five which preferred Jews) and a third
of the remainder specified, or implied a preference for,
people without children. In these circumstances a council
house is often the only hope for decent accommodation.
Just how remote a hope is this?

Since April 1965, the London boroughs at least have had
to open their housing lists to anyone who wishes to apply.
Before then, Bethnal Green had for some years tacitly closed
its list in order to deal exclusively with slum clearance.[14]
The attitude of the former Stepney Borough Council is
implicit in a council memorandum of 1964:

Many families [in the borough] come from Scotland, the
North of England, from Northern Ireland and from the Commonwealth countries. These families obviously do not qualify
for accommodation from the Council, and as a consequence
may have to reside in overcrowded furnished accommodation
paying, in many cases, a high rent for such accommodation . . .
In the case of Pakistanis the greater number would appear to
be young single men who are quite content to live two, three or
four to a room in houses in multiple occupation.

[14] D. V. Donnison, V. Chapman, and others, *Studies in Social Administration*, London, Allen and Unwin, 1965.

In March 1967 there were 7,500 applicants on the Tower Hamlets waiting list. It was assumed, because this was open to all and the list was new in 1965, that this was an up-to-date indication of housing need. But was this really so, when so little prospect was held out of getting a tenancy that many must have been totally discouraged? And when five years' residence in the borough itself was necessary before qualifying at all for housing points? Tower Hamlets did not fall in with the majority of London boroughs who require only one year's residence in the borough and five spent in Greater London as a whole. Explanation from a senior Tower Hamlet councillor: 'We've got all sorts of immigrants coming in and they're not all very desirable people.'

The borough at least has the chance to dispose of some of its less 'desirable people' through the quota of tenancies granted by the G.L.C. to each of the London boroughs which need housing help. Since April 1965 the G.L.C. has had no housing list of its own, but accepts a limited number of nominations from the boroughs and also relieves them of some of their socially or medically needy cases. Special allocations are made in this way for homeless families, 'problem' families, and families which might break up owing to their living conditions. Similar 'special quotas' are generally operated in the allocation of borough tenancies too. When, as in Tower Hamlets, the majority of the borough's own efforts are being turned towards rehousing people from redevelopment sites, the G.L.C. allocation and the specific routes of the 'special quotas' become jealously watched; it was interesting to find that by early 1967 political control over the process was being tightened in Tower Hamlets by the new requirement that all the committees concerned approve each name that went forward.

In 1966–7, only 220 families were housed from Tower Hamlets' waiting-list, compared with eighty-five from the various special quotas, and 618 from clearance areas which were the borough's responsibility (the G.L.C. cleared many more). A specimen list of new tenancies prepared for the Housing Committee (which sees the name and address in every case) in the winter of 1966–7 reveals that, although Tower Hamlets runs a 'points' system which is supposed to indicate priority according to need, it is purely notional. Quite clearly the availability of certain types of accommodation is the governing factor. The building programme and the conversion of old property provides mainly one- and two-bedroom flats. This makes statistical sense but should be accompanied by a much stronger effort to transfer existing tenants out of under-used larger dwellings. At present, if any family needs more than three bedrooms (as 500 on the waiting list in early 1967 did), it has to amass far more than the average points before it can be housed. There is no meaningful average when a childless couple are given a one-bedroomed flat after gaining only fifteen points, and while a family of seven had 129 points when they were at last given a four-bedroomed flat. This bears hard on many immigrants—Cypriots, Maltese, West Indians, and Irish all tend to have large families.

Housing immigrants has so far been almost entirely a G.L.C. affair. The G.L.C. is by far the bigger housing authority in this part of London, and has borne the brunt of the more densely occupied clearance sites. In contrast, the residential qualifications of the borough and its selection of redevelopment sites have not brought it many immigrant tenants. A senior official, in 1966, guessed that at most a dozen coloured families were borough tenants. Even if he was wrong the low estimate is revealing. Some West Indians were expected to be rehoused from sites currently awaiting clearance in north Poplar. Whatever reluctance there is to house immigrants is due to a suspicion of outsiders which has not acquired specifically racial overtones in Tower Hamlets—except in so far as race or colour gets mixed up with the anti-vice campaign, which will be discussed presently. The history of the area must have a lot to do with this. Local hostilities have narrow religious or topographical bounds. The instance is often cited of some old flats in Wapping which the L.C.C. and subsequently the G.L.C. used for housing large families of homeless and 'problem' people, who were thrust into a sort of black sheep's pen. The entire character of the neighbourhood, which was only a few years ago a small solid dockland community, has changed to a neighbourhood known for delinquency and disturbance. The fact that some of the people put there were coloured may have helped to identify coloured families with the rough elements.

But the importance of the episode is that it has confirmed everybody's worst fears about putting 'outsiders' into hitherto unpolluted areas. In this sense immigrants of all kinds may be at a disadvantage in the type of accommodation they are offered; this is impossible to prove without extensive survey, apart from the knowledge that the less attractive pre-war estates are simply those where immigrants are more in evidence—though again, the size of their families and incomes may be the deciding factor. A G.L.C. official says he gets to know the odd spots where definite racial prejudice exists: 'It's like a creaking board, you just learn to step over it.' He also says he has difficulty in getting coloured people to trust him. A good deal of hostility was being expressed as a result of immigrants being housed from clearance areas before local people on the waiting list. Apparently the people who had campaigned against slums of vice and violence had not realized that clearance of the slums meant that at least some of the inhabitants would be rehoused by the Council, even some of those they disapproved of.

Nearly all rehousing revolves around the most extensive slum-clearance programme in London, the great bulk of which (nine-tenths in 1966) is being handled by the G.L.C. In January 1967 one-third of those on the housing waiting list lived within areas due for clearance by the G.L.C. or the borough by 1971. For them the waiting list was a mere dead letter, for the Borough Council had quietly decided not to touch anybody from the list whose home was due for demolition within the current programme. Although there is ample power to rehouse from particularly bad conditions in advance of the clearance programme, both the G.L.C. and the borough are very reluctant to use them. The exceptions are certain tenement flats, which will be discussed later. The G.L.C. does take a more reasonable view than the borough of its rehousing commitment at the point of redevelopment; being prepared to acknowledge that, because large schemes can take years to go through, it is absurd to limit rehousing to people who came into the area at one stage or another of the administrative process. It likes to keep its options open, but roughly speaking no family who has lived in a house for at least a year before it is pulled down by the G.L.C. will be refused. In individual cases the period may be shorter. Tower Hamlets Borough Council, on the other hand, decided after some experiment to rehouse on council estates only those who had occupied their house since the declaration of the clearance area—which could easily be three or four years before demolition. Anyone in residence between that date and the confirmation of the order will be offered a 'half-way house'—such as an un-modernized tenement flat in council ownership. Neither authority rehouses single people from slum clearance, and the borough rarely accepts people from furnished lettings, although since the 1965 Rent Act furnished accommodation has replaced much unfurnished.

There is a good deal of flexibility as to which authority deals with particular sites. It would be perfectly possible for the borough and the G.L.C. to clear two sides of the same street and apply different rehousing criteria to each. Small pockets of slum can be dealt with outside the programme under the public health acts or by a closing order or a demolition order under the 1957 Housing Act. These small-scale operations are normally a borough rather than a G.L.C. responsibility. Closing orders are unpopular with the authorities because they say it is impossible to prevent people breaking in again and using the unfit houses and perhaps having eventually to be rehoused by the Council. Early in 1967 Tower Hamlets Housing Committee was considering a proposal that it should rehouse families only where the Council itself had put a Housing Act order, not where the magistrate had ordered closure under the Public Health Acts—which if implemented would give power to deal with grossly unhealthy conditions whilst ignoring the people suffering from them.

An interesting exception to the dictates of programmed redevelopment has been made in the case of certain Victorian tenement blocks which offer some of the grimmest living conditions in the borough. This is partly the story of pressure-group tactics operated in these blocks, all over inner London, through tenant associations organized by the Communist Party. It is also partly due to the fact that Mr. Robert Mellish, the Labour Government's watchdog on London housing, represents Southwark which also possesses many slum tenements. Tower Hamlets had in 1967 over 8,000 tenement dwellings recognized as substandard, of which the G.L.C. reckoned about half capable of improvement, and the rest suitably only for demolition. The current clearance programme embraced 2,400 of these, of which all but 236 were to be dealt with by the G.L.C. Four hundred more were already subject to clearance procedure. The borough Medical Officer of Health had by now embraced the cause of the tenement dwellings enough to urge that more should be condemned and that 500 be added to the current programme by the borough itself. This contrasts with the Stepney Medical Officer's opinion in the late 1950s, that of the ninety tenement blocks in that borough only one was unfit.

The whole question of the London tenements was by this time being dealt with as a separate programme, outside the slum clearance programme itself. Exceedingly high densities are involved—sometimes over 500 an acre—and this is the main reason for the large G.L.C. participation. However, the G.L.C. did not want to be jumped into management responsibility for the individual blocks before it had to, and was in favour wherever possible of getting together with the landlords to encourage improvements. Tenant pressure had already forced the advance purchase of a particularly notorious block, Grosvenor Buildings, by agreement from the landlord, in 1965. Up to the very last minute tenants were being admitted who wanted to claim rehousing from the G.L.C.: substantial key money was paid by poor families for this privilege. 'Fifty pounds to whites and a hundred to coloureds' was said to be the going rate. Over the years there are terrifying stories of exploitation of desperate people of all kinds by the landlords of some of these blocks, resulting in a large turnover of tenants which left space for immigrants to come in at high rents for the quality of accommodation provided. The 1965 Rent Act has reduced some rents but not improved conditions: it remains to be seen whether the apparent success of the pressure groups in hastening the day of demolition will do much to make life tolerable in the tenement blocks until that day comes; and also whether, as people are gradually rehoused from them, they get anything much better than a near-tenement of an old council flat. The attitude of the authorities to the many 'problem' families in places like Grosvenor Buildings may, unfortunately, rub off on some of their immigrant neighbours even when these have reasonably high standards.

To what extent does the redevelopment programme itself embrace the main pockets of immigrant settlement in Tower Hamlets? This is inseparable from the problems of zoning and density already touched on. The west end of the borough, with the worst overcrowding and the greatest concentration of immigrants—and also the most sordid reputation—derives its character from the intense mixture of uses: shops, cafés, dwellings, markets, factories, workshops, warehouses, churches, synagogues, schools, and slaughterhouses. Zoning involves unscrambling, the antiseptic segregation of uses lamented by Jane Jacobs.[15] Most of western Stepney is, or was in the original post-war plan, zoned for light industry and commerce. There is therefore less priority for redevelopment than in housing areas.

With about half the borough lying within areas planned for almost total redevelopment, and with at least 30 per cent of its housing stock in slums, the biggest lottery of all is the point at which the bulldozer moves in on any par-

[15] Jane Jacobs, *The Death and Life of Great American Cities*, New York, Random House, 1961; London, Jonathan Cape, 1962, and Penguin Books, 1964.

ticular site. When so much of the environment and housing fabric is rotten, a policy of 'worst first' would make hay of any attempt to rebuild according to an efficient programme. Behind this undoubted truth lies many an evasion of responsibility towards smallish pockets of very bad conditions which could be dealt with in advance of general redevelopment, but which nearly always hang fire until they can be brought into an overall scheme. (The history of one of the most notorious of these is related on pages 103-9.) Large-scale planning has a built-in rigidity which does not easily respond to immediate social need.

A large part of the borough (see map on page 80) is embraced by the 1,300-acre comprehensive redevelopment area created by the L.C.C. after the war to deal with the long-term rebuilding of the blitz-shattered districts around the docks.[16] This is still entirely in G.L.C. hands. It has transformed large districts by such famous schemes as the Lansbury estate in Poplar; it is concerned not only with housing but with schools, parks, roads, and relocation of industry and commerce. Because these have lagged behind housing, the extent of new development is masked to the casual passer-by, and its total effect marred by an admixture of old and derelict sites. More recently, two other G.L.C. comprehensive development areas have been declared, in west Bethnal Green and Mile End New Town, making a total of 1,550 acres, or nearly one-third of the borough in which the G.L.C. has the sole planning responsibility. Additional to most of this are the sites earmarked by Tower Hamlets Borough Council for its own housing programme: these are mainly concentrated in north Poplar in a district of small terrace housing containing few actual slums and not as much overcrowding as in the westernmost part of the borough. This was a deliberate choice, so as to give leeway for dealing with the more difficult areas later.

The slum programme is in theory separate from all this, but in practice slums are rarely dealt with until the architects and planners are ready to include the sites in their schemes. Thankfully the authorities can set aside some of

[16] Known as the 'Stepney–Poplar C.D.A.'.

the most densely crowded streets in the borough for the time being. Thankfully they can put off the day when they have to pay £250,000 per acre for acquiring mixed commercial sites (this was the figure paid by the G.L.C. in the Black Lion Yard area of Whitechapel). And although the 'clean-up' campaigners and others press for action, when action is threatened there may be equally fierce opposition, such as that aroused in Black Lion Yard from the many small shopkeepers, jewellers, and café-proprietors whose premises were being acquired at slum prices and who were unlikely to be able to afford anything the G.L.C. could offer them.[17] Since many of the shops and cafés in this area are owned by Pakistanis, Maltese, and other immigrants, it is worth recording the point that, in the course of improvement of the living conditions of the immigrants in slum areas, the entrepreneurs among them—good and bad alike —may be ruined economically.

It ought to be obvious by now that whether and when particular streets containing particular groups of immigrants are redeveloped depends on large-scale, cumbersome planning factors. Only in response to pressure to divert the machine may arguments be wheeled out which look discriminatory. For example, the local clergy in Spitalfields have long campaigned to get this commercially zoned area declared a slum. The Valuer to the L.C.C. was of the opinion in 1963 that '. . . most of the overcrowding is caused by immigrants who are often used to a different way of life. It does not follow that the houses they occupy are unfit or that their demolition would solve any of the problems [of drugs and prostitution].' True enough. Yet this area, west of Brick Lane, is now acknowledged by borough councillors and officials to be their worst and most neglected district—which they say they must leave for at least ten years because of the overspill it would create. The discovery that one tenement block in the neighbourhood

[17] A shopkeeper who is a tenant, not an owner of his shop, only gets an *ex gratia* payment for loss of business, value of fixtures and fittings, and removal expenses if he is setting up elsewhere. The G.L.C. finds that this usually averages about £500.

H

was occupied at a density of 500 to the acre has been mis-
quoted as though it applied to the whole of Spitalfields.
Yet so great is the admixture of commercial uses that
although Spitalfields has one of the highest ratios of overcrowding in London—28.6 per cent of the 1961 population
lived at 1½ persons per room—the overall density per acre,
66.3 persons, was easily outstripped by the whole of Paddington, Southwark, Kensington, Islington, and Chelsea.

Princelet Street, the majority of whose inhabitants are
Sikhs and Pakistanis, contains numerous small workshops:
it is zoned for commerce and industry and the only section
marked for slum clearance is a tenement block about 150
years younger than the rest of the street. Gradually new
initiatives are being taken. At the time of writing some
limited rezoning in the streets around Christ Church,
Spitalfields, was under consideration which would include
part of Princelet Street and other Pakistani lodgings. The
authorities need not worry about this: they do not rehouse
single men.

Old Montague Street, in nearby Whitechapel, is the
centre of two census districts in which a coloured population of about 20 per cent was counted in 1961; it also has
an old-established Jewish community. By 1967 it was about
half cleared of inhabitants under a G.L.C. redevelopment
scheme. New flats were going up at one end of the street.
There was no doubt of encroaching redevelopment in this
part of cosmopolitan Stepney. Until 1962 Old Montague
Street was the border between a housing redevelopment
area and the commercial zoning adjoining Whitechapel
Road. This would have meant only one side of the street
would be cleared. Then a ministerial decision—against
G.L.C. advice—altered the commerce to housing, thus
bringing the whole street into clearance plans. Such is the
luck of the draw.

Tredegar Square, along the Mile End Road, is a very
different environment from Whitechapel. A rather peaceful, decaying early-nineteenth-century square of fairly large
terrace houses, it has been one of the favourite spots for
West Indian house purchase in Tower Hamlets. Several

eccentrically painted houses and miscellaneous drawn curtains stamp it at once as a coloured neighbourhood. It would certainly look more elegant if all the houses were painted alike. In fact the borough has its eye on Tredegar Square as one of the few neighbourhoods which would repay 'rehabilitation'. As houses come on the market there, the Council buys them. The square is surrounded by the major portion of the sites for the Council's ten-year programme and it will, it is thought, do very nicely when rehabilitated, for old people's flats. So it will, and the flats are badly needed. But what might have been a constructive opportunity for the Council to work with immigrant owners on a 'self-improvement' basis has been lost. It probably never occurred to anybody to try.

The most outstanding occasion when the presence of immigrants did have an effect on redevelopment policy within the borough, it was hardly a flattering association. It also illustrates how the official machine responded to a particularly strong pressure group, and forms a fitting end to this chapter.

Early in 1961 public indignation was focused, not for the first time, on a long, narrow street of low houses, riddled with cafés, shops, and workshops, lying parallel with the docks in Stepney. Outwardly harmless-looking, and typical of dozens of streets in the East End of London, Cable Street, or rather the western section of it and the adjoining alleys and two once elegant squares covering an area of about twenty acres, had acquired a national infamy. Much that went on there then also went on in other streets, had been going on for many years, and still goes on today. Michael Banton's excellent study of the area in the early 1950s analysed precisely how its physical character and location coincided with the mixed, shifting population arising primarily from the docks and secondarily from the facilities, legitimate and illegitimate, catering for seamen and others.[18] Cable Street life was, and still is in early 1967, a café society, and by the late 1950s it was the number of

---

[18] *The Coloured Quarter*, London, Jonathan Cape, 1955.

cafés and the nature of many of them as sources of sex, drugs, and violence that in popular view made Cable Street to vice what Carnaby Street is today to fashion—a reputation which certainly encouraged its exploitation to a degree which had not been apparent a few years earlier. Besides this, most of the buildings also provided living accommodation for many people who could find nothing better and who were bringing up families, surrounded by squalor.

Slums, vice, and colour provided those who were justly indignant about Cable Street with emotionally explosive material, sometimes unscrupulously exploited by popular writers. The following is an extract from a long feature on Cable Street by Beverley Nicholls in the *Sunday Dispatch* of 5 March 1961:

This is a black problem. It is a black problem in more senses than one.

It is black because through all the squalid tangle of this dust-bin drama stalks the figure of the coloured man. Of the tens of thousands of coloured men from all over the Commonwealth who have flocked to the shelter of the Welfare State.

This is the land of liberty and the vast majority of decent citizens, from a racial point of view, are 'colour-blind'. But—and it is a big, black, BUT—is there such a thing as being a little too colour-blind?

Too blind to the fact that there are practically no checks on the other end to this swirling flood of immigrants.

Nobody at the gang plank to put his hand on the shoulder of a convicted criminal and say 'Just a minute mate. You're a ponce. And you've got quite a record for robbery with assault. Do you think the Queen of England really wants you?'

This sort of racist talk helped to pass the Commonwealth Immigration Act a year later. But the truth remained that many immigrants, of all colours, were both exploiters and exploited in Cable Street. Maltese had a particularly bad name: in August 1961, of thirty-five recent convictions for living on immoral earnings,[19] twenty-

[19] *The Economist*, 19 August 1961.

seven had been for Maltese. The chief protagonist in the campaign against vice was Father Joe Williamson, the histrionic and determined Anglican priest who became a national figure in his publicity efforts. He and his fellow-campaigners did not mince their words against 'immigrant vice-pedlars' to whom they attributed what they saw as a sudden decline in moral standards. But as it gathered momentum the campaign wisely focused on the indisputably rotten housing and environment. Some of what was said then and since displays a rather naïve equation of physical and moral 'dirt': but the point was that the publicity went home, in the quarters that counted for action.

Whereas to begin with criticism had been directed at the police and the Home Office for failing to control vice and, specifically, for not limiting the number and opening hours of the Maltese cafés, it later concentrated on the L.C.C. in whose redevelopment area the 'vice quarter' lay. No doubt wise to the fact that the Conservatives hoped to win the L.C.C. elections in 1961, Father Joe took Sir Percy Rugg, leader of the L.C.C. Conservative opposition, on a tour of streets of ill-fame which so shocked Sir Percy that he initiated a council debate in March 1961 which lasted all night. The previous month, Father Joe had launched a well-timed bombshell in the London Diocesan Conference which projected the campaign into the heart of the Establishment; bishops, M.P.s and *The Times* joined in. The Minister of Housing soon wanted to know what the L.C.C. and the Borough Council were doing about it.

The situation was precisely that which still exists in parts of Whitechapel and Spitalfields: town planning did not give priority to redevelopment on account of commercial zoning, and very little was being done to clear patches of slum meanwhile. Although the main responsibility lay with the L.C.C. the Borough Council was not blameless, since it had power to deal with slums independently. At this time all London boroughs were guided by the fact that if they cleared less than ten houses in a group, the L.C.C. did the rehousing for them. Consequently they never cleared on a

larger scale. Further complications included the presence
of two sites intended for schools in part of the worst neighbourhood; and indecisiveness over road improvements. If
Cable Street were widened under a 'minor road' scheme
(which would effectively sweep away the offending cafés),
it would be the Borough's responsibility, including the rehousing of occupants. If it were in a major road scheme, the
L.C.C. would do the dirty work.

As the campaign mounted in the early months of 1961,
the first reaction of the L.C.C. officials, after hastily totting
up what they were doing in the area in the way of occasional rehousing, was to point out, truthfully but uncon-
structively, that vice was not invariably associated with
slums and that in fact it was more usual for brothels to be
rather better set up than in Sander Street, where Sir Percy
Rugg had been solicited. However, they got a move on
and by 24 April seventeen houses in Sander Street and fifty-
seven in Pell Street had been cleared. Under pressure from
the Ministry and the Borough Council, the overall plan for
the area was being reconsidered.

A counter-campaign in Stepney Council sought to dissociate the borough as a whole from the 'vice area'. A more
positive line was taken with the L.C.C.—the Borough
even, at one stage, offered to build houses itself on an L.C.C.
housing site adjacent to the 'vice area', so as to rehouse
people from Cable Street. Perhaps it knew there was no
chance of this being accepted. The L.C.C. in fact under-
took to rehouse Cable Street even if the Borough did the
road-widening.

Plans were pushed through hastily and by June 1961 the
L.C.C. announced a revised comprehensive development
scheme for twenty-four acres bounded by Cable Street,
Cannon Street Road, Ensign Street, and the Highway. It
would provide wider streets, 1,400 houses, and two schools.
This seemed a triumph for the campaigners. Father Joe
was photographed kneeling in thanks before a demolished
brothel. His point seemed to have been finally accepted
by the L.C.C. when at the public inquiry into the Compulsory Purchase Order the Council's representative stated:

Redevelopment of the whole land within the Order is imperative to secure the removal of old properties in the area, the continued existence of which has given rise to the unsavoury conditions which have been the subject of so much criticism and publicity in recent years. Nothing but complete clearance and rehousing of all the occupants will effectively secure this.

Yet how is it that in early 1967, six years after the official machine was galvanized into action on Cable Street, the district remains outwardly very much as it has always been? Quieter perhaps—Brick Lane is the new focus of vice-spotters, and some Cable Street cafés have reopened up there. But as far as the houses and many of their occupants are concerned, Cable Street is little changed. The answer to this lies in the unconscionable time it takes to mount a large Compulsory Purchase Order, especially when many small owners are to be traced and treated with—even though demolition can proceed while compensation arguments go on. In this case some owners, once immigrants themselves, had retired to more salubrious parts of London and almost lost interest. They had to be given time to raise objections. A complex net of sub-letting had also to be penetrated. Notices had to be personally served on occupants as well as owners: these too were not always easy to identify. On top of all this, the Architect's Department had to fit in their own building plans to the revised planning schedule. These, for one thing, were hampered by a contractor's bankruptcy on the adjacent Crowder Street site, which logically had to be completed before work could go on to the next neighbourhood. None of these things excuse, but they do help to explain, the following time-table:

June 1961   L.C.C. announce decision to rezone, redevelop for housing.

July 1962   Resolution passed by Council to acquire the land in the last and biggest Compulsory Purchase Order in the redevelopment area, covering the west end of Cable Street and the west side of Swedenborg Square (known as the 'Grace's Alley Compulsory Purchase Order'). Cost: £600,000.

September 1963 Compulsory Purchase Order made: submission to Ministry for approval.

September 1964 Public inquiry held before Ministry of Housing Inspector. Thirty-three objections heard.

August 1965 Order confirmed by Ministry of Housing.

September 1965 Rezoning inquiry (change from commercial to residential) held.

December 1965 Notices served on owners and occupiers. G.L.C. Housing Department investigates rehousing needs and eligibility.

December 1966 G.L.C. architect obtains extended contract from Crowder Street site to enable continuity of development in Cable Street.

Sched. January 1968 Work to start on first new block of flats.

August 1968 Demolition complete.

? ? ? Rebuilding complete.

The people of Cable Street—English, Maltese, Pakistani, Polish, Cypriot, Irish, West Indian, East and West African —with their occupations and recreations as various as a scene from Damon Runyon provided a nightmare for the G.L.C. housing officials. Though many were recognizably settled, new characters constantly appeared on the scene. No sooner was a house cleared of its inhabitants than a fresh lot broke in. One notorious Maltese landlord, in Swedenborg Square, employing strong-arm men, kept control of several houses months after the G.L.C. was supposed to have cleared them, whipping his tenants in and out of empty rooms. Since most of them were single people who knew they were ineligible for rehousing, why should they not accept a roof while they could? Where families were concerned, the officials were as lenient as they felt they could be. Even so, of the 300 or so families who reached the record, about 60 per cent still awaited clearance by February 1967. Perhaps a hundred of these were eligible for rehousing; seventy or eighty more might, when it came to the point, have to move on, along with all the single people. Not exactly the 'complete clearance and rehousing of all the occupants' described in the public inquiry in 1964. The line does, of course, have to be drawn somewhere. But it is so often drawn in front of the same people, who never settle anywhere long enough to gain any rights. All over East London there must be a floating mass of human flotsam always one step ahead of the bulldozer. At least some of them gain a respite when the bulldozer moves as slowly as it has in Cable Street.

V | The Lambeth Story

Lambeth, like Tower Hamlets, is an inner London borough with a heavy housing problem and marked immigrant settlement. But there the likeness ends. In the nature of its problems, and its approach to them, Lambeth offers a completely different picture. Other boroughs say wryly that the only thing wrong with Lambeth is the fuss it makes about it; and certainly it has a flair, sometimes misapplied, for publicizing its difficulties. But in recent years the inheritance of rather sleepy policy and administration has, in several places, been sloughed off. The borough has begun to earn the progressive image which, particularly in housing, it likes to project. The changes include attempts to establish more constructive relations with its coloured minority: for instance a liaison committee for immigrants was set up in 1966.

By this time, Lambeth had been a centre for coloured immigration for well over ten years. Eleven thousand West Indians arrived in the borough between 1951 and 1961, according to the Census. Brixton, the central residential district of Lambeth and also one of south London's main shopping and communications centres, became synonymous with its coloured inhabitants. Today nobody thinks twice to see the green bananas, saltfish, and yams cramming the famous Brixton street market alongside traditional English produce. English and West Indian housewives shop together, push each other's prams and generally take each other for granted. Ten years ago things were rather different. Sheila Patterson's well-known study of Brixton[1] gives a sensitive picture of the two communities in process of adjustment to each other; while this process is today still far from complete, it has been peaceful enough to confound the gloomy forebodings of hostile critics in the early years.

As Mrs. Patterson has shown, it was the availability of lodgings and ease of communications which were mainly responsible for the initial coloured settlement in Brixton. There are many less flattering local versions of how the immigrants came to Brixton; such as: 'The stowaways were sent to Brixton gaol and when they were let out they just walked down the road to the labour exchange.' Most of the anecdotes reflect the rather disreputable label which was attached to the newcomers by locals, who saw that West Indians took lodgings in streets which already contained brothels; took up with stray white girls; and ran basement clubs which attracted unfavourable attention from the police. The familiar syndrome includes the very houses into which they moved—large Victorian terraced or semi-detached houses originally built for middle-class families, long since let in furnished lodgings which became translated into the standard immigrant pattern of multiple occupation. The way had already been laid by Polish and Cypriot immigrants who immediately preceded the West Indians in Brixton. Like them, the West Indians found they could sometimes buy large houses themselves on short leases which they then sub-let in rooms, often unaware of the legal and economic pitfalls connected with this kind of property.

From the start Lambeth's (Labour) Council adopted a defeatist attitude towards the housing of the new coloured population. Although all over London strangers were arriving daily and looking for homes in just the same sort of conditions as were to be found in Brixton, the fact that some of the newcomers to Lambeth were dark was taken to be a reason for treating the situation as something unique. As Mrs. Patterson has said: 'the council seems to have

[1] *Dark Strangers: A Study of West Indians in London*, London, Tavistock Publications 1963; Penguin Books (abridged), 1965.

been concerned not so much with discriminating against the few coloured applicants on the housing list as with persuading the local ratepayers and voters that they were not in fact discriminating in favour of recently arrived coloured immigrants.'[2] In January 1955 Councillor (later Mayor) Nathan Marock was reported as saying that about twelve coloured families had been rehoused in requisitioned property but none in permanent accommodation: 'even though some [coloured families] are living in miserable conditions they will get no more housing priority than the people of Lambeth'.[3] This was meant as reassurance. Panic hit some local leaders: in 1954 the then Mayor (Councillor White) described Brixton as a 'transit camp' for Jamaicans and spoke of reopening the underground shelters in Clapham to house the invaders.

The conviction grew that Lambeth was in a special position and should get special consideration from the Government since it could not possibly be expected to deal with the newcomers through the normal channels without creating ungovernable fury among the native population—although it is far from clear why such strong hostility should have been presumed to exist. While this talk went on it is hardly surprising that such official efforts as were made to set up contact with the immigrants, ended in failure and were abandoned.

In 1955 Lambeth Borough Council made the first of its intermittent approaches to the Ministry of Housing with a plea for emergency help. It could not, it said, hope to house either its present or any future immigrants, and was therefore severely hampered in trying to curb overcrowding. Mr. Duncan Sandys, Minister of Housing, replied:

The Minister is of course aware that this immigration is creating special difficulties for certain housing authorities—of whom your Council is one. He appreciates that the strict application of the provisions for dealing with overcrowding which are contained in the Housing Acts would be difficult in the

---

[2] *Dark Strangers* (Penguin edition), p. 59.
[3] *South London Press*, 28 January 1955.

present circumstances. But this duty to deal with the housing problems which have already resulted from immigration remains with the housing authority.[4]

Thus handed ministerial permission for *laissez-faire* (and having received equally dusty answers from other Ministries and the London County Council), Lambeth Borough Council settled down for the next few years to do nothing whatsoever about its immigrants: even mention of the subject became a politically dirty word, infecting the administration with the spirit of 'hear no evil, see no evil, speak no evil'. (This contrasted with the active and outspoken record of the Labour Member of Parliament for Lambeth, Mr. Marcus Lipton.) No records were supposed to be kept which would raise the accusation of discrimination; because nothing was officially recorded by the housing department, they officially could not tell whether they were doing nothing. The sole stroke of involvement by the Town Hall, undertaken in blissful ignorance of the consequences, was the purchase in 1957 of the freeholds of two streets of houses which contained some of the heaviest coloured multiple occupation. More will be told of this episode presently.

By 1965, the year of the borough's aggrandisement under the new shape of London government,[5] some key changes had taken place in the context of housing and town-planning in the borough. But the Council and its chief officers still subscribed to the well-established view that, with the best will in the world, their housing situation was so acute that they could do very little to help the coloured population in the near future without causing trouble, and that they deserved special help from the Government and the Greater London Council in view of their peculiar problems as an area which attracted immi-

---

[4] *South London Press*, 23 April 1955.

[5] Under the London Government Act of 1963, which took effect in April 1965, the London boroughs were given greater powers and several of them were amalgamated or enlarged. Lambeth's population increased from 223,763 in 1961 to 340,762 in 1965, and its area from 4,087 acres to 6,727 acres.

grants of all races but had no spare room for new housing and a long queue for council houses.

This view was supported, up to a point, by the Milner Holland Committee's report, published in March 1965. Lambeth was considerably better off than some boroughs in terms of the state of its housing stock. And no pockets of acute overcrowding appeared, when the statistics were broken down on a ward basis, to compare with those revealed in north Paddington and west Stepney. Nevertheless the figures did reveal some deterioration in the various indices of multiple occupation since 1951, for which reason the Milner Holland Committee listed Lambeth with, but after, seven other boroughs said to display the worst deterioration in London.[6] The list was concerned with the *degree of change* rather than the degree of badness. In the same period, 1951–61, Lambeth had increased its resident foreign population—those born outside the British Isles— from 70 to 138 per 1,000: the fifth biggest increase in London. The other boroughs on the 'deterioration' list also came high on the table of immigrant increase. These facts help to put the attitude of the Lambeth authorities in perspective.

In the early days of the new Labour Government the borough had high hopes of getting the extra consideration it wanted. In his first Press conference as Minister of Housing, Mr. Richard Crossman had spoken sympathetically of the special assistance needed for the 'twilight areas' of cities. Mr. Robert Mellish of the London Labour Party was appointed the Minister's right-hand man for housing in the London boroughs (which had yet to sort out their new relationship with the Greater London Council). On 31 March 1965, shortly after the publication of Milner Holland's report, Mr. Mellish visited Lambeth, together with Mr. Maurice Foley who was the Minister at the Home Office responsible for race relations. The borough representatives stated their case: they had a large coloured population which must be integrated; this could be done

6 The other seven being Hackney, Hornsey, Kensington, Stoke Newington, Willesden, Islington, and Hammersmith.

only by rehousing a small fixed percentage at a time on council estates—the figure of 5 per cent for any one estate was given as the safe maximum (which is now admitted to have been pure guesswork). Therefore the speed of integration depended solely on the speed of council-house building and the size of the redevelopment programme. In other words, more money please.

The meeting covered a lot of ground. Afterwards the Council recorded that the following conclusions, among others, had been reached:

(1) Enlarge Lambeth's housing programme and through national policies reduce the regional pressures that caused each housing space to be refilled as soon as it was emptied by council rehousing.

(2) The Government should sponsor research programmes into areas with special immigrant problems.

(3) Such areas should be defined as 'areas of special housing need'. In such areas all housing should be owned and managed by the local authority in order to reduce overcrowding, control lettings, modernize and rehabilitate until eventual redevelopment. Such redevelopment to be carried out under the procedure for comprehensive redevelopment, not a slum-clearance programme.

(4) A five-year residential qualification for housing was essential to 'avoid anti-racial disturbances'.

(5) Housing management should recruit trained social workers with knowledge of immigrants' countries of origin.

(6) The Government would decide if special legislation was needed after it had examined other immigrant areas. Lambeth's plea for a subsidy of £60 a head for everybody rehoused from 'areas of special housing need' and for an improved Exchequer grant for rehabilitated housing were rejected, on the grounds that a new subsidy structure was in preparation (that eventually embodied in the Housing Subsidies Act of 1967).

From this it can be seen that Lambeth was playing up
its old fears of causing 'trouble' by rehousing coloured
people (lent only slender grounds by an anti-colour petition
on an L.C.C. housing estate in the borough at the time of
the 1964 election) to give urgency to some fairly serious
thinking about ways of dealing with a housing situation
which was due not to colour but to immigration in the
broadest sense—caused by the regional imbalance between
London and the rest of the country.

It proved a mistake to have forged a policy link between
race and housing. The Government, as it turned out,
decided not to recognize any special need arising from the
presence of a coloured population—and Lambeth could
justly be held to have made a great deal of fuss over the subject backed by very little evidence or effort of its own. But
in course of turning this down, the much more justifiable
plea for a special policy to deal with some of the particular
housing problems outlined in the Milner Holland report
went by the board also. After months of argument Lambeth
were told in the autumn of 1965 they would not even get
Government help for the statistical survey they had commissioned on their coloured population. This was regarded
as the last straw. In a fit of defiance, or defeatism, the
Council published a pamphlet entitled *Immigration from
the Commonwealth* in which it set out a picture of an
intolerable housing shortage, exacerbated by immigration,
with which it was powerless to deal without the Government help which had been persistently refused. Whatever
the reasons of those responsible for this document, it came
over as an old-fashioned racist blast—and as such was
interpreted by the Sunday paper which leaked the con-
tents in banner headlines.[7]

This pronouncement threw a polemical smokescreen
over a whole range of specific problems with which, for one
reason or other, the local authority had not the power or
the will to cope. Its meeting of March 1965 with the
Government representatives had shown that at least in
some quarters there was a more subtle grasp of the main

[7] *The People*, 21 November 1965.

influences on the housing situation than the pamphlet of November 1965 revealed. No headlines would have been raised if the facts had been presented thus:

Along with the rest of inner London (the old metropolitan area) the population of Lambeth has been declining. Many sizeable houses of six to eight rooms contain ageing controlled tenants or owner-occupiers who have not followed their sons and daughters into the suburbs. Many similar houses have over the years fallen vacant, or partially vacant, and have been let off room by room to young workers and their families who have come to fill jobs in central London but cannot get a council house or any other adequate accommodation. They have growing families and easily become overcrowded; they have to share lavatories, cooking facilities, etc., with other households under the same roof. Their high fertility may well halt the decline in population: but they do not overcrowd the borough as a whole. They are simply obliged to live in houses which become individually overcrowded. These houses are mainly to be found in the central, Brixton, belt of Lambeth where the age, size, and tenure of property lends itself to this use. The borough becomes increasingly suburban towards the south and its overall density is only 50 persons per acre (compared with for example 86 persons per acre in Islington). But the Borough Council cannot make full use of this fact owing to overall density zoning decreed by the Greater London Council which forbids it to build new housing sites in the south of the borough at more than 70 per acre (net). It is also powerless to prevent new families filling up room spaces which have been vacated by families rehoused by the Council. Until it has powers to close this open-ended situation it is most reluctant to rehouse anybody from houses in multiple-occupation.

But for the fact that a visible minority of newcomers to the borough had coloured skins, this situation could never have been given the threatening overtones which were projected on to it. The only justification for linking race and housing would have been to point out that, as was undoubtedly true, the coloured minority as a group had to put up with worse living conditions at relatively more cost than the white majority group. But then the same point could no doubt have been made about other minori-

I

ties in Lambeth: for instance the low-income, large families, among whom many coloured immigrants could be
numbered. This situation has been apparent for years in
Lambeth: more recently statistical backing has been
obtained from detailed analysis of the Census, and from a
housing occupancy survey carried out in 1966.[8] On top of
this a good deal of statistical material is available in various
local authority departments, to some of which the author
has had access. From these sources and from general inquiries and observation a fairly accurate sketch of the
living conditions of Lambeth's coloured population in the
1960s can be drawn. Then the effect of various local authority policies and practices can be understood.

Lambeth Borough runs south from the Thames in a long,
thin strip which is a precise segment of South London,
stretching from the Royal Festival Hall to the Crystal
Palace. The northern, Thames-side tip, the Vauxhall–
Waterloo area, has the remains of a nineteenth-century
working-class environment, much cut about with industry
and transport routes. Then comes the broad middle segment, containing some spaciously laid out Victorian middle-
class stucco, and other streets of smaller and more meanly
endowed terraces built at various stages in the second half
of the nineteenth century. In the centre of this segment is
the focal point of the borough, Brixton. Round its cross-
roads, market, town hall, and shops many activities revolve.
Not far west of this (and formerly in the metropolitan
borough of Wandsworth) is Clapham, with Junction and
Common (half of the latter lies in Lambeth's boundary).
Various other districts with district names and characters of
their own lie south of Brixton—Herne Hill, Tulse Hill,
Streatham Hill, Gypsy Hill. Streatham, like Brixton a
shopping centre of some importance, is the most modern
and 'suburban' of Lambeth's districts, containing much
inter-war development and a more middle-class population.
Norwood, in the south-east, was a fashionable Victorian
villa suburb. Large private gardens have here recently pro-

[8] This was the survey mentioned on page 117, commissioned by
Lambeth Borough Council from Research Services Ltd.

vided the Borough Council with some of its main building sites.

The 1961 Census showed a population in the old borough of 223,763, of which 5.6 per cent were identifiably coloured, 4.6 being West Indians. In the relative size of its coloured population, Lambeth came fifth in the list of London boroughs after Paddington (7.5 per cent), Willesden and Stoke Newington (6.7 per cent) and Kensington (6.6 per cent).[9] But there was not (proportionately) so great an admixture of non-coloured immigrants in Lambeth as in these other boroughs, although the Irish formed 5 per cent of the population and there were substantial numbers of Poles and Cypriots who had arrived during or after the war. The fifty-six enumeration districts with more than 10 per cent of persons born in the coloured Commonwealth were scattered fairly evenly over the broad central belt, and this area corresponded roughly, but not completely, to the districts with the most shared dwellings and over-crowding.

Five years later, the borough's own sample housing survey[10] gave a rather more detailed picture. Households with coloured heads were 8.7 per cent of the whole. Coloured households were almost all in the child-bearing group, with proportionately more young children, and their average size was 3.6 persons compared with 2.7 in white households. This would suggest a total coloured population, including children, of nearly 13 per cent. Its Brixton focus was borne out by the area breakdown, shown on the chart.

This broad breakdown does not reveal the visible local contrasts between the crowded patches, containing high

[9] *London's Housing Needs*, p. 67.
[10] The (unweighted) sample of 1,344 households were selected from the valuation register. The weighted figure of 2,882 is the base for percentages. For reasons which are not entirely clear, the sample when grossed up appears to cover only 80 per cent of the population when compared with estimates based on the Census. But this need not cast doubt on the general accuracy of characteristics recorded for the white and coloured population as a whole. 'Coloured' households were those with a coloured head.

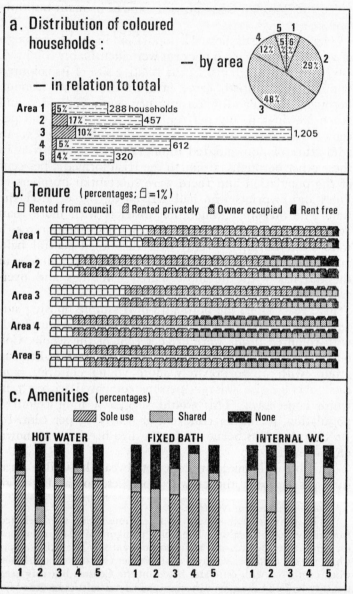

1. Lambeth households: area survey, 1966. Weighted sample 2882 households, of which 251 coloured

Source: Research Services Ltd.

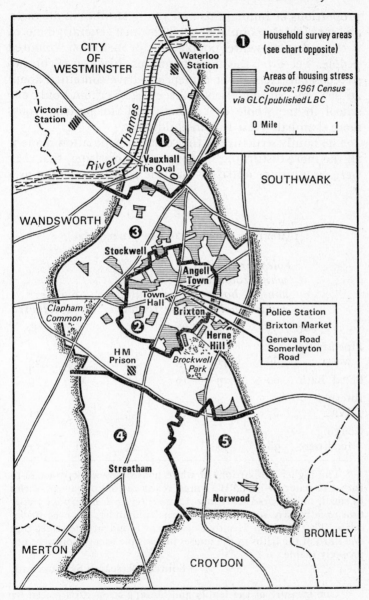

II. London Borough of Lambeth

proportions of immigrants and young families of all races, and more thinly populated patches which generally denoted a more settled white population, or better-off coloured people. Yet even the most notorious 'black area' of two streets seems from other evidence to have contained about 40 per cent white households (see page 141), and only one school in the whole of Lambeth had (in January 1967) more than half West Indian children.

The family structure of the coloured population made it all the more disturbing[11] (though less surprising) that they were, as a group, worse off than the white population as a

TABLE 8

LAMBETH: HOUSEHOLD AMENITIES, 1966

| | Sole use of facility: | | | | | |
	white house-holds	coloured house-holds	Shared use: white	coloured	No use:* white	coloured
	%	%	%	%	%	%
Piped hot water	66	41	5	34	29	25
Fixed Bath	60	29	19	62	21	9
Internal W.C.	67	34	18	55	14	11
Cooking facilities	98	76	1	23	1	1

* The higher proportions of white households without access to bath, hot water, or inside W.C. must reflect the old private tenancies in small, unimproved dwellings. Larger houses in multiple occupation usually have some sort of internal plumbing, however inadequate. The Lambeth Health Department found in one street that one third of the baths in the houses in multiple occupation were not properly usable.

Source: Research Services Ltd.

[11] One measure of the family and housing stress experienced by immigrants was the number of immigrant children in local authority care—in 1966 nearly a quarter of the total.

whole in the tenure, stability, and amenities of their homes. They moved more often, had much fewer household amenities between them (for example, shared cookers were an almost exclusively coloured experience) and depended much more on the insecure private rented market. Evidence abounds that coloured families tend to have furnished lettings and frequently lacked rent books—so that they have gained little from the 1965 Rent Act.[12] Some of the differences—for instance, in rents paid—reflects the fact that the white population includes older, less mobile age groups, often in statutory tenancies. But the way in which the coloured population contrasted most sadly with the white was in the respective share in council housing: only 5 per cent of coloured households were council tenants, compared with 20 per cent of white households.[13] This will be discussed in more detail later.

This discrepancy must help to explain the fact that in one way—ownership of their own houses—the coloured population was marginally in advance of the white majority —if owner-occupation is considered a privilege. In an area like Lambeth it can be a mixed blessing—the rotten fabric, short lease, and sitting tenant in the house 'going for a song' which may still require purchase at a price and rate of interest far beyond the easy means of the buyer. In the early days of settlement, as Dr. Davison's analysis of the Census shows, house purchase was a particularly Jamaican practice.[14] The level of owner-occupation among all coloured people cannot be divorced from the question of

[12] The Health Department found that in one particularly notorious street (see below) whereas only 13 per cent of English tenants lacked rent books (nearly all of those being sub-tenants), 80 per cent of West Indian and African households were without rent books. In the borough household survey, 35 per cent of coloured tenants lack rent books, compared with 14 per cent of white.

[13] Greater London Council and Lambeth Borough Council.

[14] Jamaican households in Lambeth in 1961 were 38 per cent owner-occupied. In some other boroughs the percentage was still higher: for example 55 per cent in Deptford (R. B. Davison, *Black British*, London, Oxford University Press for the Institute of Race Relations, 1966, p. 55).

council mortgages, which, especially since 1963, have gone some way to make up for the lack of council housing. One of the most interesting facts to emerge from the 1966 survey was that half the coloured owner-occupiers possessed a mortgage from the G.L.C. or Lambeth Borough. This, too, will be commented upon in more detail later, for it reveals the background to an interesting episode in bureaucratic cross-purposes.

In the southern half of the borough there are numerous streets of medium-sized Victorian and Edwardian houses, solidly built, which can provide decent homes at a cost of £4,000 upwards (cheaper ones are suspect). They must seem paradise after the stress of the multi-family house. The spread of immigrant settlement in the 1960s can roughly be traced according to the distance of these houses from the original 'hub' of rented accommodation in Brixton. Where the house is of modest size and financial pressures not too great, there is no reason to believe that the spread of owner-occupation by coloured people into areas where single-family houses have been the rule means that the rule will be broken. In areas where multiple occupation is already the rule, the owner-occupier may be more inclined to continue the trend by sub-letting (see below, pages 127-8). Most house-buyers who move out of central Brixton must be in search of an improved environment.

Take the case of Mrs. A, a Jamaican, who after nine and a half years of living in two small damp rooms in her brother-in-law's house, with her husband and three growing boys, was near the end of her tether. Application to the council list in 1958 produced no response other than one call four years later from a housing visitor who agreed that 'it was disgusting for the children'. A house on which they got a 90 per cent council mortgage fell through. Finally they acquired their present home, a six-roomed house in a seventy-year-old terrace in the Brixton Hill area. Council mortgages were unavailable at that time (January 1966) and eventually on the £4,500 house, with only fifteen years of a leasehold to go, they obtained a private mortgage at the repayment rate of £36 a month. A loan raised for £300 of

Houses in Multiple Occupation: Abandoned Car in Play Occupation

This family of five had been without electricity for five months (the landlord having failed to pay the bill). Because of the small space, the bed is a table at mealtimes, and storage (of the bicycle for instance) demands ingenuity.

Left and above : Family Life in One Room: Two Versions

The Rare Solution—Council-House Tenants

Owner-Occupation 1:
Two Sikh Brothers and
their Families (four adults,
five children) share a Victorian middle-class house

Owner-Occupation 2:
A Small Indian Family, an
industrial terraced cottage

the £800 deposit required had to be repaid within three years. These commitments weigh very heavily on Mrs. A's mind, but she rejoices in the freedom of their own house. Their only lodger is her husband's nephew, and it would go against all she has struggled for to revert to the cramped life of sharing with another family.

At the opposite extreme are certain houses in African ownership which serve as hostels for a succession of students or kinsmen. The coloured student in London is in an especially trying position; not only does he have to face the appalling combination of high prices and colour bar in accommodation, but he does not even have a wage behind him. The good work done by the British Council cannot possibly cover all. When coloured students are married, as many are, the position is nearly desperate. The Nigerian Government has been worried about the increase in uncontrolled baby-farming among student families in London, for often the wife must work to support her husband. Such families are not uncommon in Brixton, where not only the accommodation but various institutions (such as the Brixton School of Building) bring them to the area. Sometimes, they even end up in the hostel for the homeless, and very often at the furnished rent tribunal. They seem to have a gift for quarrelling with their Jamaican landlords; perhaps not surprisingly when they are anxiously swotting and scraping at the same time.

The rather intelligent solution found in Lambeth to have been adopted by a few lucky students with grants is to use the grant to put the deposit on a house, and then live by letting rooms to their fellow-countrymen. When they return home they may loosely pass on responsibility for the house to another student. Although the author has never seen such a house, the public health inspectors know a few, and say the idea is catching on among Africans. Another instance was given of a house in Clapham bought with money said to have been provided as a community effort by a West African village, to shelter its sons when they came to study in London. The trouble with these arrangements is that no one has very much permanent interest in keeping up the house, or in the daily running of it. Conditions are said to be very bad indeed. Lambeth Borough Council, which early in 1967 was considering how to make best use of the increased aid for hostel-building, and for housing associations, promised in the Housing Subsidies Act, may eventually try to help students through one or both of these means; but it would be hard to keep costs to the level of the poorest. A good many of the students must come grossly ill-prepared and provided, and it might be better if they were given a clearer idea beforehand of what to expect. But until the local authorities and the educational world face up to the implications of housing London's vast student population (or decentralizing their education) the most vulnerable among that population will live impossible lives and perpetually run into trouble with the health authorities.

While this sorry stress may produce the worst kind of multiple occupation, there is good reason to argue that what Lambeth needs is not less multiple occupation but more—in order to make best use of its large-sized houses. Many streets which have only recently gone into multiple occupation as immigrants move into new districts are perfectly suited to the purpose provided the division of the house is carried out properly. A typical street of substantial Edwardian houses just south of Clapham Common in the extreme west of Lambeth borough has a number of houses up for sale. In late 1966 a survey by the Public Health Department revealed that, out of seventy-nine houses in the street, thirty housed one family, and thirty-six contained two families. In the view of the department these were reasonable two-family houses, given the proper conversion and facilities. The worry was caused by the remaining thirteen houses: seven of these were occupied by three families; three by four families, and three by as many as five families. The Health Department felt that if it had the same powers as Birmingham to control multiple occupation in advance of its occurrence, it would use these powers not to prevent people sharing in areas where sharing was a new phenomenon but more constructively, to make sure that only suitable houses, suitably adapted, were so used. At present there is only a registration scheme (under the 1961 Housing Act) covering the six central wards of the borough, under which houses occupied by more than two families are supposed to be registered by the owner for approval of numbers and amenities by the Health Department. In spite of extensive publicity, this scheme, launched in October 1966, had very limited response in its early months—hardly any from coloured owners 'unless we stand over them while they fill in the form'. This is hardly surprising, since it is estimated that the great majority of people in these lettings are coloured immigrants and so are many of their landlords. An effective registration scheme, with the concomitant thinning-out of lettings, would bear directly on coloured immigrant families.

TABLE 9

HOUSES IN MULTIPLE OCCUPATION IN ONE LAMBETH STREET,
BY NUMBER OF LETTINGS AND NATIONALITY

	Number of lettings per house						
*Nationality of occupants**	2	3	4	5	6	9	
British	74	10	1	–	1	–	
West Indian	18	24	17	7	6	1	
African	–	3	3	1	2	–	
Other or mixed	3	3	–	3	–	–	TOTALS
Total houses	95	40	21	11	9	1	177
Total lettings	190	120	84	55	54	9	512

Source: Lambeth Health Department.

* The dominant nationality of the house was recorded. Very little mingling of nationalities was found, but the record may not be completely reliable in this respect.

This was confirmed by a survey carried out by the Health Department in one street of more or less identical six-roomed houses in central Brixton. Some houses had been in two-family occupation since before the war. Whilst many houses with English occupants were in the two-family category, the more fragmented and congested lettings were overwhelmingly West Indian or African (see Table 9).

The figures were bumped up by a few very bad houses. One of the worst offenders was the absentee landlord of eight crowded and run-down houses: this landlord had a Muslim name and lived in a London suburb. His four worst houses contained fifty-three people, with a top rent of £5 for one room (possibly charged to a prostitute). He was getting about £19 a week per house.

By attacking bad landlords, and bad conditions, the authorities inevitably dislodge tenants who have then to find accommodation elsewhere—perhaps in even more crowded circumstances. This is a longstanding dilemma and obviously cannot be escaped until public housing (or sufficient private rented accommodation) is available to all and sundry. This has given the London boroughs every encouragement to adopt a *laissez-faire* policy towards multiple occupation. At one extreme an eviction order may mean that they have reluctantly to rehouse the affected family; at the other, the enhanced protection from eviction available to tenants since December 1964 means that their efforts may be nullified anyway. Despite these drawbacks Lambeth decided in 1965, having strengthened its formerly very weak Health Department, that it would press ahead with 'de-crowding' houses in multiple occupation. The new Chief Public Health Inspector, who came from Islington where his hands had been severely tied, was delighted: it was the first time any borough had given him *carte blanche* on 'de-crowding'.

What gave the Department courage was the knowledge that across the border in Wandsworth a *laissez-faire* policy was in action: if they acted quickly the worst landlords and their luckless tenants would simply disappear from Lambeth. Estate agents and worried public health inspectors from neighbouring boroughs (including Croydon in the south) began to report an increase in multiple occupation which was believed to be at least partly due to the efforts of the Lambeth Health Department. Nevertheless, really bad landlords could still get away with flouting orders, since the Council was very reluctant to take them to court without watertight evidence. The one and only attempt to prosecute for breach of an order to cease letting to new tenants had ended in a fiasco, after an official was floored in court by confrontation with a row of coloured faces which he could not swear were not those he saw at the time of his inspection.

One unforeseen weapon fell into the hands of the Health Department in its crusade against multiple occupation. It soon became apparent that quite often houses financed by local authority mortgages contained tenants; occasionally the owner did not even live in the house. This was against the terms of the mortgage and pressure could be brought to bear through the mortgagees—Lambeth Borough Council and the G.L.C. It has been described in an earlier chapter how the G.L.C. has had to tighten up on abuses in this field: Lambeth Health Department prides itself on having been instrumental in bringing this about. Inspection of houses became almost entirely based on the list of mortgages obtained from the two councils. In the first six months of 1966 the Health Department successfully 'de-crowded' 141 excess people from houses in the borough: 125 of these came from houses on which there were G.L.C. mortgages; six from houses mortgaged to Lambeth Borough Council; and ten from houses inspected in the ordinary way because they were known to be in multiple occupation. The G.L.C. and its coloured borrowers were recognized as the chief targets in this campaign, simply because this was a combination which did often produce illegal tenancies and consequent overcrowding in terms of the numbers using sparse household amenities. The Health Department was aware of criticism that its efforts were tantamount to picking on the coloured man; but, it said, its job was to administer certain laws and if this was a sure-fire method of doing at least a fraction of the job, why not use it?

One can feel sympathy for public servants who are paid to apply a certain standard, and who measure achievement in terms of the number of times that standard can be enforced. But although the Lambeth Health Department acted as though the game was 'Oranges and Lemons' (where the numbers are gradually 'chopped' down) in fact it was 'tag'—a constant number of people taking it in turn to be chased. If their operation were successful, there would be three alternative results. When brought to book by the G.L.C., the mortgages would either get rid of their tenants (who would then have to squeeze in somewhere else) or lose their mortgages. In the latter case they would either have to sell—a difficult task if there were sitting tenants—or they would then have to raise another mortgage on the private market, at high interest rates, and perhaps be forced to take even more lodgers to pay it off. There would be no overall reduction in crowding (except perhaps in the narrow terms of Lambeth's own boundary) and there might even be an increase. This is a criticism of the whole situation rather than the Health Department alone; but the department can be criticized for choosing a ready-made formula that did not necessarily include the worst land-lords at all. One cannot help feeling that this was the result of its defeat in court which undermined confidence in its ultimate power against landlords who deliberately defied the law.

As the result of this campaign, a great many houses which had been deprived of G.L.C. mortgages came on the market. The street described on page 128 is a case in point. Thirty houses were up for sale at the time of the survey and thirteen of these had council mortgages; some of the others may have had building society or private mortgages also withdrawn when the Health Department drew attention to conditions. Thirty-nine other houses with council mortgages were in multiple occupation, thirty-two of which belonged to West Indians, and only one to an Englishman. Twenty-three of these West Indian houses were shared by more than two households, and only nine of them were 'satisfactory' by health department standards for houses in multiple occupation. In four cases the owner did not live in the house. One man had six G.L.C. mortgages in other people's names. The Greater London Council was to be blamed for not making its rules plainer, and for not realizing sooner what was going on. But it gives generous mortgages and it is unlikely that many of the transgressing owners were actually desperate for the extra money from tenants, as they might have been with an expensive private mortgage. To explain why West Indians were prone to this particular misdemeanour one has to recall a great many things: their attitude to authority, their inexperience in housing and law, the needs of the other West Indians to whom they offered a roof. In other words, the immigrant situation. It would be wrong to treat immigrants unequally by allowing them to get away with breaking rules which other people have to keep; on the other hand, in Lambeth in 1966 there were other houses, and other rules, which needed more urgent attention. No problems were solved by playing tag.

Thirty thousand dwellings, one quarter of the total stock, were in permanent public ownership in Lambeth at the end of 1966. Several thousand more publicly acquired houses (not part of this stock) awaited demolition in redevelopment areas. The Greater London Council owned 57 per cent of the total public stock, and nearly two-thirds of the dwellings on purpose-built council estates. Over a quarter of Lambeth Borough Council's stock (3,400 dwellings) is in formerly private houses and blocks of flats acquired for rehabilitation or conversion. The borough has a particularly strong policy of rehabilitation, and would like to do more; this is allied with active encouragement of improvement grants to private owners. The treatment given to the acquired houses ranges from complete conversion and modernization (to a standard which compares very favourably with the similar houses bought and done up by the young professional people who are moving into the borough), to the minimum repair and provision of amenities for houses with a shorter 'life'. This is not to be confused with the temporary use of houses in demolition areas—many of which are not actually unfit—which provide an extra, submerged pool of tenancies for as long as they stand. This pool does not appear in the figures of housing stock or of annual lettings, since it is mostly occupied by the people who were in the houses when they were first acquired by the Council; and if the occupants are swopped around from one house to another awaiting demolition it counts as a 'transfer' rather than a new tenancy.

Nearly all Lambeth Borough's pool of houses in re-development areas—known on the job as 'mucky property' —are in the Brixton area. For management purposes Lambeth housing department divides the borough into four areas, and Brixton is the central area. The central area office administers over 2,300 'mucky' houses and these, as opposed to the houses on the borough's estates within the area, can be let and swopped around freely without instructions from headquarters. The central housing area covers the district of most intense coloured settlement and much of its manipulation of tenancies within redevelopment districts affects coloured people—without appearing on the permanent record.

From the record, however, it is quite clear that as far as the Borough Council is concerned, at any rate, the housing of coloured families follows a markedly different pattern from lettings as a whole. Table 10 shows the breakdown of the tenancies granted in different categories of property by Lambeth Borough Council in 1966.

It is impossible to argue accurately from these bare figures how far the housing of coloured families is *qualitatively* different from that of council tenants as a whole. For instance eleven out of the twenty-nine coloured families housed in acquired property went into converted dwellings, which might well have been, to many people's taste, a lot more pleasant than an early post-war flat. Nor, with such small numbers involved, can much be argued

TABLE 10

LETTINGS: LAMBETH BOROUGH COUNCIL, 1966

Percentage Breakdown by Type of Dwelling and Colour of Tenant:

	All tenants	Coloured tenants	All tenants from redevelopment areas	Coloured tenants from redevelopment areas
	%	%	%	%
New flats	40	22	32	10
Post-war flats	26	9	31	8
Pre-war flats	6	8	6	8
Prefabs	–	2	–	3
Total % on estates	72	41	69	29
Acquired/converted property	28	59	30	72
	100%	100%	99*%	101*%
Total numbers	683	49	458	39

* Discrepancy due to rounding.

Source: Lambeth Housing Department

from the smaller proportion of coloured tenants allotted new flats. What is clear is that coloured people as a group predominated in acquired property outside the estates and in this they went contrary to the general pattern. This was particularly marked in the case of families housed from redevelopment areas, which accounted for three-quarters of all the coloured families housed. There can be little doubt that these trends are influenced by Lambeth's often expressed fear of trouble if immigrants are housed too obviously on estates. By putting them in houses in an

K

ordinary private street, nobody can recognize them as
council tenants.

During 1965, in its argument with the Government,
Lambeth Housing Department suggested, in a figure
snatched from the air, that it was dangerous to let more
than 5 per cent of the dwellings on any one estate to
coloured families. In 1966 only 4 per cent of all new tenancies on estates went to coloured families and, as this year
was believed to be one in which a record number of coloured families (forty-nine) had been housed, it does not
look as though any great risks are yet being run. The
Housing Department is still coy of counting up exactly how
many coloured tenants it has amassed over the years: 1966
was the first year in which any records were officially kept.
But it is obvious that the lettings section has always had
a pretty clear idea whom it is dealing with. The G.L.C., on
the other hand, seems rather more ready to put coloured
families on to its estates in Lambeth, and its large stock of
pre-war housing is found convenient for the purpose. The
general practice is to disperse coloured families around the
less attractive estates, in the belief that they will encounter
a more tolerant atmosphere there; although this is not
always the case, the belief is encouraged by the occasional
over-publicized protests against coloured tenants on modern
estates, such as the Loughborough Estate in central
Brixton.

The G.L.C.'s tenants in Lambeth come from all over
London, although a great number of them are local, and
some originate directly from the 'quota' accepted from
Lambeth Borough itself. Two hundred tenants (additional
to those shown on the table) were accepted in the G.L.C.
quota in 1966, and these included a few more coloured
families. Over the next few years the annual G.L.C. quota
may rise in support of Lambeth's ambitious building programme, which will involve the displacement of thousands
of families. As in many areas of this type, the order in
which the redevelopment sites are tackled has aroused some
controversy, including the allegation that bad housing
containing immigrants is left standing in preference to

redeveloping sound houses with white inhabitants. True as this is, the Borough Council has a watertight alibi: the plea that low-density sites must first be developed in order to provide leeway for clearing densely occupied houses. The reasoning is genuine. Whatever Lambeth's faults, trimming its clearance programme in order to avoid immigrant areas is not one of them. In fact some of the large houses and gardens which provide comparatively low-density sites early in the programme are in the Angell Town area of Brixton, on which clearance has already begun, and from which sixteen coloured families were rehoused from one site in 1966.

Even the comparatively modest number of immigrant families being rehoused by 1966 was apparently enough of a novelty to stimulate interest in the waiting list. This, anyway, was the Housing Department's explanation of the fact that by mid-1966 the rate of coloured applications was running at about five times the rate of two or three years previously, and coloured applicants formed one-sixth of a total list of 13,350. The Department at about this time sensibly installed a West Indian counter clerk. Unfortunately, there was an ever-decreasing chance of benefit from the waiting list owing to the claims of redevelopment. It makes little difference that the rules have a rather heavier weighting in favour of Lambeth residents than the recommended standard for London boroughs; for everybody can expect to wait a very long time. The waiting list is not even an accurate measure of need, for in recent clearance areas at most only 14 per cent of families have been found to be on the waiting list. There is in fact little point in being on the list at all if you live in a clearance area, since the Borough is unwilling to house even acute cases in advance of general clearance—especially if it is one of the many areas due to be dealt with by the G.L.C. Take the case of Mrs. T., a Jamaican lady who has lived for four years with her husband and four children in one room (shared cooker, lavatory, and water) in a house acquired by the G.L.C. through its purchase of the Church Commissioners' Brixton estate, which it will eventually redevelop. She has been on Lambeth's list for five years and goes regularly to the Town Hall to inquire about her chances. Nobody has thought to disillusion her. The G.L.C. has not even reduced the £3-a-week rent she was paying to the previous landlord.

In a policy announcement of September 1966 Lambeth warned waiting-list applicants of the small chance they would have in future of being housed. Only a hiatus in the Government approvals of compulsory purchase orders for clearance areas gave space for 300 families (including the G.L.C. quota) to be housed from the lost in 1966. There was an added reason given by the Council for its reluctance to allot many spaces to the waiting list: '. . . where families are rehoused from privately owned premises there is no guarantee that the rooms will not be relet to a family or families coming into the borough for the first time, thus defeating the whole purpose of such rehousing.' The *whole* purpose? This looked like the old invasion complex at work again—although in fact *net* migration was expected to depress, rather than inflate, the population rise forecast for Lambeth.[15] While the priority given to redevelopment was a valid one, it also offered a way out of rehousing processes over which the Council had less control.

In one context at least Lambeth showed much more generosity than most boroughs towards people whose housing difficulties it could have shut its eyes to—the homeless. The Housing Department works closely with the welfare officers and is itself responsible for homeless families in the later stages of their progress through the hostel system. It rehouses most of them eventually as permanent council tenants. With the help of the G.L.C., seventy-five homeless families were rehoused in 1966. Humane treatment—for instance the acceptance of husbands in hostels as well as

[15] The Registrar General estimated at the end of 1966 that by 1971 the borough's population would be 363,700, compared with 341,976 in the same area in 1961. Without migration, the estimate would be 378,300.

wives and children—distinguishes Lambeth's approach from that of all too many other boroughs. In the autumn of 1966, over one-sixth of the families in the three hostels for the homeless run by the Housing Department were coloured—twenty-five out of 140. Most of them had four or five children, as did the many Irish families. The social workers were of the opinion that for most of the coloured homeless, unlike many of the English and Irish ones, it was bad luck rather than bad management that had put them on the street. The West Indians as a group coped well. One or two West Africans obviously found the whole experience a great strain, but the occasional law-student family were spoken of with respect as 'the only professional people we've had—very high standards'.

There is no better way of ending this chapter than by telling the story graven on the heart of many a Lambeth councillor and administrator—the story of Geneva and Somerleyton Roads, a story by no means ended yet. This was the borough's most conscious confrontation with its coloured minority; but it came about in a way that should never have happened.

Two roads of tall, dirty Victorian houses lie within the triangle formed by three converging railway lines only a quarter of a mile from Lambeth Town Hall. By 1950 the blight of many years of neglected and fragmented lease-holds and long statutory tenancies at low rents was plain to see. It was the obvious reception area for the immigrants of the 1950s, as for others before them. Most of the two-hundred-odd houses were already split into two-storey tenements or single-floor lettings. Some became still further subdivided into single-room lettings, without any addition to the household amenities; some acquired gambling clubs in the basements, or were known to the police as brothels or dope dens. A few very bad houses and the general air of dirt and neglect, plus the colour and/or poverty of many of the inhabitants, made these roads a byword for all that 'decent' people shunned—to the indignation of the many inhabitants of all races who consciously tried to keep up decent standards and felt unjustly branded.

The original ground landlord of these houses was the Beauchamp family estate,[16] whose leases were due to fall through in June 1966. The freeholders would then have full control of the properties, and would clearly have a load of trouble on their hands. But this was not as clear as it should have been in 1954, the year in which the first informal exchanges were made between the then Director of Housing for Lambeth, Mr. Carter, and Messrs. Clutton, agents for the Beauchamp Trustees. Mr. Carter had first approached Cluttons in the hope of obtaining some of the rather more attractive low-density sites in the neighbourhood which were in the freehold of the Ecclesiastical Commissioners; but he was told it was unlikely the Commissioners would sell. (The whole of the Commissioners' Brixton estate was later bought by the London County Council for £1 million). But Cluttons gladly offered Lambeth Borough Council first refusal of the freeholds of Somerleyton and Geneva Roads, with the adjacent portions of Coldharbour Lane and Sussex Grove—about 230 houses and thirteen acres in all. At first the Housing Committee were not very enthusiastic. There was uncertainty about the future of the whole Loughborough Park area in which the streets stood. (This was to prove a continual difficulty, with Lambeth at the mercy of the L.C.C./G.L.C. planning initiative.) But Cluttons pressed the issue, pointing out how inconvenient it would be for town planning if the freeholds were sold off piecemeal. And did Lambeth want the L.C.C. to buy them instead?

It was realized that the presence of many West Indians would create special problems. The idea was mooted that it would be worth buying the houses because if they were used for housing West Indians a lower than usual standard of rehabilitation would be acceptable. But how far this view underlay the Council's final decision to purchase the properties it is impossible to say. Very little attempt was

[16] Not, as has often been mis-stated, the Church Commissioners.

made to assess the extent of rehousing that might be necessary. A survey of 25 per cent of the houses undertaken in
early 1956 found them 'fairly sound except for the roofs'.
In ten years' time the Council could either convert or redevelop the property, as it saw fit. In either case, it seemed
a bargain at the price eventually agreed with the Beauchamp Trustees of £57,600. This deal went through in
late 1957. The administrators and councillors concerned
believed that they might be landed with a racial problem
in eventual rehousing, but decided not to worry about it
for the time being—it was possibly hoped that the immigrants might disperse elsewhere by June 1966.

This was not, of course, the case. The immigrants remained, and by this time many lessees were West Indians
or Africans. Little effort was made to maintain the structure of the houses although the threat of enforced repairs
was, in theory at least, hanging over the lessees. The
Council decided early on that it would not buy in any of
the leases in advance, although several people were anxious
to dispose of the responsibility. Too much might have had
to be done at the Council's expense if it became too closely
involved; so although the Health Department assiduously
served notices against the insanitary conditions, very little
was done to enforce them.

Apprehension mounted all round as the time approached
for the Council take-over. St. John's Inter-racial Club, which
represented the nearest thing to recognized West Indian
leadership, published in January 1966 a survey of the two
roads (which read in parts like an apologia for West Indian
landlords). It correctly pointed out the very great variety
of conditions inside the individual houses and put forward
a plea for council loans to the lessees of improvable houses.
It raised a storm in the Town Hall by claiming that some
landlords had been promised council houses if they got rid
of their tenants before the Council took them over. The
allegation was indignantly denied by the officials concerned.
But there is no doubt that at least the scent of favours in
store (if not that particular favour) had been imported by
the cajoling techniques adopted by public health officials in

lieu of the enforcement of notices, which had been forbidden on policy grounds.

By this time there was a strong body of technical opinion
that the majority of houses were so unsound as to justify
dealing with the whole area under slum clearance procedures—something which many members of the public had
been saying for years. Under this procedure the usual subsidy could have been obtained for rehousing; otherwise
none was to be had. But the Council would have lost face
severely by any such change of plan; and there was also in
some quarters strong feelings in favour of a rehabilitative
approach. Redevelopment was anyway only a few years off,
the main planning programme for the area having now
been agreed. It had looked at one hopeful point as though
the G.L.C.'s ring motorway, due to pass through Brixton
some time in the 1970s, would neatly obliterate Geneva and
Somerleyton Roads and land rehousing responsibility with
the G.L.C. But this was not to be. The motorway route
precisely skirted the area (following the course of the railway line) and, what was more, an intersection would gobble
up about eighteen precious acres of low-density development with which the borough had been hoping to offset
the high density of Geneva–Somerleyton. (In compensation
the borough was eventually promised other G.L.C. land
in a nearby neighbourhood.)

As midsummer 1966 approached, the Housing Department prepared for D-day—the acquisition of the whole of
Geneva and Somerleyton as part of its stock, and the inhabitants as its direct tenants. The Housing Manager, Mr.
Harry Simpson (who succeded Mr. Carter in 1962), had
always been keen to win the confidence of the coloured
population; he saw this as a challenge and an opportunity.
A big concession had been gained by obtaining council
agreement to the acceptance, as tenants, of anybody who
was in occupancy up to a few weeks before the take-over;
this was interpreted very generously when it came to the
point. The first task was to decide exactly who had claims
to what space—not at all easy when landlords were busy
shoving tenants about up to the very last minute—and

then convert numerous leaseholdings and furnished sub-tenancies into straightforward unfurnished council tenancies. People had to be shuffled about within the area to distribute space more evenly, and some moved out altogether to reduce the density. Stock had to be taken of the degree of rehabilitation that was possible. It was intended to use all but the worst houses right up to the moment of redevelopment.

It was a situation requiring careful and sympathetic, as well as firm, handling. Social problems—mental and physical illness, illegitimacy, large and penurious families —abounded. The area had become predominantly one in which growing families could find accommodation denied them elsewhere; their crowded conditions contrasted with the underoccupation of the houses still inhabited by older white people. Such extreme contrasts were to be found as, on the one hand, a West Indian family of ten in a small dripping basement; and, on the other, an English family of three, the husband blind and paralysed, in a whole house with ten rotting rooms. There were few very old people left—those that there were seemed to evoke the only inter-racial neighbourliness to be seen, for they were said to be cared for by their neighbours regardless of racial differences. Otherwise there was little evidence of mixing, though little sign of inter-racial violence. According to a 10 per cent sample survey taken by a social worker in the neighbourhood soon after the take-over, the Geneva–Somerleyton households were just over half West Indian, and nearly two-fifths English and Irish; the rest being Cypriot, Nigerian, and a miscellany of Maltese, Poles, Turks, and Indians. The West Indians and Cypriots had the largest families (an average of 3.3 children) but the rest were not far behind. Half the children were under five. The average length of residence was two and a half years, but this included some longer-stay inhabitants— there were West Indians who had lived there for as long as eight years, a few English people who had been there for very much longer—and an assortment of recent arrivals in furnished rooms with a quick turnover. Some brothels and

illicit clubs were among the fixtures, certain addresses
being favourite pick-up spots for the Brixton police.

The entire running of the physical take-over by the
Council was entrusted to the area Housing Manager for
central Lambeth, in whose territory the streets lay. Co-
operation had been obtained from the National Assistance
Board in giving loans to people who were acquiring furniture for the first time; in this and many other practical
ways the operation was launched on a sensible basis. Housing officials often had to mete out rough justice on the
spot where, for example, ex-landlords were trying to make
tenants pay through the nose for worthless sticks of furniture. The arrival of the Council was on the whole accepted
with good grace—not surprisingly, considering that many
rents were substantially reduced. Prostitutes and other
people unlikely to see eye to eye with the authorities mostly
disappeared without trace. A long-drawn-out argument
about repairs was embarked upon with certain ex-lessees by
the Town Hall; some claims were abandoned as hopeless.

Rehousing and reshuffling the inhabitants of Geneva–
Somerleyton was clearly urgent, and was treated as an
emergency military-style operation. While the iron hand
was often appropriate, the velvet glove was noticeably
lacking. Not only did the people being moved get virtually no choice—in the circumstances this was normal practice—but the handling of individuals of all races on a
personal level was often carried out in an unnecessarily
heavy-handed and unsympathetic way. A tone which can
only be described as bullying was sometimes adopted, in
circumstances where a little kindness would have gone a
long way. Maybe this was what people were, unfortunately,
prepared for. Maybe no serious harm was done. Whatever
happened, a lot of people were going to end up with more
space, and more basic amenities, than they had previously
enjoyed. Nevertheless the methods and solutions were not
very reassuring in terms of the general relationship of
authority and the coloured population.

Technically, the operation of moving people was a 'transfer' rather than 'rehousing', since they were already legally

council tenants. This mere administrative detail assumed great importance. In a clearance area (which this would have been if the houses had been legally recognized as unfit, which most of them were) people have the right to be choosey, since the council is under an obligation to them. In a transfer, the council is doing you a favour if it gives you something better than you had before.

To the initial surprise, and lasting relief, of the officials of central Lambeth Housing Area Office, it was found that West Indian families from Geneva–Somerleyton, and some of the older white people as well, could be popped into unimproved houses awaiting redevelopment without a murmur. Property usually regarded as unlettable was wheeled into action—mostly in the immediate neighbour-hood, but sometimes from distant parts of the borough. People who did murmur were either told there was no alternative or, usually, offered something worse. There was nothing intentionally unkind about this. The over-riding purpose was to get people out of foul, unhealthy, crowded conditions as quickly as possible, and to make room for the short-term improvement of such houses as were thought sound enough to be worth it. The task was made more urgent by the discovery that the worst fears about the physical state of the property were justified. A large proportion could not possibly last out the seven years by which time redevelopment was supposed to have begun. About a third of the houses in Somerleyton Road were so rotten as to be dangerous to the inhabitants—yet a matter of months after this discovery it had still not been possible to evacuate everybody. The old and sick presented particular rehousing difficulties, and were often most re-luctant to leave.

Six months after the take-over, some 150 out of the 780 households taken on as tenants in June 1966 had been moved, mostly to similar accommodation within the imme-diate area. Over half of those moved were coloured. Of the eighty-three coloured families moved by the end of 1966, only four had gone to Lambeth council estates (one, the Wyvil Estate, had its first coloured family and registered a

protest). Six coloured tenants were taken on by the G.L.C.,
and mostly sent, together with some 'poor whites' (the
Americanism is current in Lambeth) miles away to Deptford, to some old council dwellings which could not be let
to anyone else. Twelve coloured families were transferred
outside the immediate area to acquired property of various
kinds: some had fully modernized converted houses with
—luxury—baths and central heating; some went, under
protest, to some Victorian tenements acquired by the
Borough Council in the Vauxhall area. A good many went
into houses where the minimum facilities—sink, cooker,
cold water—had been installed and the minimum 'patching' done. Some houses were so decrepit that the electricity
board refused to connect the supply. 'We lean over backwards not to give them facilities that other people in
clearance areas don't have. Once you give them better
property they won't take anything else,' was the housing
officials' explanation. The policy was considered justified
even in the case of the several families recognized in housing management jargon to be 'A' or 'potentially A' class.
It seems to have been felt that all must somehow establish
their credentials by seeing how clean they kept a 'mucky'
house, and how punctually they paid the rent.

The great majority of coloured families—sixty-one of
those moved by the end of 1966—remained within the
immediate Geneva–Somerleyton area. So did several white
families, but it was more usual for white than for coloured
people to be sent to an estate outside the area. This was
not necessarily a compliment: indeed the area office rather
prided itself on having got rid of some white families, 'real
shockers—C class with a vengeance' to the northern, Vauxhall housing area, where the shabbiest old estates were sited.
The net result must, however, have been to make the
Geneva–Somerleyton area still more predominantly into a
coloured quarter.

In many ways this reflected the wishes of the inhabitants.
It would be wrong to give the impression that coloured
families all went under protest to the old houses allocated
to them, as long as this meant they could remain in the

neighbourhood. Officials were often surprised to find how a neighbourhood with such a bad name to the outside world should attract such a strong core of loyalists, of all races. It was after all a very convenient place—handy for many people's work, handy for shopping, especially in the vivid, teeming Brixton market which lay only a few hundred yards off. Many families, too, attached great importance to remaining near their children's schools and, especially, re-taining rights over one of the rare nursery school places in the immediate neighbourhood. This was said to have been a cause for which several households sacrificed the chance of better accommodation. There is a great deal that is warm, sociable and attractive about central Brixton as its West Indian inhabitants have made it; a great potential for planners to build on if only they knew how. A tenants' association had, for example, been started with the en-couragement of the Housing Department in Geneva–Somer-leyton; it got off to a shaky beginning, but at least it was the right idea.

The rebuilding of central Brixton—market, shops and all—is one of the Borough Council's most cherished plans. Much of the residential property round about it is already in phased redevelopment programmes. Nearly all the houses into which the inhabitants of Geneva–Somerleyton were being reshuffled had a 'life' of seven years or less. This could—with emphasis on the conditional—be the justifica-tion for the short-term rehousing of coloured families in the Brixton area in houses no one else would accept. A double standard is operated now; whatever happens it must not be allowed to continue to operate when redevelop-ment takes place. The vitality of the immigrant population of Brixton is one of the area's greatest assets; there is an enormous, scarcely recognized opportunity to use it con-structively, in redevelopment which takes full account of social as well as physical needs, and which recognizes the character which the immigrants have stamped on the neigh-bourhood. To concentrate the West Indians in Brixton

slums now can only be justified if they are given a full
share in the new Brixton of the future. To do so would
require new, imaginative departures in community planning. The sour American tag says that 'urban renewal
means Negro removal'. Can Lambeth, on its present record,
be trusted to prove this untrue?

VI | Manchester: Problems at the Core

The best place to start in Manchester is the bus stop by the intersection of Princess Road and Mauldeth Road. Princess Road is one of the main routes from central Manchester to the southern suburbs; further south it becomes Princess Parkway, a 1920s model approach to the model municipal suburb of Wythenshawe. Mauldeth Road runs from east to west, skirting the playing fields and inter-war council estates that form an almost continuous belt between the older, inner city—built before 1914—and the more open suburbs, mainly small houses and gardens built between the wars. The largest council estates, also dating from this period, lie in the same zone.

The bus stop around 4.30 p.m. is awash with teenagers from the nearby Secondary schools—two Grammar schools and a Secondary Modern. The bus runs in both directions, into town and out. The point of the story is that on the right-hand side of the road, among the boys and girls waiting to ride home towards the centre, there is a large proportion of coloured faces. Very few, if any, of these come from the Grammar schools. Very seldom is a coloured boy or girl to be seen waiting at the left-hand bus stop, the suburban route.

Educational distinctions will become more blurred if Manchester completes its hotly debated programme of comprehensive Secondary education for all. But the residential distinctions to which educational attainment is linked will not disappear so fast. They too are in the programme of change. Despite allegations to the contrary, Manchester City Council's slum-clearance targets do include some of

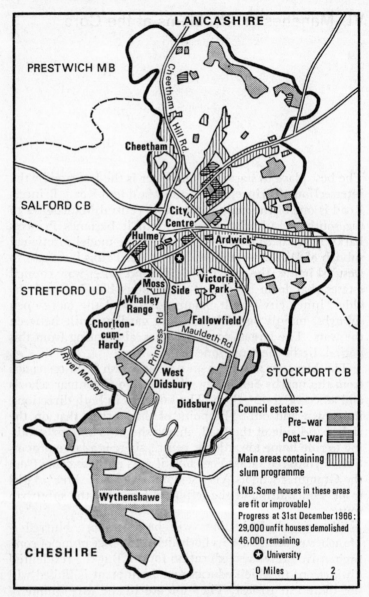

III. County Borough of Manchester

2. MANCHESTER
Council house let-
tings (net of trans-
fers) 1962–6

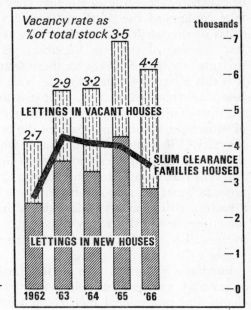

Vacancy rate as
% of total stock 3·5

thousands
—7

2·9   3·2

4·4

—6

LETTINGS IN VACANT HOUSES

—5

2·7

—4

SLUM CLEARANCE
FAMILIES HOUSED

—3

—2

LETTINGS IN NEW HOUSES

—1

Source: Manches-
ter Housing Dept

1962 '63 '64 '65 '66

—0

the main areas inhabited by its coloured population. If and
when targets are attained, almost the whole stock of old
private housing within the city boundaries—with certain
important exceptions—will be replaced by modern municipal housing, supplemented by chunks of overspill in such
out-county communities as can be prevailed upon to take
it. In the long, difficult process Manchester will be dis-
placing its oldest and its youngest, its sickest and its poorest,
its most rooted and most unsettled, and its most cosmopolitan population. For these extremes are contained among
the people who now live within two or three miles of the
city centre.

The well-to-do have always moved out, away from the
smoke and crowds. But in spite of this Victorian Manchester was built for a greater range of social classes than
inhabits it today. Consequently the range and quality of
housing, now laid under the unifying mould of decay, is
varied enough to provide today's poor with different modes

L

of existence, according to whether they inhabit the industrial cottages of the north-east sector, the once-*bourgeois*
villas of the north and south or the health-conscious 'by-
law' housing of the late Victorian period. The greatest
mixture is to be seen in the southern sector of the town, and
it is this mixture which has made Moss Side, Manchester's
legendary coloured quarter, what it is today. Here, and in
the district around the university immediately to the north
of Moss Side, within easy reach of the commercial heart of
the city, Victorian tradesmen and white-collar workers
lived with their families and servants in houses whose size
and construction reflected nice degrees of status. In between
ran smaller streets of more obviously working-class housing,
a pattern still clearly visible today although the status is
sometimes reversed—it may be smarter now to own your
own small terrace house than to live in one room in a big
house.

For those Victorians who could afford carriages as well
as servants, greater distinctions were possible. Rich merchants and professional men could withdraw a little distance, though not far by modern standards.[1] Distinctions
might not last for long unless steps were taken to ward off
the encroaching lower classes and the flow of industry
which might eventually, as in parts of Cheetham, result in
large dwelling-houses being converted into factories. The
most notable example of defensive upper-middle-classness
in Victorian Manchester was Victoria Park, developed from
the 1830s onwards, mostly with very grand detached houses
although some modest terraces crept in later. The park was
formerly enclosed with a toll gate; some roads remain un-
made-up even today. At first it was well outside the solidly
built-up area of the city, and the area to the south of it
remained relatively open until filled in by inter-war council

---

[1] Katherine Chorley, writing of the Manchester background to her
Edwardian childhood, said: 'My own grandparents typified this
process of "moving out". They moved in sequence from York Place
behind Upper Brook Street to Grove House on the Oxford Road
where the Whitworth Art Gallery now stands, and then to Bowdon
in Cheshire' (*Manchester Made Them*, London, Faber, 1950).

housing and private semis. Victoria Park had begun to lose its attraction in the Edwardian period,[2] but it retained its grand reputation much longer and some people still lament its decline, more noticeable to them since it became one of the areas in Manchester inhabited by coloured immigrants.

Manchester, the wonder of the early Victorians, was also by them regarded as a dire example of industrial urbanization run riot.[3] Engels was not alone in contrasting the utter squalor of its working classes with the comfortable indifference of their employers. But his is the most famous description of working-class housing in Manchester in the early 1840s, and one of the worst parts of the town he described was that inhabited by Irish immigrants who formed one-fifth of Manchester's labour force in 1840.

Here lie two groups of about two hundred cottages, most of which are built on the back to back principle. Some four thousand people, mostly Irish, inhabit this slum. The cottages are very small, old, and dirty, while the streets are uneven, partly unpaved, not properly drained, and full of ruts. Heaps of refuse, offal and sickening filth are everywhere interspersed with pools of stagnant liquid. The atmosphere is polluted by the stench and is darkened by the thick smoke of a dozen factory chimneys . . . On average about twenty people live in each of these little houses which at the moment consist of two rooms, an attic and a cellar. One privy—and that usually inaccessible —is shared by about one hundred and twenty people. In spite of all the warnings of the doctors and in spite of the alarm caused to the health authorities by the condition of Little Ireland during the cholera epidemic, the condition of this slum is practically the same in the year of grace 1844 as it was in 1831.[4]

Even as Engels wrote, the Manchester city authorities were making their first by-laws controlling the most outrageous housing conditions.[5] Stronger by-laws in the 1860s

[2] *Manchester Made Them*, p. 146.
[3] Asa Briggs, *Victorian Cities*, London, Odhams, 1963.
[4] Friedrich Engels, *Condition of the Working Classes in England* (trans. and ed. by W. O. Henderson and W. H. Challoner), Oxford, Basil Blackwell, 1958, pp. 71-3.
[5] *Victorian Cities*, p. 107.

and 1870s, and again in the 1890s, produced a more spacious
and regular layout of working-class terraced streets. This is
clearly visible in the street pattern of Moss Side West, built
in the 1870s. In about 1900 Manchester builders started
to use the better 'stock brick'—dark, smooth, and uniform
in appearance—in place of the more attractive but less
impervious rough brick which distinguishes houses built
before the turn of the century. Their poor durability has
given south-east Lancashire a more urgent slum problem
than some other areas with stone-built houses of equivalent
age. The stock-brick period is roughly where today's slums
stop. For example, much of Moss Side East, south of Great
Western Street, is of stock-brick construction.

By this period, local authorities were taking direct action
to house the poor by building municipal tenement blocks.
In 1904 dissatisfaction with this method was expressed by
T. R. Marr, later chairman of the Manchester Housing
Committee, who contrasted the tenements with the salubrious suburban cottage-type houses built for working-class
people by private enterprise at Bournville and Port Sun-
light.[6] Manchester's municipal Bournville, at Wythenshawe, had to await the late 1920s for realization. Meanwhile the available land within the city boundary was
purchased, as soon as possible after the war, for suburban-
style municipal estates, which soon surrounded the Victorian city.[7] The suburbanization of the working classes
had arrived, and with it the increasing contrast in amenity
and way of life between the inhabitants of the estates and
those who remained to occupy whatever was going in the
way of private housing in the inner, older city.

In all this Manchester presented an almost copybook
example of urban growth and decay, except in one respect.
The normal concentricity of city growth, the tree-trunk
principle, was badly deformed by the pressure of two neighbouring county boroughs, Salford and Stockport, and the

[6] *Housing Conditions in Manchester and Salford*, Manchester,
Sherratt and Hughes, 1904, pp. 78–9.
[7] Walter L. Creese, *The Search for Environment*, New Haven and
London, Yale University Press, 1966, p. 256.

building limits set by Mersey marshland to the south, and
Pennine escarpments to the north-east. In shape the modern
city resembles a kidney-bean with the centre on the left-
hand side. Only the narrow, filthy river Irwell divides the
centre of Manchester from Salford and the docks on the
Manchester ship canal. Salford and Prestwich form the
north-east quarter of the whole conurbation. As *The
Economist* said in 1965: 'There are few things that go on
within the compressed boundaries of Manchester itself that
can be solved satisfactorily without reference to most of the
100 other local authority areas within roughly twenty miles
of its centre.'[8] Jealousy, exclusivity, and fear of dominance
by the city inform these relationships, and the battle for
sites for Manchester's overspill estates has been the saddest
product of these ill-feelings. While the middle classes, and
increasing numbers of working-class people able to buy a
house of their own, continually migrate outwards, those
without money or initiative depend on public action to lift
them from the poor living conditions of the inner city—
action which has frequently been hampered by opposition
to overspill from the very people who have moved out
voluntarily. This is only one of the many factors which, as
will be shown later, have caused Manchester's redevelopment to move forward in such a jerky fashion.

Where people have moved out from Victorian Manchester they have, of course, left room for others to move
in. Some of these others will in turn be moved on by slum
clearance; others will find their own path to suburbia, as
earlier immigrants have done before them. How far each
generation of immigrants follows the same path is a tan-
talizing subject, which can only be touched on here. Immigrants have always been prominent among Manchester's
poorest, and most prosperous, citizens. Among the poor,
the Irish labourer is ever present. Among the prosperous,
nineteenth-century Manchester numbered many successful
German and Jewish businessmen among its leading citizens: it was always something of a cosmopolitan city and

---

[8] *The Economist*, 27 February 1965.

its strong cultural life benefited accordingly.[9] The Jewish middle classes have remained city-orientated and continue to provide some of the most active elements in Manchester life, including its government. An intelligent and liberal Jewish grip on the local Labour party has helped to maintain a high standard in the City Council—it is sometimes said that Manchester is run by its Jewish professional men, and in so far as this is true it is no bad thing.[10] Religion and culture have helped to keep less prosperous Jews (like the Irish Catholics) tied to the older residential districts of the city; Cheetham, north of the city centre, is the traditional Jewish area. (Perhaps this was an example of immigrants taking second-best—north was the smoky side.) There has long been middle-class Jewish migration to the suburbs, notably Prestwich and Didsbury. Jews still believe they are unwelcome in the 'posher' Cheshire commuter villages. But the fact that there has been little overt hostility to coloured immigrants in Manchester is often attributed to the Jews having set a good example both as well-adjusted immigrants themselves and as active proponents of tolerance—while this may not be true of all Jews, it does apply to the influential professional element.

During and after the Second World War, many European refugees arrived in Manchester, especially Poles and Ukrainians. Like the Jews, they favoured Cheetham, possibly because houses were becoming empty through Jewish movement to the suburbs at this point. West Indian immigrants were also brought by the war, mainly as munitions workers.[11] A small coloured population had in fact existed since the 1914–18 war, augmented over time by seamen, students, and some professional men. But Manchester, like the rest of the country, only acquired a recognizable coloured population in the 1950s. The 1951 Census records,

[9] *Victorian Cities*, p. 103.

[10] Written before the 1967 Borough Council elections in which the Conservatives won control of Manchester for the first time for thirty-one years.

[11] A. H. Richmond, *Colour Prejudice in Britain*, London, Routledge, 1954, p. 50.

for example, only 351 West Indians in Manchester, compared with 2,502 in 1961. As far as can be computed from country of origin, about 7,300 coloured people showed up in the 1961 Census—over 1 per cent of the total population. Since then Manchester's population has been falling, but the immigrant and coloured proportion has been rising: by how much, exactly, it is hard to say.

One measure is the school population, although even this is not clear owing to contradictory estimates which have been made by the Education Department. A probably conservative estimate in January 1966 (replacing a much more generous one which had been withdrawn) counted nearly 3,000 immigrant children of African, Asian, West Indian, and European origin in the schools. By far the largest group were 1,549 West Indian children, followed by 449 Pakistanis and 224 Indians. These three groups therefore totalled only 2,212, a smaller number than that recorded a year later in the towns of Nottingham (2,346) and Wolverhampton (3,906) (see Chapter VII). The Manchester figures will not include a number of second or third-generation coloured children; but it does seem that in Manchester there are fewer coloured immigrant families —although a greater range of immigrants of all types—than in some much smaller towns. But it is also likely that there are a good many more single immigrant workers (especially Pakistanis) and more students of overseas origin than in either Nottingham or Wolverhampton.

The 1961 Census showed up only 560 Pakistanis and 1,682 Indians in Manchester, which must have been an undercount then, and has certainly risen appreciably since. The Pakistanis, the majority of whom are from the Sylhet district of Bengal, estimated their own numbers in 1966 as 6,500; and the Sikh community (most of the Indians) has been estimated at 2,000-2,500. One should allow for exaggeration in these figures, which at their face value would suggest that the Asians equalled or outnumbered West Indians in Manchester. West Indians, too, tend to get overestimated; even the informed guesses of supposed experts in 1966 varied from 7,500 to 'at least 15,000' (includ-

ing children born here). The author is inclined to accept
as more accurate estimates in the lower half of this range,
especially in view of the school figures. Just to put the
whole thing in proportion, it is as well to bear in mind that
the Southern Irish outnumbered people of non-European
origin in the Manchester 1961 Census by three to one.

Sheer numbers are anyway of far less importance than
location and degree of concentration, and both these are a
function of housing. True to form, coloured settlement in
the Manchester area first began in the slum district around
Salford docks and in places within easy reach of there where
furnished rooms were available. This meant a movement
south-east, into Stretford and Moss Side, and north-east to
Cheetham. In the usual way the slightly larger houses suitable for letting off in rooms were those immediately available to immigrants. Multiple occupation was common in
the 1930s in districts such as Chorlton-on-Medlock (between the city centre and the University), where in 1931
houses varying in size from five to eight rooms were
inhabited by several families in very poor conditions.[12]
Moss Side had retained its respectability longer than
Chorlton-on-Medlock, but even in the 1930s had some
workmen's lodgings and some coloured inhabitants. A war-
time hostel for West Africans in Carlton Street, Moss Side,
and another for West Indians in Demesne Road, Alexandra
Park (a classier district just south of Moss Side) helped to
establish this as a favourite area for Negro immigrants.[13]

Ardwick Green, an older and more central area adjoining
Chorlton-on-Medlock, was another fairly early immigrant
area, now favoured mainly by Pakistanis. With Chorlton-
on-Medlock, it forms part of the most physically decayed
belt which lies within about a mile and a half of the city
centre—most of Moss Side lying just beyond this belt. The
Sikh community has tended to settle in little clusters all

[12] Manchester and Salford Better Housing Council, *Some Housing
Conditions in Chorlton-on-Medlock*, Manchester, 1931.
[13] C. R. Kinder, 'The Effectiveness of Voluntary Organizations in
"integrating" the West Indian immigrant in Moss Side, Manchester',
unpublished B.Litt. thesis, University of Oxford, 1966.

over this belt, following certain of their number who fairly soon established themselves as slum landlords. Both Sikhs and Pakistanis have been among the first coloured people to be affected by slum clearance. Six objections from Pakistani owners were raised at the Higher Ormond Street/ Clifford Street clearance-area inquiry in March 1966, and the Sikhs objected unsuccessfully to the demolition of their temple in a converted house in Rosamund Street West. They cut no ice with an attempt to link this with discrimination which was being shown towards them in employment on the city buses, but had a better point when they asked why the city planners could not allow space in redevelopment for a Sikh temple, as they did for other places of worship.

The 'immigrant' school population (which includes a minority of European immigrants) is at least some indication of the main centres of immigrant settlement. The Primary schools recorded in January 1966 as having over 30 per cent immigrant children were only twelve in number. They were located as follows: Moss Side, six (including three in Greenheys, the northeast corner of Moss Side); Longsight (between Ardwick and Victoria Park), three; Hulme, one; Chorlton-on-Medlock, one; Whalley Range, one.

All the main areas of coloured settlement in Manchester are also those in which anyone of limited means, especially anyone with children, has to go to seek lodgings or to buy a tumbledown house. The parallel carries through to the student and young professional classes tied to institutions in the inner city, such as the university and the hospitals. There is a substantial coloured population in this category and they cannot find accommodation easily in the suburbs. This demand helps to explain why Victoria Park, seedy but still quite decent, provides a home for the more status-conscious coloured community. West Indians have moved across the road from Moss Side, Pakistanis and Indians (sometimes as landlords rather than owner-occupiers) down from Ardwick and Longsight.

To the west of Moss Side lies Whalley Range, a late Victorian development of large detached houses shading into a smaller and more recent variety. By 1966 a noticeable quantity of coloured immigrants, having become established as lodgers in some of the bigger houses, were buying the smaller ones for single-family occupation; in the words of a disapproving local lady, Whalley Range was 'on the turn'. This south-westerly movement of the more ambitious coloured immigrants reached out to Chorlton-cum-Hardy and had echoes throughout the southern suburbs, wherever older 'village' centres have created a supply of semi-detached terraced houses or larger houses suitable for sub-letting—for instance in West Didsbury, and Levenshulme. It is, of course, possible to find examples (especially among Indian and Pakistani professional and businessmen) of coloured people buying houses in more desirable suburban districts such as Cheadle—but there are also well-attested stories of their having been refused. There has certainly been no marked exodus as yet outside the Moss Sides and Cheethams: a main reason for this must be the ease with which it is possible to buy a house of your own in a Victorian district, even if this, relatively speaking, is not as cheap an operation as buying a newer house. But the choice is not, as it is in some smaller towns, simply a small slummy old house and a post-1920 suburb: the range of older property can cater for several levels of aspiration.

Outside this range, price is a governing factor—and so is discrimination. In Chorlton-cum-Hardy, according to local estate agents, coloured immigrants are buying pre-1930 houses of the less desirable kind for £1,500–£3,000 for a four-to-six-bedroomed house. Anyone with a fair-sized family could fare a lot worse—and, incidentally, would not often find a house of this size on a council estate. But the newer, smaller, more 'conventional' houses were more expensive, probably too costly for the great majority of immigrants. And at this point opposition crept in: in fact coloured people were said to run into frequent strong resistance from vendors of anything except the older terraced houses which no one else wanted. One agent in south Manchester, however, rated this resistance fairly low—only about 10 per cent of his clients, he believed, would stand firm against selling to coloured people at any cost. A sticky market had lowered the resistance of others and, he pointed out, 'You always get the selfish ones who don't give a damn for the neighbours'.

Brand new houses in the Manchester area are also mostly too expensive for coloured buyers, so there has not been much occasion to put discrimination to the test; but it certainly exists. One leading Manchester solicitor had to resort to subterfuge to obtain a plot of land for an Indian client on an estate where a colour bar was obviously in operation. When the Indian moved in, the solicitor was soundly rated by the builder's solicitor for 'letting down the profession' and warned that unless he guaranteed to toe the line in future, the builder could not accept any customers, of whatever race, who were acting through his firm. The solicitor in question reckons he must have lost several hundred pounds in conveyancing fees as a result.

The assumption that 'black drives out white' can at least be shown not to hold good in some older but still quite decent areas, like Whalley Range, where continued sales to white buyers are reported in spite of its being a favourite area for coloured purchasers. Some of the white buyers are Irish, and some may have come from Moss Side or other more depressed districts in search of improved conditions. They may not therefore contribute much in the way of 'class' to the area. This abstract quality counts in concrete terms when it enters into the calculations of people like building-society managers. It is scarcely a coincidence that the areas where immigrants can afford to buy are precisely those where prices have been affected by the difficulty of obtaining a mortgage. The age of the house is the most limiting factor; immigrant settlement is largely confined to the pre-1920 houses which, although they still make up a majority of the present stock, are being gravely depleted by slum clearance and are mainly confined to the central belt of the city.

Building societies vary very much in the emphasis they lay on different factors, but one large society with branches all over the Manchester area summed up its own attitude in terms which agreed closely with the comments of estate agents on building societies generally:

We very seldom lend on property within about four miles from the city centre. We never lend on any 'cellar and attic' property—that means anything built before about 1916. In fact we are pretty wary of anything before 1930, though this depends on the district and the person—we might lend in a good pre-1930 area to someone like a university professor. This society gave up lending in Moss Side before the war. We don't lend at all in Cheetham now, and only occasionally in Whalley Range. Fallowfield is pretty suspect and Withington is getting that way. No one will lend on Victoria Park, because although the houses may be all right the area condemns it as a bad risk, bound to lose value.

While not all building societies in Manchester are as conservative as this one, this is a pretty fair example of the sort of self-fulfilling prophecy which sets property into a downward spiral. The remark about the area rather than the house in Victoria Park being a bad risk can only be interpreted to mean the people in the area. As long as building societies act this way there is bound to be some truth in the belief that coloured people depress prices by their presence.

How far does the local authority step in where the building societies fear to tread? Manchester Corporation lent £11,600,000 to 7,600 mortgagees between 1955 and 1966. While there is no knowing how many borrowers have been coloured immigrants, there is certainly no suggestion that coloured applicants are treated any differently from anyone else—except that more trouble is taken in explaining things to them. In contrast to many building societies, proof of long residence or employment is not required; like most local authorities Manchester is more interested in the property than the borrower, and if a man has just one week's employment as a railway porter that is accepted as his weekly wage for borrowing purposes. While aware that certain sorts of property and certain sorts of borrower may lead to multi-occupation, which is of course against the lending rules, no one has much time to find out if the rules are ever broken.

But the scheme is nevertheless of limited use to immigrants because the Corporation has fairly conventional
ideas about property, and stringent valuation standards,
reflected in the fact that only about half of all applicants
get an acceptable mortgage offer. At first the Council
refused to lend at all on pre-1914 property, and although
this is not so now, by 1966 there was relatively little property of this age not threatened by the Corporation's own
clearance plans, and therefore not eligible for a council
mortgage. Exceptionally, such property might be lent on—
with rates geared accordingly—with a very short repayment period, as little as five years. In fixing rates, the Corporation seems to regard anything pre-1940 as on the old
side. They lend rather warily in old but solid areas like
Whalley Range, where a corporation mortgage may mean
only a 60 per cent short-term loan on a valuation which has
already knocked 20 per cent off the price. They do not,
however, object to second mortgages which must often be
necessary. Loans are not normally given on houses worth
over £3,500, so there is left only a fairly narrow range of
not too old, not too expensive houses on which a corporation loan is assured, a range which must anyway overlap
considerably with the building societies' field. The Government injunction to lend to people on the waiting list has
led in 1966 to quite a lot of loans to young couples buying
fairly new houses well outside Manchester. Local agents
contrast the attitude of neighbouring Stretford Urban District, which seems to have gone to the opposite extreme and
interpreted the Government's 1966 circular in terms of
lending only on pre-1918 houses.

There is one feature of house purchase in Manchester
which deserves special mention, because of the hardship it
causes. This is the practice of selling cheap slum houses at
inflated rates of interest, on terms which offer all the disadvantages of owner-occupation without the compensating
security. Since the 1940s, at least, it has been an expedient
with the landlords of rent-controlled houses to sell cheaply
to sitting tenants on a 'buy as you rent' principle. As more
of these houses have come on the open market, usually in

a very poor state from age and neglect, they have frequently been bought by poor people under the same sort of extended hire-purchase agreement. Often this has meant that a selling price of a few hundred pounds stretches on endlessly, at so much a week, representing phenomenal rates of interest, yet without the purchaser enjoying any legal security of ownership. Until the house is fully paid for, even slum clearance compensation goes to the vendor. In the early 1950s coloured immigrants were buying this type of house in districts like Chorlton-on-Medlock and even then paying relatively high prices. For example, a West Indian lodging-house in Brunswick Street demolished under slum clearance in 1962 had been bought by a Jamaican from a Pole ten years earlier for a nominal price of £600, with a deposit of £300 and £20 per month, which was still being paid off four years later. Not surprisingly the rents, from a houseful of West Indian men, were much above the general level for the area.

Many Irish people have bought houses in the slum districts of Manchester this way; indeed to anyone with little money and many children this is practically the only way of obtaining a reasonable amount of space for a tolerable weekly outgoing. Occasionally the prices paid are nothing less than scandalous. An appeal to the furnished rent tribunal in September 1966 from a lodger brought to light that a house in North Road, Longsight, had been bought by an Irish couple in 1964 for a price of £1,800 at £200 deposit plus £5 a week on mortgage. The house was in such a deplorable state that the Tribunal considered it barely worth £200 or £300, let alone £1,800.

A similar case two months later illustrated another way in which this type of agreement was being abused. A house in Bland Street, Moss Side, had been sold to the English wife of an Indian immigrant for £10 deposit plus £490 to be paid off at £3 a week at 7 per cent interest, the interest to be calculated on the sum still due at the beginning of each year. Moreover, if the purchaser fell down on any single payment for as long as twenty-eight days she would be dispossessed forthwith and previous instalments regarded simply as 'payments in return of licence of possession'—an obvious attempt to circumvent anti-eviction legislation. This had been agreed to without consultation with any solicitor save that of the vendor. When the purchaser's mother eventually took on the responsibility which her daughter could not meet, the vendors agreed to her doing so only if the repayments were increased from £3 a week to £5 a week! One or two estate agents in Manchester, ostensibly acting for others but fairly obviously on their own behalf, are well known for this practice. It serves their purpose best if, as is often the case, the purchasers fall into arrears and are quickly turned out so that the whole cycle can begin again, under what is in effect rental without the statutory security of tenure. When this sort of thing comes before the furnished rent tribunal, it is because the hard-pressed purchaser is in turn pressing lodgers of his own. If, as is frequently judged to be the case, the lodger is paying too much for poor accommodation, all that happens is that the rent is reduced and the purchaser-landlord is worse off than ever.

Over half of all furnished lettings in Manchester in 1961 (6,707 out of 12,265) were in shared dwellings, and a very much higher proportion of those which come before the tribunal are in this category. In the great bulk of cases immigrants are involved either as landlords or tenants, or both. Applications to the tribunal give a fairly accurate picture of the geographical spread of multiple, or of two-family occupation of houses in Manchester. They also give a fascinating insight into the relationship of different immigrant groups as landlords and tenants, while the details of individual cases fill out the picture of frustration and exasperation which these relationships so often seem to involve. Of course the more successful landlord-tenant arrangements—or the ones where the tenant is in no position to make a fuss—are not likely to come before the tribunal; nevertheless it is a valuable source of light on the housing expedients of immigrants.

No less than one-sixth of the 300 applications to the tribunal made between May 1965 and the end of November

1966 came from an area of not much more than a half mile square around Cheetham Hill Road (mainly in Collegiate Church ward). Although there may have been reasons for the people in this area being particularly conscious of the tribunal, it does in fact correspond to what both the members of the tribunal and the city Health Department consider the locality of worst multiple occupation in Manchester. Its decline seems to have been more recent and more marked than that of Moss Side, perhaps because the 'original' Jewish inhabitants moved out more recently than other middle-class people. The houses are nearly all, in these particular streets, of the large Victorian *bourgeois* type, instead of being mixed with smaller terraces as they are south of the city centre. What has given the area a particularly bad name is that vagrant Irish tinker families have been attracted by empty houses where they squat and quickly reduce them to utter squalor, moving on when they have burnt every door and floorboard in the house. As in Sparkbrook, Birmingham, the tinkers provide a focus of resentment for other groups, and it is no one's business to rehabilitate them.[14]

Ownership is cosmopolitan (again, to judge from the rent tribunal records) showing evidence of the old Jewish settlement of the area, plus Polish, Pakistani, West African, and Irish landlords. West Indians would not show up on the record but may also own houses there: they are certainly represented among the tenants. A rough analysis on a surname basis does suggest a preponderance of Polish, central European, and/or Jewish landlords, and it may well be that these are people (or heirs of people) who once lived in the houses they now let but have since moved somewhere more attractive. Absentee small-landlordism does often result in neglect and rapid deterioration. The largest identifiable ethnic group of tenants applying to the tribunal from this district are West Africans, but this may tell more of West African litigiousness than of their living conditions.

In Victoria Park, much frequented by West African

---

[14] See *Race, Community, and Conflict*, pp. 98–9.

students, ten out of twenty applications to the rent tribunal in this period involved West African tenants. Several of the others were West Indians. Pakistani or Indian landlords were often involved, sometimes as owner-occupiers, sometimes simply as proprietors. Owner-occupiers often ran into trouble when they tried to give notice to a tenant in their house in order to make room for a relative from abroad. Their action might result in the tenant's appealing to the rent tribunal and obtaining the statutory six months' security of tenure and a reduction of rent into the bargain. This is a difficulty which frequently occurs with immigrant house-purchasers who do not know the law; it throws up the question of whether the safeguards for owner-occupiers who genuinely need space for their own families are strong enough.

One of the investment-landlords in Victoria Park is a young, impoverished-looking Pakistani, speaking no English, who owns at least three medium-sized respectable terrace houses. Besides his sharply dressed West Indian tenants he looks the archetypal, simple-peasant capitalist. One is very often reminded in Manchester that house-ownership has always been a common source of advancement for new immigrants, and that today's established landlords are often the family heirs of peasants or pedlars from Kilkenny, Kircudbright, or Krakow. Sometimes there are special motives involved—for example, the Pakistani shopkeepers and *restaurateurs* who have bought houses around Ardwick Green in order to lodge and control their own employees. Acquiring houses in this sort of area does not require much education or even acumen; fairly typical of many landlords must be the Irish plumber who owns about thirty houses up and down town, mainly in Moss Side, and spends his time pottering amiably from one to the other trying to make the lavatories work before the sanitary inspector comes round again.

He is not hard pressed. Because of its determined concentration on slum clearance, the Health Department has almost given up the attempt to control conditions in houses in multiple occupation. It has never (up to the end of 1966)

M

stepped in to do work in default; it has made no control orders and relatively few management orders. It very rarely prosecutes landlords, although it did do a few 'demonstration' prosecutions based on an existing Manchester Act which requires 'farmed' houses to be registered with the Corporation. In this it contrasts with its neighbours, Salford and Stretford, a fact which may have some influence in driving sloppy landlords and 'decrowded' tenants into Manchester. It is preparing another Bill, on Birmingham lines, to give it the right to refuse registration in advance; until then, sleeping dogs lie.

It might be supposed that local bureaucracy in Manchester would long since have come to terms with the fact that most of its poorer inhabitants, if they do not have access to a full private tenancy or a council house, must either rent lodgings or buy a slum house. But although the City Council is more enlightened than most, it has been very slow to admit that the type of tenure under which anyone happens to be living cannot be any reliable guide to his needs and deserts. The prejudice against sub-tenants and inhabitants of furnished rooms—by implication 'drifters' and therefore morally inferior—is very deep-seated. In Manchester families in lodgings do get considerable priority on the ordinary waiting list. But in the administration of slum clearance 'lodgers' still do not get equal rights, in spite of the very fair statement of their situation made as long ago as 1935 by an ex-chairman of the Manchester Housing Committee:

When a family comes to live in a single room in these houses let in lodgings . . . conditions are such that only a very remarkable woman can keep a family in decency, cleanliness and self respect . . . It can be reasonably assumed that there are at least 5,000–7,000 families in the city living in single room tenancies. These constitute the really disgraceful housing conditions of Manchester and . . . are the direct result of the housing shortage. The solution of the problem is simple: to provide a separate house for each family at a rent each can afford to pay. There is no other solution. Since the houses themselves are quite good they cannot be included in slum clearance areas. Slum clearance therefore can have no effect whatever on the scandal of houses let in lodgings.[15]

Thirty years later slum clearance *is* now having an effect on these houses. But the official attitude—especially among top administrators—is still one of suspicion towards their inhabitants. Here is a quotation from the Medical Officer of Health, Dr. Metcalfe Brown, reporting on the causes of the unusually high infant mortality of 1961:

Urbanization is frequently associated with atmospheric pollution and substandard housing, both having a very real influence on the infant mortality rate and all present in the Manchester area. Multiple occupation slum housing, in particular, with its inevitable overcrowding and the presence of common food preparation, lavatory, and washing accommodation encourages the spread of infection. Furthermore, bad housing conditions are not infrequently associated with unemployment, poverty, a low standard of personal cleanliness and hygiene, defective maternal care, and ignorance and fecklessness. Such conditions are especially likely to flourish among an immigrant population, irrespective of colour or creed, with defective standards of hygiene and social conduct.

The statistics showed that those parts of the city where a high birth rate (indicating a large number of young families) coincided with a high infant mortality rate, were indeed those associated with both immigrants and multiple occupation.[16] They were, predictably, also among those with the greatest proportion of people living at over one and a half persons per room. The Census recorded 6,700 households in Manchester living in furnished accommodation and in shared dwellings, and showed that overcrowding was most common in these conditions. The highest percentages of overcrowding occurred in the neighbouring wards of All Saints (where 15.1 per cent of the population were living at more than 1.5 to a room) and Moss Side East,

---

[15] E. D. Simon and J. Inman, *The Rebuilding of Manchester*. London, Longmans, 1935, p. 66.

[16] These statistics may have been influenced somewhat by the location of one or two large hospitals, but the Health Department does not think this factor played a significant part.

where the percentage was 14.7. These percentages were not nearly so large as those found in the most crowded areas of London, Birmingham, and Liverpool, and the overall densities represented an improvement on those of 1951. Nevertheless, the fact that within these areas a great deal of underoccupation, by old people, was mingled with the crowding of whole families into one or two rooms, concealed within the average the extreme maldistribution of housing space which is a characteristic of the 'twilight areas'. Besides this, in the most decrepit houses some rooms are unusable.

The attitude of the authorities towards the inhabitants of this kind of housing varies oddly according to whether they are being considered as applicants on the general housing waiting list, or as people to be rehoused through slum clearance. Over a third of the waiting list at the end of 1965, consisting of 3,266 applicants, were living in lodgings, as opposed to the remaining 6,273 who were householders—either tenants or owner-occupiers. Since applicants are supposed to reapply each year, this is considered an up-to-date picture—if people simply forget to reapply, their application is cancelled after a few months. Manchester does not operate a points scheme, as such, but classifies applicants in a hierarchy of need. Top priority, above the waiting-list itself, goes to people moved from slums. They absorbed 55 per cent of the available tenancies in 1966. Next in priority come those with high medical priority and those where medical factors are combined with serious overcrowding—the key decision here resting with the Medical Officer of Health. Then come applicants living in overcrowding of the gross kind defined by the Public Health Act of 1936, which is very bad indeed (see the Appendix to this book); they are followed by people living in lodgings under overcrowded conditions as defined by Manchester's own standard, which would cover, for example, a man, his wife, and two babies, sharing one bedroom. Various other categories follow, including provision for families living in lodgings to benefit according to their size.

Within these categories, applicants are advanced one stage for every year they have been on the list—so that provided their circumstances do not alter radically for the better the crowded lodging-house family does have quite a good chance of reaching the top of the list in a comparatively short time, particularly if they have more than one child. Once accorded priority status, position within that category counts for a lot, and is worked out in the housing office according to a complex set of calculations, depending on such things as how many other people share cooker and lavatory with the family. The result may seem hair-splitting but is intended to be fair. Under this system there is no doubt that some, at least, of the families in the worst type of multiple occupation, including coloured families, have been offered tenancies within a reasonable time of applying.

The benefits are modified in two respects. Applicants have to have lived in Manchester for two years before their application can start to become effective. And once an offer of a house is made, very little choice is allowed; indeed after two refusals of houses offered an applicant loses priority, and a third refusal is likely to send him right back to the beginning again. Moreover, given two claimants with apparently equal need, it is fairly obvious that the true Mancunian gets preference over the stranger; otherwise, why does the Housing Department require to know on the application form: 'All addresses at which you or your wife have previously resided (from birth)'? This, of course, conveniently indicates ethnic origin where this is not already obvious from the surname of the applicant. Nevertheless, although it is impossible to tell without further survey how many coloured immigrants have been housed so far by Manchester Corporation—the Housing Department simply assesses it at 'some hundreds'—it seems likely that strangers may benefit indirectly through the urge to speed up the housing process: the Housing Department is frequently impatient of individual requirements which cause delay, and these are more likely to be raised by long-standing residents who want to live near a relative or a familiar neighbourhood. This reason was put forward by a member of the Housing Committee in a letter to the Press, replying to complaints that coloured people were being preferred in rehousing.[17]

The real injustice of the waiting-list system is suffered by owner-occupiers. It has already been described how 'hire-purchase' of houses, scarcely distinguishable from rental, is common in slum districts. Yet once the occupant of a house has signed a contract, however dubious, which makes him the legal owner, even though his housing situation is not one whit better than if he had signed a tenancy agreement, he forfeits any chance of obtaining a council tenancy unless his house is actually demolished as a slum. Even more unjustly, if he owns a house which cannot be sold or occupied by him on account of a sitting tenant, he also cannot qualify for the waiting list. Or, rather, in both these cases he can put his name on the list, but as a mere formality: he will not be offered a house as long as he remains a house-owner.

Yet, under slum-clearance administration, the totally opposite philosophy prevails. Within certain time limits— in practice, dating backwards from the time of the declaration of the clearance area—all tenants and owner-occupiers are accepted without question for rehousing. Most would also be accepted who had moved in after declaration and up to the date of confirmation of the compulsory purchase order, usually a gap of about eighteen months—this would depend on whether the move was judged to be a deliberate gambit to get rehoused. But until recently a quite different set of rules applied to anybody in a slum-clearance area who was not a householder—in other words, the lodger class. Acting on the assumption that only one council tenancy could be allocated to any one house demolished, the rules were drawn up to avoid responsibility, as far as possible, for houses in multiple occupation. Officially a distinction was drawn between families who lodged with a householder, and those occupying rooms in a house where the owner or tenant did not himself live under the same

[17] *Manchester Evening News*, 26 August 1965.

roof—the so-called 'farmed' houses. This is a totally arbitrary distinction as far as the lodgers, or sub-tenants are
themselves concerned, although, as we have seen, they get
identical and quite reasonable treatment as applicants on
the waiting-list. In fact, as the rule stood until February
1966, *unless* they were also waiting-list applicants, and
already in or near the top category of the list, the occupants
of farmed houses were not rehoused at all from slum clearance. Lodger-families living with householders not only
had to be at the top of the list, but had to have been in
residence for at least two years, before they could be
considered for rehousing.

The inevitable result was that, as the slum-clearance
programme progressed, more and more families were displaced who were not eligible for rehousing. This was
officially recognized as a reason why relatively few coloured
people were being rehoused from slum clearance, even
though in certain clearance areas—particularly the Rus-
holme Road area cleared between 1961 and 1964—there
had been many lodging-houses demolished and many
English, Irish, and coloured inhabitants displaced. It
gradually dawned on the official mind that if this were to
continue, there would come a moment when clearance
suddenly caught up with an itinerant crowd of lodgers who
could be avoided no longer. Some of the councillors for
Moss Side complained that their wards were being invaded
by people displaced from neighbouring clearance areas;
refusal to accept these people, they pointed out, was only
storing up trouble for the future. The Director of Housing
was nevertheless reluctant to accept families from multiple
occupation—in the usual fear that they would be of low
standard, feckless and troublesome to house—although he
was inclined to look more favourably on 'long-term'
lodgers. But thanks to pressure from councillors the rules
were modified. But the change was only partial, and expressed in such a way that the administration could still
avoid the most troublesome cases if they so wished. As a
study of policy and administration, this is a classic.

The motion passed by the Housing Committee was

phrased with ambiguity so that the officials could, if they wished, continue to draw a distinction between 'lodgers' and the occupants of 'farmed' houses. It read:

That families (excluding widows or widowers without children) living as lodgers in houses at the time they are inspected by the Medical Officer of Health with a view to their representation for clearance purposes [i.e. at the very beginning of the clearance process], be assumed to be entered on the housing waiting list so as to qualify for rehousing if they are still in occupation when the notice of entry is served.

In fact the time limit is interpreted more liberally than this resolution implies—but the Housing Department can still fall back on it if it wants to refuse really difficult families.

But what made the housing administrators really worried was the extension of this resolution, in March 1966, to single people over 60 years old. A constant feature of poor residential districts of big cities are the elderly single or widowed people who have no homes of their own in the legal sense. When the supply of lodgings runs out through redevelopment, what solution is there for them? The council has two choices: to build houses on redevelopment sites with sufficient space for lodgers—a solution which Manchester rejected when asked to do so for the sake of the university students—or to provide hostels. This second solution was at the time of writing being strongly opposed by the officials within the Manchester Housing Department, who did not see it as part of their duty to run hostels, although they recognized that if their committee did take full responsibility for elderly, lone people, more than a mere roof would have to be provided. (Eventually, this will have to be hammered out between the Housing and the Welfare Departments). In self defence, the Housing Department was adopting the tactic of confronting its committee with housefuls of Pinter-like derelicts, saying: 'Do you really mean people like *this*?' So far, to its credit, the committee was saying 'Yes'.

The point of the story is to show that the more completely a local authority does away with cheap, decayed inner-city districts, the less it can avoid contact with poor, inconvenient, unconventional people. This is far more than a housing problem, but from the housing point of view as from any other it makes more demands on the time and understanding of administrators. For instance, a housing visitor who usually reckoned to interview the occupants of about five houses per hour, said he had achieved only half the rate in some recent clearance areas. Delaying factors are: multiple occupation; language problems of immigrants; incomprehension by the old and feeble-minded.

In one such area, due for demolition to make room for university expansion, the author called on some of the houses. Poverty was painfully obvious. Some very old people lay under blankets, too sick or poor to light a coal fire. Others sat in the dark corners of large, derelict, otherwise empty houses, whence the more active had long since departed. Similar houses, with at least the internal decoration in rather better condition, were occupied by joint Pakistani households (the families of brothers) or, more frequently, were being bought on hire-purchase by Irish families, who were taking in a variety of poor lodgers. Some rooms were taken by men working casually on surrounding redevelopment sites, but except for one old theatrical landlady, conventional lodging-houses had ceased business. Out of twenty-five households visited,[18] twelve were old-age pensioners, all living on under £6 a week.[19] Seven households were Pakistani, one West Indian, and one West African. The latter was a 74-year-old man from Sierra Leone who had lived in Manchester since the First World War. He sat in the dark (the electricity supply cut off because the landlord had not paid the bill) in one room in an otherwise empty house, curtains drawn against the broken windows. He had moved four times in two years from houses which

[18] Including those who might possibly qualify separately for council house accommodation, even though at present living jointly or as lodgers.

[19] Before the introduction of the supplementary benefit in November 1966.

had been demolished, a routine of which he spoke with quiet resignation. It was possible, under the new regulations, that he might be given a council house at last.

What sort of house? In a few local authorities widespread use is made of 'deferred demolition'—patched slums —to house those for any reason thought unsuitable for housing estates. Manchester has two streets which the housing officials find very useful for 'problem' cases—but the Health Department disapproves and the scheme has not been extended. In one of these houses a middle-aged (English) bachelor has been placed next door to a tinker family who use his back yard as a lavatory and have pinched every stick of furniture he possessed—he now sleeps on a mattress on the floor. This is the sort of problem that authorities are up against and one cannot altogether blame them for trying to escape from it.

There is however no ground for suspicion that Manchester has tried to confine coloured tenants to patched housing, or in any other way avoided giving them fair treatment. Or, if this were ever true, it is not so now. Admittedly this judgement is based on less thorough examination of records than was possible in smaller authorities. But coloured families do not in themselves present much of a problem to the Housing Department—very few, for example, fall into the category of tenants who receive supervisory visits—and as neighbours they are said not to be objected to so strongly as are problem families of obviously anti-social behaviour. If there is trouble, it does not often come to the surface—perhaps because the Housing Department is not very sensitive to complaints, reasonable or unreasonable. Although coloured families do not always get as favourable a report from the housing investigator as they would if they were white, in the vast bureaucracy of a department the size of Manchester's this may not make all that much difference in the long run. The Department is frequently criticized for not paying enough attention to personal factors—aware of this it commissioned a report from the social administration department of the University on the subject—but this failing at least has the advantage that nobody is over-finicky about putting 'suitable' tenants into 'suitable' locations.

As a result a poor family may get sent quite unreasonably to a distant overspill site with expensive fares to work and shops: but the family may be white or black. It is not revealed how many coloured people have been dispersed to overspill estates, but the number will certainly rise as slum clearance moves families from multiple occupation in Moss Side, Cheetham, and elsewhere. In 1966 about 60 per cent of overspill lettings went to people from slum clearance, although these people also had the pick of the generally more popular houses within the city boundaries.

Whether this proportion will continue as more cleared sites within the city are rebuilt with new houses remains to be seen. Certainly there is no bar in Manchester to allocating new houses to coloured people, if the family is of a suitable size. So far the colour issue has not openly arisen among the continual objections from the county districts to the reception of overspill, though it must sometimes be part of the general opposition to 'dumping the worst elements on us'. It does not help that Moss Side, known as a centre of coloured settlement, also retains in the public mind a reputation for vice and crime acquired in the 1950s.

Within Manchester itself, there are signs that some people would like to make political capital out of the inevitable discontent from those on the waiting list who see slum-dwellers given precedence, and who may be particularly resentful if such people are coloured. The Tory Councillor chosen to be chairman of the housing sub-committee of the Manchester Council for Community Relations (the body responsible for immigrant affairs) expressed to the author some sympathy for this resentment. His sub-committee had suggested that the Council should build a special block of multi-racial flats to help integration, although there were slender grounds for supposing this necessary or even desirable. It could have been interpreted as an attempt to steer coloured people away from other estates. However, the idea was safely translated into a project for a housing association.

Many delicate ratios are involved in a redevelopment programme the size of Manchester's; if one factor gets out of line, others will suffer. It is intended to clear no less than 54,000 houses between 1965 and 1974 (47,000 were still standing in September 1966) and, with rather less certainty, to build 50,000 more. At the end of 1966 the existing stock of 75,750 corporation dwellings included 17,330 on over-spill sites well outside the city; and at least 25 per cent of the current programme would be overspill. At least 3,000 overspill sites remained to be found, and many more were by no means secure: opposition was fierce and well organized in 'posh' suburbs like Wilmslow, which feared pollution by Manchester slum-dwellers. Any serious setback over overspill could still throw the programme badly off balance.

A still greater weakness in realizing the programme lies in the failure, in recent years, of the planners and builders to keep up with the demolition gangs, so that large expanses of cleared site near the city centre have lain dormant for years. This exacerbates the inevitable social and physical blight which seeps into neighbouring areas, exaggerating their existing decay. Churches, pubs, and Bingo halls loom out of a yawning rubbish-filled desert, by day a haunt for children and scrap-pickers, by night a threatening void to those who pick their way through the mud to the few new blocks now erected. In the fringing slum streets, shop-keepers eke out a trade as long as they can, and old people live fearfully on in half-deserted terraces, victims of pil-ferers and vandals. Apparently empty houses, devoid of electricity and plumbing, are homes for the homeless. At the end of one street a boarded-up butcher's shop with broken panes is placarded: 'Hooligans or! to whom it may concern there was no need to SMASH OR GRAB there is plenty of meat for all inside.'

How can the remaining members of this crumbling society be convinced there is plenty of meat for them? An alarming amount depends on the efficiency (now being rubbed up) of the redevelopment process, and how far this can be reconciled with humanity. Already the building programme is running into difficulties, though by unforeseen windfall the vacancy rate in existing council houses has been increasing sufficiently to bridge the gap between new building, and the greater number of dwellings lost through demolition. (The chart brings out the picture further.)

Would these trends continue? If something had to give, would it be the slum clearance (over the dead body of the Health Department) or the waiting list, with all the suffering, frustration, and anger this would cause? In recent clearance areas only about 15 per cent of people had been found to be also on the waiting list; over a quarter, on average, were old-age pensioners. Would the pattern alter radically as the areas of immigrant settlement and furnished lodgings were encroached upon? Would the programme prove adequate to deal with the greater proportion of lodgers now being accepted for rehousing?

All these things might affect the ability to attain the set targets, and therefore the speed at which the inhabitants of any particular area were to be rehoused. So would the nature of the redevelopment plan itself, for with housing as top priority, areas which were zoned for industry, shops, or even roads and schools, might not be cleared until last. Such areas included that part of Moss Side around the intersection of Princess Road and Moss Lane which was planned as the site of a district centre; they included some streets in St. Luke's ward much populated with Pakistanis.

None of these projects, however, could be singled out as in any way being influenced by the presence of immigrants. Indeed it seemed likely that those parts of Moss Side which at the 1961 Census showed the thickest immigrant settlement—by far the highest being one enumeration district with nearly one-third of the inhabitants born in the West Indies—would be among the first in the area to be cleared. The map on p. 148 indicates the extent of the main area containing the slum programme, which is progressing from the centre outwards. Roughly speaking, the

better-built houses less than about seventy years old are
unlikely to be affected; Victoria Park is due for long-term
rehabilitation, not redevelopment; Whalley Range will not
be touched. These, on the whole, are the areas where
coloured people have most recently settled, and which
already present a mixture of shared and single-family
dwellings. The shared dwellings are often large houses
quite suitable for the purpose provided they are suitably
looked after. As the tide of revelopment laps outwards, a
coloured population will still remain between it and the
land of Englishmen's castles, semi-detached suburbia. Who
can tell what changes in fashion and social attitudes will
prevail in Manchester and its suburbs in the mid-1970s and
beyond? But it matters for the future that where the
coloured population lives should not continue to be
equated with the slum schools, the sink on the landing, the
conditions that only the desperate or despairing will accept.

VII | Two Midland Towns: Public Policies

For two prosperous industrial towns only fifty miles apart, Nottingham and Wolverhampton present an absorbing contrast. In every respect—historical, economic, social, administrative—they have taken different turns. The effect is not merely the difference in 'feel' and character between one region of England and the next, but a different material experience for its inhabitants in many important ways. This books deals with housing, but the contrast could be drawn in other fields. Although Nottingham has fewer immigrants in proportion to its size than Wolverhampton, it cannot be only for this reason that the indigenous population and the immigrants seem to have reacted to each other so differently in each place.

If one had to define the contrast between the two towns in one word, that word would be 'class'. Nottingham in the nineteenth century grew fat on the fortunes of lace magnates, and its poor were crammed into slums which became a byword through the selfishness and neglect of its Corporation. Wolverhampton was, and is, a town of artisans making metal things in small workshops, living off each other in typical Black Country style, few obviously richer or smarter than their neighbours. Since the war this pattern has been changing, and more people are now employed in big firms; but the artisan, small-business ethos still prevails, as it does throughout the West Midlands. Nottingham has greater proportions of unskilled workers, and more women at work —statistically, and in certain quarters visibly, it is a far more working-class town than Wolverhampton; yet at the same time there are greater contrasts, and more evidence (past

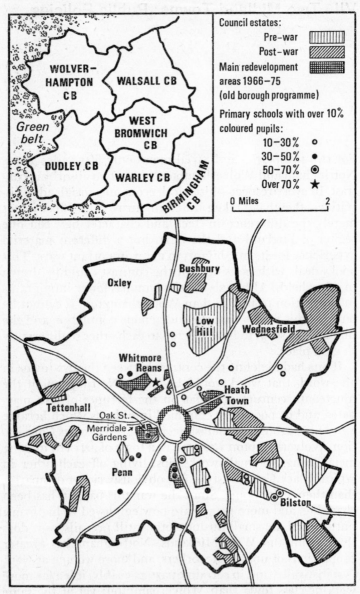

Council estates:
Pre-war
Post-war
Main redevelopment
areas 1966–75
(old borough programme)

Primary schools with over 10%
coloured pupils:
10–30%   ○
30–50%   ●
50–70%   ◉
Over 70% ★

0 Miles   2

IV. County Borough of Wolverhampton
(boundaries as from 1 April 1966)

and present) of a distinct upper crust. General housing standards are lower in Nottingham, but civic monuments are
more impressive (including the famous modern theatre).
Wolverhampton's civic pride goes into its award-winning
housing estates; its social distinctions seem narrower, but at
the same time more competitive, than in Nottingham,
where, it seems, people 'know their place'. In the 1950s, as
immigrants were arriving in visible quantities for the first
time in both towns, the following statistical differences were
recorded: the pattern is not so very different today.

TABLE 11

NOTTINGHAM AND WOLVERHAMPTON: SOCIO-ECONOMIC
COMPARISONS

*(Figures in bold type denote ranking order among 157 towns in
England and Wales of 50,000 or more population in 1951)*

	Households—		Occupation groups*	
	with all 5 standard amenities	living at more than 1½ persons per room	I+II	IV+V
	%	%	%	%
Nottingham	54 **129**	5·3 **50**	13·3 **115**	33·4 **32**
Wolverhampton	66 **76**	4·7 **67**	15·3 **86**	27·6 **63**

* I, Professional; II, Intermediate; III, Skilled; IV, Semi-skilled;
V, Unskilled.

	Labour Force—			
	in manu-turing	in services	in profes-sional services	women at work
	%	%	%	%
Nottingham	50·6 **55**	35·7 **88**	6·8 **77**	36·2 **29**
Wolverhampton	56·7 **38**	28·6 **115**	5·7 **112**	32·0 **86**

Source: C. A. Moser and Wolf Scott, *British Towns: A Statistical Study of their Social and Economic Differences*, London,
Centre for Urban Studies, 1961.

N

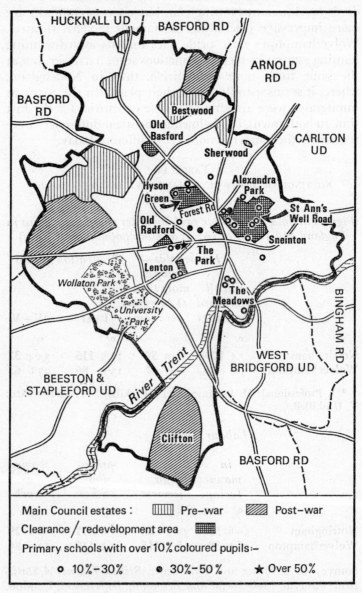

Main Council estates : ▦ Pre-war ▨ Post-war

Clearance / redevelopment area ▦

Primary schools with over 10% coloured pupils :—

○ 10%-30% ● 30%-50% ★ Over 50%

V. County Borough of Nottingham

Wolverhampton is set on a hill and the hill is in the middle of England; the sewage on the west side drains into the Atlantic and on the east side into the North Sea (passing through Nottingham, via the river Trent, *en route*). Its topography has given it a two-faced character. On the east, Wolverhampton is part of the Black Country, that undulating mass of dark-red industrial villages linked by more or less continuous 'slurb' (no other word will do). The west side, the smart side, faces the green belt and the soft Shropshire farmland. This side, people can ignore the open blast-furnaces which still smoke on the other, leeward side of the hill. Such large houses as were built in the eighteenth and nineteenth centuries were built on this side; but there were never many of them, for the rich industrialists either did not exist, or lived elsewhere. The most favoured council estates today are those built on the western fringe, scarcely distinguishable from the private developments around them. But the bulk of council housing is in the vast low-density inter-war estates on the less attractive northern outskirts—just on the 'wrong' side of the railway line and industrial belt which divides Wolverhampton vertically. At the same time as these estates were built there was the usual extension of private suburbia, but on a rather mean scale; one reason being that the small firm structure inhibited the growth of a managerial class with higher housing standards.

Today, the main demand for new private housing comes from the growing white-collared class and from the many factory workers who can now afford a house of their own— at least if it is a new one, demanding the minimum deposit. To satisfy this demand, private builders, inhibited by the green belt, have had to turn back into the interstices of the Black Country itself to look for sites. Because many of these houses have to be built next door to the old depressed environment from which their owners are trying to escape, the status distinctions between the two become enhanced, as it were in self-defence. You have paid for something better and you want to make sure that it remains better. This seems one plausible explanation for the determination with which coloured immigrants are prevented from moving into the

newer parts of Wolverhampton, as described in the next
chapter.

Another explanation for the markedly unfriendly attitudes towards immigrants found throughout the Black
Country is the adherence to local distinctions which cause
people even from neighbouring towns to regard one another
as strangers. It is no coincidence that the amalgamation of
boroughs in the West Midlands which took place on 1 April
1966 was carried out in the teeth of strong resentment.[1]
Although this can be overstated, individual histories of industrial specialization do help to explain why exclusive
attitudes survive, although nowadays all are contained
within one continuous conurbation. An extreme, not entirely apocryphal, example is that of Lower Gornal, a speck
on the map only five miles out of Wolverhampton, once the
home of a salt-mining industry. Lower Gornalese, a medi-
aeval throwback, is a dialect so distinct that people swear the
men from Lower Gornal have to court Wolverhampton
girls through interpreters.

A characteristic of the Black Country is this network of
separate centres. Wolverhampton is the most important
centre (serving the neighbouring rural areas too), but its
own shopping and civic centre (now undergoing ambitious
redevelopment) is on a small-town scale. The reorganization of the West Midland boroughs in April 1966 brought
other centres, like Bilston and Tettenhall, within the Wolverhampton boundary, and enlarged the administrative
population from 150,000 to 270,000. The central shopping
area of Wolverhampton serves its immigrants, who mostly
live within little more than a mile from it; their impact is at
once more obvious, and more intensely local, than their
sheer numbers in the total population would suggest. There
are probably not more than 4 per cent of Commonwealth
immigrants (including their children) in the enlarged

---

[1] The amalgamation of seventeen West Midland local authorities
created five enlarged county boroughs: Dudley, Walsall, Warley,
West Bromwich, and Wolverhampton. Warley was a new name,
replacing the county borough of Smethwick and the boroughs of
Oldbury and Rowley Regis.

borough, and this percentage is equivalent to that recorded in the 1961 Census for Commonwealth-born people in the old borough of Wolverhampton in 1961. In spite of a concentration, mainly of Sikhs, in the old part of Bilston, the enlargement of the boundaries has not brought anything like a proportionate increase in the coloured population. The 1961 Census recorded 7,554 people born in the Commonwealth and colonies who were living in the area now enclosed within the new borough boundaries (3·4 per cent of the total), compared with the 5,887 counted within the old borough boundaries, equivalent to 3·9 per cent of the people living within those boundaries. Immigrants from Eire were 1·6 per cent of the 1961 (old borough) population and those from foreign countries—including recognized groups of Poles, Ukrainians, Italians, and Hungarians—were 2·3 per cent of the total; in fact there were roughly as many of white as coloured immigrants.

There was a marked imbalance between men and women among the immigrant groups which, in the case of the Commonwealth immigrants, began visibly to redress itself after 1961 as more wives and children came over to join their families. By 1967, the coloured population of the enlarged borough of Wolverhampton—counting babies born there, and taking into account a coloured school population of 3,900—might have been as high as 19,000. The majority of these are West Indians, mainly Jamaicans from two rural parishes; the rest are mainly Sikhs and Pakistanis from the Punjab, with some Gujarati Indians—it is the Asian groups which appear to have been increasing most rapidly. They find work as foundry-workers, tyre-moulders, and in public transport; the foundries, in characteristic Black Country style, lend themselves to operation by small groups of immigrants, working night shifts and scarcely coming in contact with their fellow-employees. Plenty of nasty jobs, unpopular with locals, were filled by coloured immigrants, thereby perhaps reinforcing local opinion of their low status.

In Nottingham, coloured immigrants have arrived in not very much smaller numbers into a town which, administratively, is not very much bigger than the new Wolverhampton (estimated at 310,000 in 1966). According to the 1961 Census Commonwealth immigrants, the large majority West Indian, formed under 2 per cent of population. The 1967 school population, however, suggested that the coloured total might have reached 15,000. But Nottingham is the focus for a growing suburban area, and rural hinterland, which makes it of far more importance as a centre than Wolverhampton. Proposals for boundary extensions rejected in 1965 would have increased the administrative population to 469,000. The character of the town is moulded by its regional significance and by an industrial and social history of greater variety than anywhere in the Black Country. This profoundly affects the environment and choice of housing available, which have also been moulded by the strange nature of the town's growth. Up to the Enclosure Act of 1845, Nottingham was hemmed in on three sides by large private estates and by grazing land, 'The Meadows', belonging to the freemen of the city. The boom in the lace industry doubled the population in fifty years without any increase in building land; the resulting slums were as gruesome as anything produced by much larger industrial cities. When land was gradually released, it was at a high premium. Where it was used for workers' dwellings, they were still small and cramped—as in 'The Meadows' itself, which is now one of Nottingham's main slum districts. Where the land was used for the middle and upper classes, the houses were grand and expensive, as in the exclusive 'Park', belonging to the Duke of Newcastle, where huge merchants' mansions were built on a steep site near the city centre (reminiscent of Knob Hill in San Francisco). To this day The Park is still enclosed and hangs on to its exclusivity by the skin of its teeth. Not until after 1918 were large private estates developed for a greater social range of dwellings. The most recent of such developments, the Clifton estate, is Nottingham's major post-war council house development, out on a limb in the south of the city.

Unlike Wolverhampton, the class and employment structure in Nottingham was sufficiently varied to provide a sustained demand for suburban housing in the inter-war period, and to protect that demand from any drastic economic cycles. At the same time, working-class housing standards, and wages, remained comparatively low. The poorest sort of housing was, and is, very poor indeed, and there is a great deal of it, as the statistics show.[2] In the late 1920s and 1930s great efforts were made to rid the city of its most squalid housing; the Chief Public Health Inspector's office still contains a framed *Punch* cartoon of the period showing Robin Hood, Nottingham's hero, aiming his shaft at the 'target' of slum clearance. This aim produced a characteristic flood of low-density council housing on the city outskirts. But the trouble was that clearance of the worst slums still left Nottingham with thousands of others as bad as the worst in many other towns (including Wolverhampton). The sheer bulk of the old poor environment must be one reason why there is not the same urge to escape from this environment as there is in Wolverhampton.

Another significant difference is the employment structure. There are more unskilled jobs in Nottingham (in knitwear, food and tobacco, drugs, and many other industries) and more factory jobs for women. Much of the industry is very localized, embedded in the working-class districts—where many small clothing firms keep going only because they are so close to people's homes that the women workers can drop in and out as they please. Even in the northern parts of the city, where the Nottinghamshire coalfield provides high wages, miners continue to live in old slum cottages even though they could afford (and obtain) something better. In the slum districts of central Nottingham, not even the wages are enough to give anyone big ideas—and anyway, outside these districts the women could not find the same easy casual employment. The effect is almost uncanny: a slice of old-fashioned proletarian life right next to the tidy commercial heart of the city centre, like a strip of old film cut into a modern 'glossy'.

It was in these districts that the coloured immigrants of Nottingham first arrived, and it was here that they obtained unskilled, low-paid employment. Cheap housing, as the

[2] See Table on p. 181.

next chapter will show, has made it possible for many of them to obtain the space they need in the poor areas, at the same time as being able to disperse, if they wish, to rather bigger or better houses in less slummy districts. Perhaps it is because there is not such a marked distinction in status between old and new in Nottingham as there is in Wolverhampton that the coloured inhabitants of the former are the more content, or at least less vocally discontent, with their housing lot. And although Nottingham has a reputation for racial violence on the basis of some widely publicized gang fights which took place in August 1958, this is an undeserved reputation. Racial feeling does not, in the mid-1960s, run nearly so high as it does in Wolverhampton, which has all the same never erupted into violence. The differing attitudes to housing may very well have something to do with this.

Politically, Nottingham and Wolverhampton are more similar than on most other things: they both in 1966 had Labour Councils of long standing whose position had been recently eaten into by the Tory opposition. Most Labour councils make a habit of resolutely ignoring the subject of immigration, to the extent of, whenever possible, ignoring the presence of the immigrants. These two are no exception. Nottingham some years ago appointed a Jamaican, Mr. Eric Irons, to its Adult Education Department (Mr. Irons later became a magistrate); having made this appointment and having given a little money to the voluntary Commonwealth Citizens' Consultative Committee, the Council appeared to think no other action on its part was necessary. Wolverhampton's first official effort to help its immigrants came with two similar appointments, of a West Indian and a Pakistani, in 1965. The English-language classes being run for Indian and Pakistani women are a vital, but isolated, contribution to integration on the part of the local authority.

More characteristic, unfortunately, of the mood in which the subject of immigration is approached in Wolverhampton was shown by the reaction to the annual report of the Medical Officer of Health, Dr. James Galloway, for the year 1963 (published in April 1964). In this he pointed out that Commonwealth immigrants, who numbered (two years previously) 3.9 per cent of the population were producing 22.7 per cent of the babies. These facts were seized upon without any background understanding of the number of Commonwealth wives who had recently joined their husbands, or the fact that the immigrants were concentrated in the child-bearing age. They evoked national headlines, including a splash in the *News of the World*, and a local Tory campaign to show that 'in some areas there could be a coloured majority within twenty-five years'. While the Medical Officer probably intended to show that his department—the health visitors and midwives—were being unduly overworked because other departments did not provide better housing conditions for immigrant mothers, the chairman of his committee took the point the way most other people took it: 'The immigrant population will soon be governed by the availability of accommodation for them. If they can't get places to live they won't come.'[3]

Usually such issues get public mention in Wolverhampton only at election time, and even then they have apparently very little bearing on the result. Although Smethwick (now part of Warley) is only the next-door-but-one borough, Smethwick-type racial nastiness has made hardly any headway in Wolverhampton politics. A racialist right-winger was elected councillor in one of the immigrant wards in 1965, but dropped the following year. Maybe the generally dim and apathetic standard of local politics in Wolverhampton does not even give scope for the more unpleasant types of controversy, or maybe the fact that immigrants are unwelcome is so universally accepted as to be no subject for controversy.

The housing-immigration issue sparks up occasionally: as in early 1967 when Wolverhampton's new immigrant liaison officer, a Trinidadian, having been refused by over fifty private landlords, was at last granted a flat, as a key worker, by the council Housing Committee. The previous year, one of the successful Tory councillors who had got in in Blakenhall Ward, had declared during the campaign that

[3] *Wolverhampton Express and Star*, 20 April 1964.

the Tories would see to it that no coloured tenants occupied the new council flats, Blakenhall Gardens. Subsequently the chairman of the Housing Committee, Alderman Lane, a Labour stalwart, dispelled controversy by declaring:

It is the practice of the Housing Committee which consists of both Tories and Socialists to disperse Commonwealth tenants—and this applies particularly to coloured tenants—through the council estates. Since the majority of vacancies occur in existing dwellings, as opposed to new houses and flats, it is possible to avoid concentration in particular areas.[4]

In fact this sort of thing is, in Wolverhaampton, very much in the hands of the administrators, led by a widely respected Town Clerk, Mr. R. J. Meddings. The Housing Department, under Mr. M. C. Barton, is in many ways a model of efficiency. Everything is very cut, dried, and according to the book, since there is no pressure to keep the allocation of houses under a cloak of obscurity and patronage. Good records are kept and research inquiries dealt with in detail; it has therefore been possible to give a much more accurate picture than in most other places of the quantitative effect on coloured immigrants of housing policies. Where this has produced material for criticism, it should be remembered that other authorities, less frank, may have had still less to show or more to hide.

In 1966, the new borough of Wolverhampton owned some 31,000 houses, or about 40 per cent of the total housing stock. The annual building rate fluctuated, but several very ambitious schemes were in hand. In the nine months from 1 April 1966 there were 600 new council dwellings completed and 420 vacancies available in existing houses. This is a net figure, allowing for the fact that the department was also very active in encouraging transfers from under-occupied to smaller council property, which often means to a new flat. Nearly 40 per cent of the net vacancies were filled from slum clearance and redevelopment. The waiting list stood at 6,200 at mid-1966, including those waiting for transfers. (Six months later it had increased by 10 per cent.)

[4] *Wolverhampton Express and Star*, 24 January 1966.

There were 368 coloured applicants; 125 coloured tenants already occupied council property—not all of it, however, in purpose-built council houses. The Housing Department likes to know exactly who is who, unlike some local authorities who hide behind deliberate ignorance. There is in fact some official uneasiness at the low number of coloured tenants, and the figure of 125 in July 1966 had for some months been quoted as 'about 150' to make it sound a bit better.

The obvious reasons for the small number of coloured tenants are, first, the small number of applicants; and, second, the fact that slum clearance has not, so far, taken in significant numbers of immigrant houses. But both these statements need qualification. In the first place, Wolverhampton deliberately discriminates against applications where neither husband nor wife is a native of Great Britain or Northern Ireland, by requiring them to wait twice as long as anyone else before their application starts to count for points. This rule was introduced shortly after the war when Southern Irish, Poles, and other European immigrants were settling in the borough, and were obliged to live in crowded rooms, thereby earning high scores in housing points—a condition interpreted officially as being 'because of their lower standards'. Everybody else, at that time, waited eighteen months for their application to become effective; immigrants had to wait three years. In 1964 the waiting period for natives was reduced to one year, but it was not until December 1967 that the rule for immigrants was reduced to two years—a motion in the Council calling for uniformity having been defeated.

In practice few people were likely to be offered a tenancy after less than three years on the list, so the rule is not so harsh as it sounds. Overcrowding is allowed for fairly generously in the points system, although multiple occupation without overcrowding does not earn very high marks. Medical priority is awarded through the points system— there is no extra quota—and four points are given for every year on the list. Any change in circumstances which increases overcrowding (other than the birth of a baby or eviction through a court order) does not count for extra points until a year after the housing department has been notified; so that an immigrant who brought over two children from abroad and failed to inform the housing department at once could not expect any consideration for some time. The system is complex but carefully weighed to achieve what is intended to be a fair balance; it is very strictly and conscientiously applied, with no allowances or exceptions made. Complaints from immigrants that they have to earn more points than anybody else before being offered a house most likely arise from their own misunderstanding of a very complex system which(though published for general use) is not set forth in easily comprehensible language.

Slum clearance is well advanced in Wolverhampton but is still going on in patches of small terraced streets within about a mile of the town centre—the area occupied by immigrants. Whitmore Reans, a major immigrant centre, is scheduled for extensive comprehensive redevelopment. So far, however, immigrants have been a small minority of the people cleared, or at least a minority of those who qualify for rehousing through having been in occupation before the confirmation of the compulsory purchase order. An impression is current among some immigrants that 'we are just told we must be out by a certain date and not that we will be offered a council house'; if true, this may help to account for the fact that in 1966 as many as 26 per cent of those eligible for rehousing found their own accommodation. It may also arise from a deliberate vagueness on the part of the Housing Department as to whether people qualify for rehousing who have moved in *before* the confirmation of the compulsory purchase order and after it has actually been made—often a gap of about a year. 'Each case is treated on its merits.' Immigrants, who move about more than other people, are most likely to be found lacking in merit. They also suffer from the empirical approach to rehousing families from houses in multiple occupation; the general practice has been to provide one council tenancy for each house cleared, but families sharing houses are treated 'on their merits'. This may have to become more precise as clearance of the Oak Street area will cover houses of which, in 1966, nearly one-sixth were occupied by coloured families, and about half of these were in multiple occupation, or 'extended family' occupation.

Single people and cohabiting couples are not rehoused from clearance areas; owner-occupiers, however, do get the offer of council accommodation. Much indignation is caused by the fact that, however bad the individual houses within a clearance area, people do not 'normally' get rehoused until the area is dealt with as a whole, even if they are near the top of the waiting-list. There are families, white and coloured, who have been hanging on in really appalling houses, in the Oak Street area, some with all but one room unusable through damp, while the processes of clearance grind into action.[5]

The most interesting aspect of the Housing Department's dealings with its coloured tenants is their processing through the very fine filtering system used to ensure that suitable people fill the more valuable post-war property, especially new high flats. The department sets much store by good management, and has, by dint of careful preparation and selection, 'sold' the idea of living in high flats much more successfully than any other West Midland authority. This means, among other things, picking tenants who are not going to upset each other. Since the flats are nearly all one- and two-bedroomed, the new blocks are often filled at least partially with people who have moved from larger houses on other council estates (transfers get priority, after slum clearance, over people on the waiting list). Vacancies suitable for the size of most immigrant families are, indeed, most likely to occur on the older estates. Sometimes it is true that the best solution for an 'extended' Indian family is a large old house near the town centre: this is said to be what many immigrants choose.

Nevertheless, it would be most unusual in Wolverhampton to find any council property occupied by a tenant who did not match up to what the Housing Department thought

[5] The Oak Street clearance area was declared in November 1964. Rehousing was expected to begin some time in 1967.

was appropriate. Home interviews are conducted by 'welfare visitors'; but the title does not necessary imply any social work background, but it does indicate that much trouble is taken to ascertain a family's needs. During the interview the visitor plays a definite line in directing the prospective tenant's choice—much more so than is the case in less status-conscious authorities. The visitor's responsibility is formidable, for in a few minutes she has to sum up the applicant, or slum-dweller, and grade him in one of nine categories, from A1 to C3. A new three-piece suite earns good marks, torn wallpaper or weeds in the garden can tip the balance downwards. Any mark below B2 disqualifies the candidate for a post-war house. It is rare for a coloured person to get a high mark; particularly rare for Indians, with their frequent disdain for outward show.

The consequences are revealed in the following table of distribution of coloured tenants. The breakdown may not be completely accurate owing to the fact that some estates contain both pre-war and post-war houses; but if anything the error overstates the number in post-war property.

TABLE 12

NON-EUROPEAN* COUNCIL TENANTS: WOLVERHAMPTON, MID-1966

	Pre-war estates	Post-war estates	Miscellaneous (acquired houses)	Total
	Numbers:			
West Indian	44	21	27	92
Asian	15	4	11	30
TOTAL:	59	25	38	122

Percentage of total council tenancies in category:

38,400 = 100 per cent

* Including mixed marriages.

Source: Wolverhampton Housing Department

ERRATUM

(p. 194, Table 12)

Percentage of total council tenancies in category
should read

(Pre-war estates)	(Post-war estates)	(Miscellaneous acquired houses)
33	64	3

38,400 = 100 per cent

Of the sixty or so coloured tenants in pre-war estates, thirty-three were on one huge estate, Low Hill, with the worst reputation and tattiest appearance. Low Hill was the scene of a so-called 'race riot' in August 1965, caused by the fact that a West Indian salesman with an English wife was placed next-door to a hot-tempered Irishman, in a road used to housing 'problem' families, and where fights were frequent. Tenants of all races on this side of the Low Hill estate complain of the 'rough' Irish lads. Of the six coloured families interviewed at random on this estate, five lived close to the 'rough' quarter and mostly complained of the neighbourhood: two had asked for transfers for this reason. The trouble was recognized as general rather than racial: 'It's not only us who get our windows broken and the washing trodden in the mud.'

The Housing Department is more careful now than it used to be about whom it places coloured tenants next door to, and how closely it groups them; wherever possible, dispersal is practised, but this would not take precedence over 'suitability' for a particular type of accommodation. It is encouraging that the occasions when a coloured tenant is greeted with organized protest are rare: only two such incidents had up to 1967 reached the Press (one in the old borough of Wednesfield) and both were dealt with firmly by the housing manager. The second incident, in June 1966, in a block of walk-up flats in Bilston, for the first time produced a flood of letters to the local paper condemning the woman who had said she could not bear to have a West Indian 'only eighteen inches from her door'. Not one racialist letter was received.

It should also be reported that the handful of coloured families living on the most up-to-date council estates appear to be content, although like everyone else they keep themselves to themselves. One of the West Indian families interviewed was a model of the successful council house applicant: articulate; dazzlingly clean; only two children, both sons, with the eldest at technical college; and sufficient knowledge of the system to support their application with letters from doctors and social workers. Very few immigrants know how to turn the system to their own advantage; if they did, there would certainly be more coloured faces on the Wolverhampton council estates.

The small provision for immigrants on council estates has not so far been compensated by generosity in council mortgage-lending. Up to 1961 the Borough operated a very limited fixed-interest-rate lending scheme; high interest rates then caused it to be suspended, but it was not renewed and by March 1967 no alternative scheme had as yet been provided. Reluctance to do so was largely due to the fear of encouraging immigrants to buy houses in the borough. The Council had been disturbed to find that from 1959 onwards immigrants had increasingly outnumbered other borrowers. The help given them was on a very small and cautious scale: a total of 133 loans averaging £780 each, compared with an average loan of £917 to others. Pre-1914 houses had accounted for 120 of the immigrant loans and, as the Borough Treasurer reported in 1961 to a sub-committee on the subject: 'Advances on pre-1914 property are generally restricted to, say, 65 per cent of the Borough Engineer's valuation (which itself is a mortgage valuation below the current selling value of the property) while the periods have also been restricted. There is therefore an immediate margin of, say, 35 per cent on all these properties if a forced sale is made.' This policy was justified by the fear that recession might force the immigrants to return home, leaving property of reduced value in the Council's hands. The report went on to point out 'the need at the present time for immigrant labour in this area to carry out essential work and the fact that, in having loans to purchase houses they solve their own housing problem without causing an immediate financial burden on the community'. (In other words, without the Council's having to give them a council house.)

Nevertheless, although it recognized that the demand for council mortgages from immigrants was due to the fact that they, and they alone, were not getting sufficient help from building societies, the Council continued to withhold help itself. Once it became clear that there was no flood of immigrants into council houses, the arguments in favour of reviving the mortgage scheme lost their appeal. In March 1967 the Council was still studying the ministerial circular of April 1966 recommending help to people buying older houses unlikely to attract a commercial mortgage.

Houses mortgaged to coloured immigrants are subject to annual inspections by the Public Health Inspectors to make sure that there is no multiple occupation. This is admitted to be a precaution only applied to coloured people. While the suspicion may be founded on good evidence, no attempt is made to distinguish good and bad risks other than in terms of race. Much offence has been given to the householders concerned, whose families have been knocked up in the middle of the night, and who cannot even have a house-guest without being accused of illegal sub-letting. In contrast, the pursuit of multiple occupation through any other means has been comparatively mild, in recognition of the fact that there is not much to be gained by pushing people around from one crowded house to another. Severe staff shortages in the borough Health Department have made it difficult to eradicate even some of the really shocking conditions of some very ill-kept houses in multiple occupation. In 1966 the first systematic pursuit of bad multiple occupation began, based on a list of 700 houses which was recognized as very incomplete; some direction and management orders were made and a few immigrant landlords were prosecuted. By this time crowding in the borough was not so severe as it had been in the early days of immigration, so there was more scope for closing basements and attics (the latter as a fire risk). Nevertheless there were a number of houses in multiple occupation in such a bad condition that it was hard to see that any treatment other than complete closure could be satisfactory. In the words of the Medical Officer of Health: 'There are three or four thousand people in Wolverhampton living in squalor.' No policy implemented by his or any other department seems likely to put an end to this quickly.

If it still needed proving that the council house lottery is everywhere played according to different local rules, the differences between Wolverhampton and Nottingham

o

should prove it. Where Wolverhampton's standards of house-building and slum clearance have been high, along with the costs, Nottingham's have been low, and financial caution has been paramount; where Wolverhampton has an elaborate set of rules governing the allocation of council houses, according to set measures of need, Nottingham has only a few general criteria which either rule people out completely, or accept them on rather free-and-easy terms. A good many changes were going on in the administrative structure in Nottingham at the time of investigation and a more rational set of policies was beginning to emerge. But it is the record that is under examination. The truth is that for years Nottingham has ruled out of consideration for a council house thousands of families living in the worst conditions. It is against this that its policy towards coloured tenants must be understood.

The background to housing policies in Nottingham is rather unusual. About half the land, and about 40 per cent of the 102,000 houses within the city boundary, are owned by Nottingham Corporation. This property includes three ancient and valuable estates in the city centre which have been let most profitably on commercial building leases. The administration of these estates led, in the late nineteenth century, to the creation of the office of the City Estate Surveyor and Valuer, which has had only three incumbents—including the present one, Mr. E. W. S. Martin—in all its long history. Until very recently all aspects of council property—buying and selling, surveying, designing, building, maintaining, and letting—were all the responsibility of Mr. Martin. Newly formed Architect's and Planning Departments had, by 1966, taken some of the load off the Estates Surveyor, but he still had (together with the Borough Engineer) a big say in planning decisions, and still ran all the housing estates, through a housing manager who was directly subordinate to him.[6] In other words, for a city the size of Nottingham the administrative machine was still a fairly primitive one, with a few of the advantages or disadvantages

* In January 1967 a separate Housing Department was formed for the first time.

of departmental interplay in the housing and planning field.

Sound stewardship is the keynote of all the Council's property transactions. Skilful as this has been, where it has conflicted with social priorities it is not always the latter which have won. A strong business sense has allied with the political inclinations of the Council to keep as much industry as possible within the city, for the sake of its ratepaying capacity. In return, ratepayers have not been burdened with any responsibility for council housing, in spite of the size of the estates and the fact that nobody earning more than a basic £16 a week is accepted as a council tenant.[7] Financially sound as this policy may be, it has been maintained only by means of severely limiting the number of people eligible for council housing, and by going very slow on slum clearance. Some changes in leadership of the local Labour Party, and some prodding from the Ministry of Housing and Local Government, had begun by 1966 to produce results, in terms of a revived council house-building programme and a corresponding slum clearance drive. But, because slum clearance was obviously going to take up more and more council lettings for many years to come, the Council were still not prepared to extend the narrow eligibility for the waiting-list.

On the face of it, the housing rules in Nottingham favour a type of person often insufficiently catered for on council-house lists—the young married couple living with their in-laws or in lodgings. A young man can put his name down at eighteen and can get a house at any time after five years on the list, provided by then he is married. But nobody can remain on the list at all who is living in self-contained accommodation, whether rented or owner-occupied; so that if in the course of the five years the applicant moves to one of the cheap terraced houses which form the bulk of working-class accommodation in Nottingham, he loses a chance of a council house, however inadequate his present home. The only other route would be if he has a large enough family to gain a place on a separate overcrowding register: after at least a year on this a council house might be offered—pro-

[7] Increased to £20 a week in January 1967.

vided, of course, that the applicant was not earning more than the top limit.

Apart from the five-year waiting period, which applies equally to everybody on the general list, this system has the appearance of one which would favour immigrants: they are likely to have large families, low wages, and to live in non-self-contained accommodation. Many of them, particularly in the early stages, are or were single men waiting to be united with their families. How is it, then, that, questioned about the number of coloured tenants on council estates, the Housing Department (which keeps no record of race) can only say vaguely that it believes there are 'about twenty'? (The only coloured estate tenant who could be produced by the Housing Department for the purpose of an interview turned out to be a lady who had been born and bred in Nottingham.) The first reason for this undoubtedly the extraordinary ignorance of immigrants—far more marked than in Wolverhampton—of the council house system. In 1966 even the active Pakistan Friends' League, for example, did not know the unusually generous rules for single men, although many of its members could have profited by them. No official effort was made to inform immigrants of the normal council housing procedures, even at the stage, early in 1965, when the 'live' waiting list had shrunk to only 2,000, and slum clearance had not begun to take up the slack.

The other reason for the absence of coloured people on council estates is a deliberate policy of housing them in old terraced houses acquired especially for the purpose. Just as some immigrants began to wake up to the possibilities of the council waiting-list, this policy was launched, and has been expanding ever since. It is presented as a useful emergency method of housing any needy people, especially newcomers to the city, without having to wait for the normal five years to elapse. So indeed it is, although it would be still more helpful to reduce the five-year waiting period, and release to immigrants some of the 1,100 estate houses which fall vacant each year. There are several causes for uneasiness over the way in which the Corporation uses its growing stock of old houses. In the first place about 60 per cent of these are unfit and the bulk lack amenities such as inside lavatories and hot water; the minimum is spent on making them habitable. Secondly, they reinforce the tendency for immigrants to live in a sub-standard way in the decaying central districts—and for other people to move out to make way for them. Local people who want to move out to a council estate are encouraged to sell their houses cheaply to the Corporation, especially if they have health or 'environmental' reasons for wanting to move. Does living next door to a coloured family constitute an 'environmental' reason? In some people's eyes it may. The policy does provide a sensible way of redistributing housing space—especially where old people live alone in over-large houses they cannot get rid of—but undoubtedly it reinforces racial segregation.

This is all the more true in that, although everybody in bad housing need can, after a year on the list, become eligible for a council-owned sub-standard house, the native population is much more chary of accepting an offer of an old house at the cost of priority in the queue for an estate house. Although this is not readily admitted, English tenants frequently accept a sub-standard house in the belief that after they have completed their five-year stint they will be moved to an estate—only to find afterwards that no such move is possible, except through a transfer, rarely granted. Coloured applicants are usually completely unaware that any other alternative exists; they are just handed the keys of a terraced house without any suggestion of choice. Undoubtedly many of them are thereby relieved from overcrowded and relatively expensive lodgings. The rents of the old corporation-owned houses are often very low—only about 15s. a week—and so they must enable immigrants to save up more quickly for their own house.[8] But they represent a very low standard of living, and as long as these are virtually the only houses offered to coloured people, it cannot be said that Nottingham's housing policy is free from discrimination.

Nottingham Corporation runs a mortgage scheme which

[8] See next chapter.

is of some help to immigrants. A fairly generous variable-interest rate scheme has been in operation since January 1965, with the usual 'squeeze' gap between August 1965 and March 1966. (An earlier, more limited scheme had virtually ceased in 1957, and cannot by that time have been of use to very many immigrants.) In the three months up to June 1966, since the Council published the fact that it was lending on older houses, 500 applications had been made, of which 10 per cent were from coloured people, mainly Jamaicans. Immigrant applications are scrutinized rather carefully. Although the committee which passes the final approval does not know the colour of applicants, this is known to the Estates Surveyor, who in the normal course of events has to approve the property in question. If he considers the house is in an area or of a size which risks multiple occupation, the application is refused.

In practice this means that virtually no coloured person, and especially no Indian or Pakistani, has been able to get a council loan on anything other than a small house. The Corporation has taken cautiously to the Government's recommendation (Circular 24/66) that it should lend on older houses and to people refused by building societies. With an eye on the value and security of mortgaged property, it has preferred to spread into more modern houses by concentrating on another of the Ministry's recommendations— loans to existing council tenants. As a result, by mid-1966, as many as 30 or 40 per cent of loans had been going to purchasers of new houses, and only 20 per cent to pre-1914 property.

From the public health angle, multiple occupation has received very little attention in Nottingham. The machinery is felt to be too cumbersome, and by 1966 there was nobody in the public health inspectorate whose duty it was to use it. An inspector who had been previously on the job got through 200 houses and took action on half of them before he left. It was felt that overcrowding had eased of its own accord very markedly since the 1950s; and that anyway all resources must be directed on the new slum clearance drive which had suddenly emerged after years of sitting back on the pre-war record.[9] It is through this programme that Nottingham is likely to be housing more coloured people than ever before, as well as far greater numbers of white people who would otherwise not be eligible for council accommodation at all.

In 1965 it was reckoned that Nottingham would have to condemn as slums some 22,000 houses, over one-fifth of its stock, in the next nine years—this target being related to what was then thought possible in the way of replacement. A very large programme of modernization and improvement was also necessary, although this aspect received little attention. In 1966, it was proposed to condemn 11,500 houses by 1970, which with the addition of adjacent properties would mean the demolition of 16,000 houses. But doubts were growing as to whether the building programme would keep pace sufficiently to rehouse all the occupants within anything like the same period. Many variables were involved—including the amount of industry to be relocated within the city boundary, a matter of much concern, further complicated by the unknown future of the boundary itself.

The industrial aspect was particularly important in the St. Ann's Well Road area, in which the bulk of the immediate programme lay. Here was one of the main working-class districts of central Nottingham, and also one of its main centres of coloured settlement. Here and in similar areas—especially 'The Meadows', south of the city centre— was the vast pool of cheap poor housing which for the past ten years had cushioned the absorption of immigrants and shielded the authorities from having to deal with them or with a much larger number of non-immigrant families living in self-contained accommodation and therefore disqualified for a council house. Here, too, were many of the houses acquired by the Corporation for letting to immigrants and unsatisfactory local people.

It would be wrong to suggest that the presence of coloured immigrants has had anything to do with the tardiness of slum clearance in central Nottingham. Far more influential

[9] From November 1955 to the end of 1965 only 3,225 slum houses were demolished in Nottingham.

is the reluctance to disturb industry, and this, too, is one of the main factors influencing the phasing of the programme. In the St. Anne's Well Road redevelopment area of 300 acres, there are 29,700 people and 4,900 jobs, in about 200 different firms. Most of the employment—about 2,600 jobs, according to a survey carried out by the Town Planning Department—is in clothing and textiles, and about 75 per cent of the people, mainly women, working in these firms live within five minutes' walk of their job. Such is the socio-economic weave which has somehow to be unravelled and knit up again. In early 1967 it was beginning to be suggested that it was also necessary to involve the people of the area themselves and to think of their special needs: for instance the Commonwealth Citizens' Consultative Committee raised with the City Architect the question of whether some houses could be built of a size to suit extended Indian families.

The characteristic development of the area is the steep cobbled street running slap across the contour, with narrow brick terraces and common back-yards leading off it at right angles. A fringe of once better-class houses lining some of the main thoroughfares are gloomy with the tatty dress of unmistakable multi-occupation. This district got a bad name for the so-called race riots of 1958. Some streets, especially those where the Corporation puts its 'problem' families, have a sullen air of broken windows and writing on the wall; these houses contrast sharply with the paintbox colours of those which obviously belong to immigrant owner-occupiers. The immigrants appear more numerous than they are. Only one school serving the redevelopment area has more than 30 per cent of coloured children.[10] Excluding English-born children, the 1961 Census showed that only 10.5 per cent of the inhabitants of the redevelopment area were foreign, of which a quarter (831) were Irish. Nearly 4 per cent, 1,161, of the total population were Commonwealth immigrants, and of these 751 were born in the West Indies, and 331 in India, Pakistan, and Ceylon. Household tenure, in 1961, still followed the old working-class

[10] School survey, January 1967 (Nottingham Education Department).

pattern: 64 per cent of households in unfurnished lettings, 17 per cent owner-occupied, and only 9 per cent of furnished lettings. Well after the announcement of redevelopment plans houses were changing hands, frequently changing over from renting to owner-occupation. The change very often marks the death of an old statutory tenant and the sale to a young family. In 1961 the population of the area as a whole was younger than that of the rest of Nottingham—11 per cent were under 5 years old and 27 per cent under 15. This tendency could be expected to continue. It is not only the fact that there is nowhere to play but the street that gives the St. Anne's Well Road district the air of teeming with children.

The clearance programme is phased in eleven stages, of which the second and sixth, respectively, will cover the main concentration of multiple occupation, and therefore of coloured immigrant settlement, as recorded in the Census— the greatest concentration recorded being only 17 per cent of the population in any phase. The pattern will have altered as more immigrants have bought their own houses (as described in the next chapter), but there is no reason to suppose that the number of coloured people whom the Corporation will have to rehouse at any one time will appear large except in comparison with the very inadequate provision made for them hitherto. The process is not expected to begin until 1968 and it is hard, at present rates of progress, to imagine it complete before the mid-1970s at the earliest.

That still leaves Nottingham's second large area of substandard housing and immigrant settlement, 'The Meadows', completely untouched. This is precisely the sort of area where, with imagination and a generous improvement grant policy, the co-operation of the inhabitants could be sought in modernizing and sustaining the area for as long as it was realistically expected to stand. There is, unfortunately, little indication so far that this is likely to happen.

VIII | Two Midland Towns: Private Tastes

It is meaningless to criticize local authorities for their lack of provision for immigrants without also giving some idea of how far conventional local authority housing matches up to the immigrant's own preferences; and how far he can get what he wants in the private sector. This chapter will attempt an assessment of this side of the situation in Nottingham and Wolverhampton.

In the words of an estate agent in Wolverhampton: 'The coloured chap's the same as you and me: all he wants is something a bit better than he's got.' That just about sums up the state of knowledge of consumer preferences in housing. Whether the consumer is English, Indian, or Jamaican, all that one can safely assume is that his point of reference is the type of house he is accustomed to, and that his first idea of improvement is 'something better than he's got', rather than something different altogether. The average council house tenant will think in terms of a better council house; and owner-occupier in terms of a better house of his own or a better area. Habit is the strongest influence of all; how many people, asked to describe their ideal house, would describe variations on their own home?

Therefore, in order to understand how immigrants are likely to react to the various opportunities open to them in housing, one really has to understand their indigenous housing habits, as well as the environment they may have become accustomed to in Britain. This requires very much more detailed understanding of the differences between housing in Britain and in the various countries of immigrant origin; and of the differences between the countries themselves, and different groups within those countries, than the author can lay claim to. However, drawing evidence from immigrants in Wolverhampton and Nottingham alone, one can at least point to various clues, without necessarily being able to give each one its due weight. In these two towns we collected as many housing histories of immigrants as was possible in a short time, as well as assessing local reactions both directly, and through estate agents, social workers and so forth.[1] What follows is a commonsensical but not a statistical evaluation. It may not satisfy the expert but should help the layman in understanding the background to this book as far as the immigrant himself is concerned.

The very first point, which is both obvious and fundamental, is that the immigrant has come from overseas and may never envisage the future without the possibility of returning home. How definitely he intends to do so, or how strong his ties remain, depends on both national and individual circumstances. It is safe to say that East Pakistanis, for example, are likely to be here as lone men, earning all they can as quickly as they can, and fully intending to return home to the families they have left behind. Whereas a West Indian is far more likely to be in two minds about which side of the ocean he intends to remain, and even if he believes he is not in Britain for good, he is more likely to bring children or wife with him. West Indian women, with or without children, often come to Britain on their own; Pakistani women virtually never. All these things affect the type of housing needed, and may be affected by it.

How, too, is the house regarded by people of different ethnic origins? A place for husband, wife, and children to be together? A shelter for all kinsmen? An object of proud possession? A manifestation of dynastic wealth? A source of income? In Nottingham and Wolverhampton it was possible to discern all these attitudes among various immigrants. It has often been pointed out that West Indians conform to a more English idea of the 'family', and therefore of

[1] The author was lucky to obtain the full-time help of Miss Margaret Etherington, a trained social worker, for a month of interviewing during the summer of 1966.

the family home, than do Asian or African people where the
unit may be the larger kin or 'extended' family. But here
again, a distinction has to be made when it comes to housing: does the kinship idea extend to living under the same
roof as, say, your father, brother-in-law, nephews, and
cousins, or merely in the same neighbourhood? An Indian
family in Wolverhampton provided a perfect example of
the first type of kinship in action: a son got married, and
instead of the young couple moving, English-fashion, into a
house of their own, the entire family, including the newly-
weds, moved to a larger house. In Nottingham, the greater
supply of large houses intended for large Victorian families
makes such arrangements still more feasible. But the even
easier supply of very cheap small terraced housing offers
another alternative which appeals particularly to the Pun-
jabi peasants—they seem to acquire family houses much as
they might acquire fields at home, and one might be told
that Mr. Singh owned more than one house in the street,
Mr. Singh's brother yet another, and his cousin another
again. Maybe, if what you are used to is a family compound
with separate dwellings inside a shared enclosure for different members of the family (which is a common Indian and
Pakistani village pattern), it does not make much difference
whether the English version is a group of houses in one
street, or a group of rooms in one large house.

The strongest attitude to the home shared by all immigrants is that no kinsmen in need of shelter can be refused.
This is far more important than any number of sanitary
notices served against overcrowding; and it often creates an
atmosphere of coming and going which leads the neighbours and public health inspectors to exaggerated conclusions about the numbers in one house. Visiting family and
friends at weekends and holidays is an important activity—
witness the number of cars laden with West Indian and
Asian parties on the M.1 on a Saturday morning. Carried to
its logical conclusion the habit should mean that immigrants actually need more spare space in their homes than
English people do: indeed the absence of a spare room has
once or twice been put forward to the author by immigrants

as a reason for not wanting a council house. Other social customs may be space-consuming: for instance, one Pakistani house in Wolverhampton had had a room built on for the women and children.

It has been remarked earlier that West Indians, on the whole, showed far more interest in the idea of becoming council house tenants than any Asian immigrants: in fact we never once met personally any Asian immigrant with his name on the housing list in Nottingham or Wolverhampton unless his wife was English. This can be explained in terms of the generally more anglicized attitudes of West Indians (with the exception perhaps of certain upper-class Indians— but then upper-class English people do not think in terms of council houses either). But it is perhaps possible to draw a further distinction between the West Indian love of possessing *things*—cars, new furniture, television sets—and the Asian attitude to *property*, in which outward show may not play much part although the urge to acquire is intense. The difference between people of slave origin and people of landed peasant origin must lie behind this. The result does seem to be that the West Indian's first desire is for possessions to put into the home, while the Indian or Pakistani may primarily wish to possess the house itself, without much interest in its decoration and furnishing. Such, at least, is the impression gained from visiting immigrant homes. It may explain the greater willingness of West Indians to rent rather than buy their homes—although it also explains why, once a West Indian has acquired a house of his own, it then becomes a prized object in itself, on which care and attention are lavished.

The attitudes to housing which an immigrant brings with him are immediately subject to modification in the light of his experience in Britain, and in the particular part of Britain where he happens to live. Sometimes the search for a house determines the region where he eventually settles; for example we met immigrants in Nottingham who said they had come there because it was easy to buy a house, but impossible to do so in London.[2] Most strikingly, too, the

[2] In 1961 a survey of Commonwealth immigrants in different

differences in the local attitude towards immigrants in the
two towns of Nottingham and Wolverhampton, mentioned
in the last chapter, made its mark on the ambitions and ex-
pectations in housing of the respective immigrant populations, and their willingness to discuss their difficulties.

In Wolverhampton, where racial consciousness was open,
and where every few months the local Press carried some
story of colour prejudice or discrimination in housing, immigrants were quick to discern obstacles and ready to talk
about them. In Nottingham, there was possibly more sense,
among the articulate, that adjustment was a two-way process
requiring good sense, restraint, education, and courage on
the part of the immigrant himself. Within the inevitable
limitations, there is more established immigrant leadership
—and therefore more reaction to it from the immigrants
who resent being 'led'—in Nottingham than in Wolverhampton. In Nottingham, spokesmen who felt responsibility as leaders tended to emphasize the success of the more
competent members of their community in settling down
and adapting themselves; failures were not readily mentioned. In Wolverhampton, any failure at all tended to be
ascribed to racial discrimination. It would be wrong to make
too much of this contrast which is mainly a difference of
emphasis—for both towns abound in stories of refusal to let
or sell houses on grounds of colour, and in evidence that
immigrants are very ignorant of the ways of the housing
market and their opportunities and rights in the public
sector.

Since so much discussion centres on the subject of dispersing immigrants from the inner cities where most of
them live, it is important to be aware of the many personal
influences which may keep them there, quite apart from the
effect of public policy or pressure. Some of the influences
met in Nottingham and Wolverhampton were (in no par-

---

towns found that in Nottingham 72 per cent said they intended to
remain permanently—the second highest percentage after Liverpool
(73 per cent) and over twice that in London (35 per cent). (Economist Intelligence Unit, *Studies in Immigration from the Commonwealth*, No. 3, *Social Integration and Housing*.)

ticular order of importance): transport facilities, to reach work or friends in another part of the town; easy access to work for night-shift workers (especially Indian and Pakistani men in Wolverhampton) and for women workers (West Indian women in Nottingham); education, especially reluctance to move a child once he has settled in a new school in a new country; shops accustomed to immigrants or catering especially for them, in food and/or language. Other ties include attachment to institutions—clubs, places of worship —similar to those found among the Irish in most English cities. Although immigrants by definition do not have the same roots as English slum-dwellers (who may be even more reluctant to move from the inner city) the sense of strangeness of the world outside the known neighbourhood may be more acute, especially in the extreme case of Asian women, who may lack any communication or contact save with surrounding compatriots or relatives. At least the twilight areas offer an anonymous kind of security, summed up in the West Indian refrain: 'Nobody bother you here.'

Since most council housing estates are out on the borough boundaries, their location alone may scare off all but the most confident immigrants, quite apart from whether they want to become council tenants at all. This is a natural reluctance which has to be overcome by many English people. Unless immigrants are helped to overcome it, the combination of what they can afford and what the private sector is prepared to let them have, may oblige them to continue living in the diminishing stock of decayed old private housing until the last roof is pulled down over their heads.

It is surely significant that in Nottingham, where the huge stock of slum houses (mainly, of course, occupied by English families) provided some kind of solution to the initial immigrant housing problem, there was very little evidence of immigrant interest in council estates. It was, anyway, possible to obtain something better without recourse to a council tenancy. In Wolverhampton, on the other hand, where immigrants were confined to often better-quality, but less plentiful, and price-inflated, old terraced housing (nearly all a mile to a mile and a half from Wolverhampton town centre), they were far more obviously keen to get out, as they could see English people were doing all the time. The coloured population is more concentrated than it is in Nottingham—one in seven schools contain over 30 per cent coloured pupils compared with one in thirty in Nottingham—and its attempts at dispersal are more fiercely resisted. Some immigrants are beginning to realize that a council house may be the only way to obtain better living standards, since suburban owner-occupation is almost completely inaccessible owing to local prejudice. But it should not be left to them by themselves to grope towards this solution.

It is worth elaborating on the kind of difficulties coloured people are up against in private housing in Wolverhampton. Having started by concentrating in a few large lodging-houses lining the main roads leading to the two centre, they have since spread into smaller rented and owner-occupied dwellings in the side streets linking the main roads. But outward movement is limited to those areas where fingers of pre-1914 property reach towards the suburbs—and on this property mortgages are either very expensive or unobtainable. The houses themselves have increased greatly in price under immigrant demand. Southwest, in the Penn direction, immigrants have been able to move furthest, but according to local estate agents they meet with stiffer resistance the further out they go, and the same applies in the north-west of the borough. Certain residents' associations are suspected of organizing resistance to coloured house-purchasers, for example by banding together to buy a house as it comes on the market and then finding a white purchaser. One association which says it does not attempt any such thing is the Clairegate and Blakely District Residents Association: the views of its chairman, Mr. H. S. C. Rhodes (who lives in a small 1930-ish semi-detached house in north-west Wolverhampton) are none the less interesting:

I come from Dudley and twelve years ago we moved to Wolverhampton—Whitmore Reans. It was a lovely street until the coloureds moved in and we had to go. I lost a lot of money on that house. We came here two years ago and I started the residents' association last year: we've got 300 members and a good renewal rate. The aim is to keep up the amenities—that means stopping the neighbourhood going downhill. It *will* go down of course, but we may delay it. Oh, it means agreeing to maintain our gardens, and lobbying the council to mend the pavement. Keeping out coloureds? No, we couldn't do it. They're bound to come. Other associations have tried, but they've failed because people turn round and say 'You give me so much or I'll sell to coloureds'.

I've got strong personal views you know, but they're my own views . . . You can't live in the same street as them. If you've got a daughter she can't go out . . . and if they're next door the other side of the wall it's a thousand times worse. You see them every time you walk down the path, you smell their food, the mice start coming . . . You may say what's the difference except skin, but I tell you they *are* different in ways we don't understand. You don't know what's going on in their heads. But I can tell you they breed on purpose; they plan to outnumber us . . . People are moving out of Wolverhampton as fast as they can. They don't want to but they're forced out.

Maybe only a minority of Wolverhampton people would express themselves as strongly as this—but open disapproval of coloured people is often evident, typified by the woman who glared across at some turbanned Sikhs talking loudly in their own language in the park and burst out angrily to her friend: 'If only they would *conform*!' It seems that many of the inhabitants of Wolverhampton regard the presence of coloured people as degrading, or in some way threatening. It is true they do have a decidedly higher coloured ratio, in a somewhat smaller total population, than does Nottingham. Nevertheless some local reactions have been quite unbalanced. The scare resulting from the findings of the M.O.H.'s report in 1963 produced a proposal from the Conservative Association in south-west Wolverhampton that the Government should ban all further coloured movement into the area, 'to preserve local culture'. A Labour Councillor later suggested that locals should be given cheap plots of land if they would agree to live next door to coloured neigh-

P

bours—hardly a happy basis for race relations. Yet it is important to remember that strong words, however unpleasant, are not the same as strong-arm action. It is difficult to envisage the people of Wolverhampton banding together to offer physical obstruction to coloured house-buyers, as reported from the white suburbs of America.

Although the hard core of resistance may not be large or even, in the last resort, very fierce, it strengthens the resolution of those builders who refuse to sell new houses to coloured people. A spokesman for William Whittingham Ltd, a prominent local building firm, believed that the immigrants had indirectly done the business a good turn by helping to boost demand for new houses from white people fleeing from the older areas. The firm used to sell to the occasional coloured person, 'but we gradually tightened up when it became clear that 10 to 15 per cent of buyers wanted the assurance that they would not risk coloured neighbours'. This policy was challenged, to no avail, when in August 1965 Whittingham's refused to sell a house to a Sikh bus-conductor. In the firm's opinion the publicity of this incident did them more good than harm, since it reassured white buyers.

The opposite line was taken by another large Wolverhampton firm, Macleans, who built an estate of low-priced houses, Merridale Gardens, just off a Victorian road partly occupied by immigrants. In the second phase of development, when several English families were already well settled in, coloured buyers started to show an interest. Macleans decided they could not refuse them. Many English residents then complained they should have been warned of this; a few were very angry indeed. (Race-consciousness was not limited to the English: an Indian purchaser, for example, asked if he could be sure of having English neighbours in order to avoid noisy Jamaicans.) The episode appears to have had no ill effects on subsequent Macleans sales on other estates (most of which, admittedly, were too remote or too expensive for immigrants). But gradually English owners have been moving out, and making no bones of the fact it is because they object to coloured neighbours—

although the coloured families interviewed here seemed outwardly more English than the English. Perhaps it was significant that one Indian family had erected a nine-foot fence
all round their plot, in defiance of the open-play layout. But
they professed to be content enough—after all, this was
probably the only place in Wolverhampton where a coloured
person could buy a £2,780 houses with £275 deposit. No
English people interviewed complained of losing value on
their houses—most likely they have done better than they
might, since this is still virtually the only modern housing in
Wolverhampton available to coloured buyers.[3]

Decent rented accommodation is extremely scarce for
anybody in Wolverhampton. For anyone with children, it is
almost impossible. Sometimes childless coloured people are
preferred to English families with children; coloured families with children are the worst-off of all. As elsewhere, it is
coloured landlords—here, especially, Sikhs—who provide
most of the rented rooms available to other immigrants.
They are nevertheless far from popular. The most bitter
complaints come from the middle-class Indians who are
obliged to seek shelter from peasant fellow-countrymen
whom they despise and whose standards of living and cleanliness are markedly lower than their own. The continued
shortage makes it possible to charge rents of about £2 10s.
to £3 a room, which is steep for the amenities provided and
often goes with irksome rules enforced by the landlord. (But
appeals to the furnished rent tribunal increased rapidly in
1966.) The worst case we came across was of an Irish couple
who paid £4 to an Indian landlord for one small room, on
top of which they paid extra for baths and did all the cleaning.

The cramped, ill-equipped lodgings in which many
coloured people live in Wolverhampton, are directly reflected in their share of the maternity beds allocated by the

[3] According to the local agent, in the three and a half years the
market price of houses in Merridale Gardens increased by 11 per
cent, which was admittedly less than many other price increases. But
the houses were known to be of a type which normally might not sell
very easily.

Health Department on 'social' grounds. 'Social grounds' tend to mean housing, although they also include illegitimacy. One-third of these beds in 1966 were going to coloured mothers: an analysis of one month's bookings (June 1966) actually showed two-thirds of the beds allocated to West Indians and Indians.

In Nottingham, things are not so bad. Not only is there a far greater choice of older houses to satisfy various levels of immigrant ambition, but there is also far less open resistance to coloured house-purchase—although renting to immigrants is still mainly confined to other immigrants among private landlords. Reluctance to sell suburban houses to coloured people there is, although it far more often takes the form of evasion rather than open operation of a colour bar, such as is common in Wolverhampton. This can be just as irritating to a coloured purchaser: several people interviewed had had sales withdrawn just as they were on the point of signing, as though the vendor had suddenly yielded to pressure from neighbours. There was a widespread, and probably correct, belief that immigrants were often expected to pay slightly higher prices for conventional houses. 'Unconventional'—that is, slum-houses, have most certainly increased in value since immigrant demand began to make itself felt some ten years ago.

The relative ease with which slum houses, and even quite decent pre-1914 houses, can be bought in Nottingham helps to explain why the pressure on rented rooms is no longer as great as it used to be. Immigrants pay £1 10s. to £2 10s. for a furnished room—very often less if the landlord is a relative. These prices (allowing for inflation) are considerably lower than those of the mid-1950s. Lodgings are far less crowded than they used to be—although there is still a shortage of good-quality rented rooms. The few major Indian landlords have been selling off some houses—business is not what it used to be, especially since the Rent Act of 1965. One of the most respected members of the Indian community, inside and outside Nottingham, is Mr. J. S. Nehra, who is also one of the very biggest landlords. In 1966 he owned 100 houses and four garages in Nottingham (as well as other houses in London, Birmingham, and else-where). But he too felt that the new legislation had made landlordism scarcely worth while, especially because of the difficulty of getting rid of bad tenants. He classes West Indians in this category, and, although at the time of inter-view he had twenty West Indian tenants, he had decided on principle not to take on any more. He owns a few self-contained flats and lets them at modest rents (£2 10s.) to families with children, 'even if other people offer more'.

Mr. Nehra, who lives simply in a large, bare Victorian house in the Forest Road area (a part of town favoured by Indians), is in many ways characteristic of the benevolent, paternalistic immigrant leader. Although not all his fellow-countrymen in Nottingham see eye-to-eye with him, he is frequently a tower of strength to those in need. He presides over the Indian Association, through which he personally guarantees bank loans to house-purchasers: 'If a man falls down on his payments we go and talk to the bank manager and then we talk to him and tell him not to do such a silly thing again.' Until the squeeze put a temporary end to the system early in 1966, some £500,000 of finance had been arranged in three or four years. Legal advice is available to house-buyers with one of the leading Nottingham solicitors; advice on tactics and deportment in house purchase is also given, and Mr. Nehra is convinced that no Indian need have difficulty buying any house in Nottingham, provided that he is a 'decent, sensible' sort of person. As a landlord Mr. Nehra understands very well that unreliable people are not welcome in the housing market: through him and the In-dian Association the influence on the Indian house-pur-chaser to strive after certain standards of behaviour in order, as it were, to qualify as a house-buyer, must be strong.

Improved standards, in the sense of higher housing ex-pectations, among immigrants in Nottingham, are demon-strated by the experience of the Coloured People's Housing Association. The Association started in 1956 as an alliance of social workers and professional advisers, backed by loan stock from private investors and Nottingham Corporation.

It came into being at a time of urgent need: for instance in 1958, the year of the so-called race riots in St. Ann's Well Road, the Association housed a family of five who had been sharing a six-roomed house with six other families, paying £2 a week. From the Association they could rent a whole house for £1 12s. 6d. By dint of buying up old terraced houses at low prices the Association eventually acquired about twenty-two houses. In the first few years the houses were much in demand, but by the mid-1960s the Association had begun to outgrow its usefulness. The money that coloured people could pay had increased, but the quality of the Association's accommodation had not. Immigrants could buy similar houses themselves for little more per week than the rent of one of the Association's sub-standard properties. If they wanted to rent, they could get a similar house from the Corporation for less money. The Association could not afford to improve its houses, but immigrants spoke of them disparagingly: 'They think slums are good enough for us.' The name, even, implying a special type of housing for coloured people, was dated. By 1967, the Association was beginning to realize that a turning-point had come in its career. What Nottingham really needed was not a cheap source of poor housing for immigrants, who could easily obtain that by other means, but a source of decent, rented self-contained accommodation for both English and immigrant families who could pay more for something better. It seemed the obvious setting for a medium-rent housing association; possibly by the time this is published something of the kind may have begun.

Standards are rising, too, in the type of house which some immigrants want for their own. There must be those for whom a small damp terraced house without bath or inside lavatory was always a temporary expedient, on the way to something better. For example, in The Meadows district, where about 200 of the 6,500 houses are occupied by coloured immigrants (nearly all West Indians from Jamaica, and one small island, St. Kitts), several of the original owners have moved out to better areas within or just outside. Nottingham—to better-quality fairly old houses in West Bridgford, just across the Trent, or even to more modern property in the north-eastern suburbs. It is not unknown for coloured immigrants to buy brand-new houses in the outlying areas, but they are not welcomed by builders; some refuse to sell entirely. A colour bar has also been confirmed on a caravan site. It is not nearly so impossible to move from the centre of Nottingham as it is from the centre of Wolverhampton—but it is not at all easy to go just anywhere.

In future the distinction may lie more and more between those who can make the grade according to English standards, and therefore are accepted, however reluctantly, in the suburbs—and those who cannot, or do not want to, and who therefore remain in the slums or the in-between twilight areas. Already districts like The Meadows are becoming receptacles for those members of the host community (who far outnumber the immigrants) who are too poor or too ill-educated or in other ways incapable of living anywhere better. At the pace at which slum clearance is at present envisaged—possibly another twenty years before The Meadows is cleared away—it is frightening to think of these people, and the less capable of the coloured population, left in a standard of living and environment which marks them as third-class citizens today, and will do so twenty times more in twenty years' time.

There is much that could be done to improve the area meanwhile—not all the houses are slums, overcrowding has spontaneously thinned, and even a few of the larger houses in multiple occupation are going over to single-family occupation by large Sikh households. Several immigrant owner-occupiers are putting in bathrooms and new kitchens; they would do more if improvement grants could be given without constant reference to the fifteen-year limit. But will the most improvement-minded immigrants see out The Meadows? It is those with the shiniest, starchiest parlours, and the most obvious home-making inclinations, who already want to move to 'a nicer area'. If something is to be done, it must be done quickly: and the people must be involved. With the backing of an active local Methodist church, an Amenities Committee has been started, to encourage local pride in the area and to act as spokesman to the authorities. Only on these lines can hope for the future lie.

This chapter has only touched on the many conflicting forces, internal and external, which may keep an immigrant in the depressed inner city, inspire him to get out, help or discourage him when he tries to do so. Perhaps a fitting end is to point out a further source of conflict: that between the generations, between parents who are genuinely immigrant, and children, who by habit and education or even birth are Englishmen. Some Sikh friends in Wolverhampton, a middle-class family living in a small terraced house, were moving house. The mother, a forceful and energetic woman who ran a small shop, had ambitions as a landlady; it was she who decided they should all move back into a large house in Waterloo Road, the original immigrant lodging-house area. But the older children, in their teens and twenties, protested —they knew the reputation of Waterloo Road and saw the move as a retrograde step. One teenage daughter declared she was going to devote herself to domestic science, 'because many Indian people need to learn how to use a house'. By English housekeeping standards, with which she identified herself, she was right. By her mother's standards, she may not have been. But the standard by which the English themselves should be judged is whether, when girls like her want to marry and set up house of their own (perhaps in so doing consciously escaping from family ties), they are given the acceptance by the community which they have every right to expect.

It is a good rule of journalism never to ask a question which can be answered with a straight 'yes' or 'no'. There would have been no point in writing this book if the question posed had been simply: 'Do local authorities discriminate against coloured people in matters of housing?' This could have been answered with equal truth in the affirmative or the negative according to context. There is no room for complacency as long as there are any affirmative answers to such a question. But it is far more illuminating and useful to everybody concerned with improving matters if, as far as possible, the questions asked begin with 'how?' The previous five chapters have put a series of mainly 'how' questions to five different local authorities; although incomplete, the answers should help to further understanding of the very wide range of conditions which create, or reduce, the scope for discrimination.

The results are not in every case strictly comparable. This was partly unavoidable, but partly deliberate, since different contexts assume different degrees of importance in each place. For instance, the obvious reluctance (in practice if not now in principle) of Lambeth Borough Council to place coloured tenants on housing estates is to some extent mitigated by the presence of the G.L.C. as a first-tier housing authority. Because it is more remote from public opinion, the G.L.C. may be able to take action which, rightly or wrongly, is regarded by the boroughs as inviting public disapproval. In much the same way, the sheer size of the city of Manchester and of its public housing commitments makes its government more immune to pressures which, in a

smaller town like Wolverhampton, encourage the adoption
of policies (on the waiting-list, on mortgages) designed to
prevent the immigrant from gaining benefits commensurate
with his needs.

But racial consciousness is not to be confused with racially
prejudiced behaviour; towns where race is a hot topic do not
necessarily treat other races worse in the course of administration. Thus Wolverhampton's self-imposed task of identifying the race of council applicants and tenants, which is
partly the result of a negative policy towards foreigners,
also has an important positive potential which should not be
overlooked. This was the only authority out of the five which
was able and willing to supply precise statistics as to the
number of coloured applicants on the council waiting-list
and the number who had been housed in council estates.
Through these figures, responsible people were made well
aware that the coloured races had not been obtaining council houses in proportion to their numbers in the town or to
their housing need: without this knowledge it would be
very easy to use the housing of comparatively few families as
evidence that the problem was being met. In Nottingham,
where council house rules of allocation were few and somewhat arbitrary, nothing in the rule-book suggested discrimination—yet in fact coloured people were receiving manifestly less equal treatment than they were in Wolverhampton.

Ignorance in the Nottingham Housing Department of any
figures relating to coloured tenants or applicants was not a
matter of policy (as in Lambeth) but was chiefly the result
of the underdeveloped state of the housing department itself. In Manchester, on the other hand, a similar ignorance
could not be attributed to lack of information, all of which
was there on the files, but to lack of any motive, either good
or bad, for analysing the situation in these terms. It would
no doubt be an extremely tedious job to go through the files
extracting information on the race or any other individual
characteristic of the hundreds of thousands of Manchester
families in the Department's records. Yet this sort of exercise is one which more and more authorities will have to

3. BEDFORD
Population of
houses in mul-
tiple occupation
1955–66

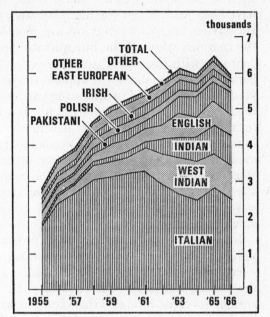

Source:
Bedford
Health Dept.

undertake in future if they are to do their job properly, as
suggested in the next chapter. The commonly held belief
that the keeping of records of the race or origin of applicants is in itself a racialist practice to be deplored was dis-
puted by the P.E.P. report on discrimination; the author
heartily agrees with P.E.P. on this point. Knowledge must
always precede effective action.

Without too much recapitulation, or too many statements
of the obvious, it may be useful here to run over the other
main conclusions arising from the previous chapter. The
first conclusion which anybody studying the private and
public sectors side by side is almost bound to reach is that,
although the private sector offers much more scope for open
discrimination on racial grounds, the public sector is more
prone to 'accidental' discrimination arising from the way it
tackles priorities, formulates its rules, or generally presents

itself to the public. A great many of the allegations which have been made about the discriminatory attitudes of local authorities towards immigrants are rooted in ignorance of the complex stages of the bureaucratic process; results are confused with intentions, and vice versa. Thus in Wolverhampton and Lambeth, the apparently 'impartial' management criteria applied in allocating particular houses to particular people, more often than not resulted in coloured tenants obtaining something manifestly different, if not immeasurably inferior, to the accommodation allocated to most non-coloured tenants. On the other hand in Cable Street, Stepney, although immigration contributed emotionally a great deal to the clearance issue, in practical terms it was the inherent inflexibility of a large redevelopment scheme which held up public action for so long.

In judging the effect of clearance programmes, a distinction has to be made between discrimination based on the selection of particular areas for clearance, and that based on the selection of people for rehousing. In none of the five authorities could it be said that clearance areas were defined in terms of avoiding coloured people, although the possibility of having to rehouse immigrants on a large scale was everywhere regarded with considerable trepidation because of the feared effect on public opinion. Problems of population density and the relocation of industry were the paramount considerations where large redevelopment programmes were in progress or under consideration.

In the two authorities—Manchester and (through the G.L.C.) Tower Hamlets—which were in the midst of really vast slum clearance schemes, it was obvious that the physical demands of the programme were very difficult to reconcile with the great variety of human needs thrown up by it. The natural reaction of the authorities was to define their rehousing commitment as strictly as possible so as not to impede progress or to deprive people on the waiting-list of all priority. In both places the natural victims were the inhabitants of lodging-house accommodation. In Manchester, however, the Council had recently undertaken greater responsibility towards this class of people, and it was significant that this was partly because it had become apparent that many coloured people and other immigrants were being pushed from one clearance area to another as their furnished lodgings were demolished.

(Manchester and East London) with the biggest slum pro-
It is, incidentally, no coincidence that these two areas grammes were also those with the longest history of overseas immigration; for the Victorian slums were largely created by the over-rapid expansion of towns to accommodate the industrial workers who, *a priori*, were newcomers, many of whom originated from Ireland or Europe. But it would be impossible to argue that these traditions of immigration have had any uniform effect on official attitudes towards modern immigrants. The stated council housing policy in Manchester has comparatively little bias against strangers, while in Tower Hamlets (for instance in the adoption of the five-year residential rule) it is on the strict side. These differences could be explained in terms of the particular influence which the descendants of immigrants in each place have in local politics; they could also be explained in terms of class, of physical environment, of the greater housing shortage in Tower Hamlets as compared with Manchester. No one explanation will suffice.

Everywhere, the greatest local variations are to be found in the rules concerning eligibility for council housing. Wolverhampton was the only one of the five boroughs with any rule which specifically put foreign-born applicants at a disadvantage; but there was no system which did not either deliberately or in practice produce some sort of difficulty for newcomers. It requires considerable finesse to evolve a system of allocation which is impartial as well as humane; probably the only hope, even in the most well-intentioned authorities, is a constant feed-back of results and some deliberate knowledge of the people who for one reason or another are being excluded from the public housing system. There is no housing authority at present which would regard such analysis as being within the scope of its duties.

There was also extremely wide variation among the different local authorities in the application of public health laws, and in the use made of loan schemes for house purchase. In most of the authorities studied, public health legislation was not pursued with vigour, because of the impossibility of doing so with a limited staff at the same time as carrying out slum clearance duties; and/or because of a reluctance to do anything which might involve the council in rehousing responsibilities. In Manchester and Nottingham virtually no attempt was made to control houses in multiple occupation—but these were also the two towns with the least severe overcrowding owing to the supply of cheap old terrace housing. Elsewhere, control of multiple occupation was in one way or another defined in terms of the coloured population, partly because this was one easy way of identifying the problem. Even Wolverhampton, where officials in principle did not believe in pushing people round from one house to another, there was strict prevention of multiple occupation in the houses on which loans had been made to coloured purchasers.

It is evident that, out of convenience, and sometimes out of the desire to maintain property values, mortgage policies and public health policies to a certain extent go hand in hand. In Nottingham, where there was virtually no action taken against multiple occupation, the mortgage scheme was, at the time of investigation, administered in a way that was intended to prevent multiple occupation from spreading: in practice this meant being cautious with loans to immigrants. In Manchester no such deliberate attempt was made, but the Corporation was partly protected by its strict valuation standards, which reduced the proportion of council mortgages on older property which might risk multiple occupation. In London, the extremely liberal lending policy of the G.L.C. would undoubtedly have been more restrained, and therefore of less help to immigrants, had the same authority carried public health responsibility for the mortgaged houses. Nowhere else in the country are these two functions divorced, since nowhere else has London's particular allocation of responsibilities between the boroughs and the overall metropolitan authority.

The five local authorities described so far are all large

towns, or parts of big conurbations, where housing conditions in one form or another are at their most acute, although the population itself may be decreasing. This is a
deliberate bias, since coloured immigrants mostly live in
such places, and since it is in areas of stress that housing
policies in general must stand or fall. Nevertheless, according to the 1961 Census, about one-third of Commonwealth
immigrants lived outside the main conurbations. Although
this third is situated mainly in sizeable self-contained towns
like Nottingham which reflect many of the housing problems of the conurbations, some of the remainder live in
smaller places, where neither in terms of quantity nor of
quality can there be said to be a serious housing problem,
although population growth may create new difficulties, if
house-building does not keep pace. In future, as more industry moves out from the conurbations to overspill sites,
and as the immigrants or their children become less big-city-
minded, it can reasonably be expected that the immigrant
and/or coloured population of Britain will increasingly be
found in smaller towns and expanding population centres
where housing problems, if they exist at all, are of a more
manageable nature. Therefore, before going on in the final
chapter to make some recommendations for future policy,
let us look briefly at one such town which has already had
experience of a wide range of immigrants. It may hold some
clues for the future.

The town chosen is Bedford. Apart from its small size and
relatively easy housing situation, it provides a useful contrast to the previous five local authorities in two other ways.
As a non-county borough it does not (except through dele-
gation) have responsibility for the first-tier functions of
education, town-planning, children and welfare (including
homelessness, although this scarcely arises). And, from the
immigration point of view, it is of particular interest as a
town whose main experience has been of a group of European immigrants—south Italians—to whom it had begun to
be adjusted before any coloured Commonwealth immigrants arrived. While the first of these points may have a

significance in the context of this inquiry, it is not an obvious one; the second point however is of considerable interest.

Bedford in 1967 is a town of some 66,000 people, and has been growing steadily, at the rate of about 1,000 a year, for over fifteen years. Although its character remains that of a country market town and service centre, new offices and science-based industries have been attracted to it by its convenient situation and excellent rail and motorway connections with London. By the same token Government planners have suggested that it should grow still faster in the 1970s and beyond, which could mean the planned intake of London overspill rather than the present purely voluntary movement of population into the area. Thus, although Bedford is not a 'new town', it has some of the characteristics of one, and may acquire still more in the future.[1]

In contrast to the white-collar, white-coat character of much of Bedford's new population, the presence of overseas immigrants in the town is due to the old traditional heavy industry of the area, the brickfields. Work in the kilns is hard, physically unpleasant and not usually very well paid; it is also very vulnerable to fluctuations in the economy. After the war difficulties in attracting local labour were first solved by employing European refugees, but in 1954 employers imported the first of successive batches of south Italians. At first these workers came without their families and lived in hostels provided by the brick companies; but soon they began to be joined by wives and children and moved out to private rooms, thus for the first time creating a noticeable problem of multiple occupation in the town. In 1955 the authorities counted 1,699 Italians; adults and children, living in multiple occupation; they formed the bulk of the 2,699 individuals in Bedford living in this way.

The town Council seethed with indignation that local industry should have foisted these foreigners with their

[1] At the time of writing, the most definite proposal of growth for Bedford was still that made in the South-East Study (London, H.M.S.O., 1964). This mooted an intake of at least 30,000 (exclusive of natural increase) in the period 1971–81.

strange ways upon the town without consulting the Council first. An alien group that might have gone unnoticed in a large town attracted a disproportionate amount of attention, mostly at first unfavourable, in a small country town with very little experience of anything more foreign than a Welshman. With the help of the local M.P., Mr. Christopher Soames, the Bedford Council obtained the support of the Government in insisting that, in future, employers should obtain council agreement to the recruitment of Italian labour. For about three years in the early 1960s, the Council imposed a ban, on the grounds that the Italians already in the town had achieved a decent housing standard which would be impaired by the arrival of more of their fellow-countrymen. In 1964 the ban was lifted to allow in a hundred more Italian workers. Throughout, this system has been backed up by the issue of accommodation certificates to Italians who want to bring their families to Bedford: if the accommodation is not approved by the Health Department, the family cannot come. On these grounds, in the years 1956–66 entry was refused to 240 out of 1,150 Italian families who applied to come to Bedford.

At about the time the first Italians were arriving, the office of Chief Public Health Inspector was filled by Mr. E. A. Avison, who still holds it.[2] He has made the Italians and subsequently the Commonwealth immigrants very much his own concern; and under him a system of control of multiple occupation has evolved to a degree which would scarcely be possible in a larger town or one in which slum clearance or other duties made greater demands on the time of public health inspectors. By Mr. Avison's own account, as his experience of the immigrant of Bedford has grown, so has his understanding of them and their ways; for the Italians in particular he has obviously developed great affection. But it is not only Italians with whom he now has to deal. First West Indians and then increasing numbers of Indians and Pakistanis have joined the European immigrants in Bedford. By 1966 the Italians and their children

[2] See E. A. Avison, 'Immigrants in a Small Borough', Institute of Race Relations *Newsletter*, October 1965.

Q

totalled over 6,000; of the coloured Commonwealth immigrants West Indians numbered well over 1,000, Indians
perhaps about 1,000 and Pakistanis nearly 600. These were
the biggest groups of immigrants; altogether, people born in
foreign and Commonwealth countries, and their children,
probably formed about 10 per cent of the town's population.

Full control of foreign immigrant entry to Bedford ceased
to be possible once Commonwealth immigrants started drift-
ing into the town from other parts of the country. Although
the system of control applied to Italians continues, most
brick-field recruitment in recent years has been of Asian
immigrants who have come in chiefly from the northern
textile towns; they seem fairly mobile, and a recession in the
brick-fields may send them off again. In contrast the West
Indians, however, have tended to work in engineering, iron
foundries, and various jobs other than the brick-fields. Over
the years, the original Italian labour force has also become
partly absorbed into other, less rigorous, and better-paid
local industry or service employment. Parallel with this has
come an improvement in living conditions marked by the
progress from single-room multi-occupation to the sharing
of two-family owner-occupied houses, and to single-family
occupation. The Pakistanis, very few indeed of whom have
brought any wives with them, are the only group of immigrants who are still almost entirely in low-grade occupations
and dormitory-style lodgings; whether they will progress in
status must depend a lot on how many of them abandon
what is generally their original intention, to stay in Britain
in a strictly migrant capacity.

The housing progress of the various nationalities can be
traced up to a point through the careful statistics published
each year by the Health Department of the nationalities of
the inhabitants of houses in multiple occupation (see chart
on p. 223). Thus the Italian multiple occupation is now
below what it was in 1956, although the number of Italians
in the town has almost trebled since then. Each minor increase represents a batch of new arrivals, which is gradually
dissipated by movement out into single-family accommodation. (Movement into a two-family house from one in mul-

tiple occupation still counts under the latter head.) The chart is also interesting in showing how, in Bedfard, multiple occupation is such a particularly immigrant phenomenon. The English and even the Irish count for relatively little, although it is noticeable that the English total of people in multiple occupation has more than doubled in ten years, presumably owing to Bedford's rapid growth. But the English newcomers were more likely to be in jobs which would enable them to buy their own houses rather than in the low-wage occupations of the overseas immigrants.

The methods devised in the early days of Italian immigration to control overcrowding and exploitation by landlords included the passing of a private Act of Parliament in 1956 to enforce the provision and inspection of rent books; and the introduction of midnight raids by public health inspectors to check the numbers sleeping in a house on Sunday night (the only time to catch all shift workers at home). But all along the preferred method of the authority has been persuasion rather than coercion, and even the night forays, so the Health Department claims, are banned in houses known to contain children. The first and only effort to use town-planning legislation to control multiple occupation by immigrants failed because an English neighbour would not testify to a 'change of use'—an episode accepted happily by the local authority as evidence of good race relations.

As the standards in Italian houses improved, so the local authority evidently acquired pride in what it regarded as its own handiwork: officials like to point out that south Italians in Bedford have achieved a way of life now that their own countrymen thought them quite incapable of ten years ago. The good nature and domestic harmony of Italian households in which two or three wives share one kitchen is a constant source of wonder. But having established an amenable, cheerful stereotype for the Italian immigrants, the local authority was unprepared for the rather different attitudes towards authority of some of the Commonwealth immigrants. Mr. Avison's reports contain occasional notes of regret at what he calls the 'colour-consciousness' and suspicion of West Indians (who object to health inspectors calling without an appointment), or the difficulties of establishing understanding with Pakistanis.

For every nationality the conclusion has been that the arrival of wives has led to an immediate rise in domestic standards. Only the Pakistanis, who were said in 1965 to number 530 men, only eight of whom had their wives with them, remain a source of difficulty to the health authority. It is clear from visiting some of their houses that the Health Department has not had very much effect except perhaps in terms of sheer overcrowding. One obstacle to improvement is the constant rate of £1 a week per bed paid by Pakistani lodgers; any landlord who makes improvements and charges more simply loses his clientèle.

Anxious as the Council is for the immigrants of all races to prove themselves fit citizens of Bedford, its own attitude seems to assume that assimilation is either impractical or undesirable. The emphasis has been on providing special facilities for each group, rather than encouraging immigrants to participate equally in the services enjoyed by the community as a whole. For example, at the instigation of the Health Department, a community centre has been provided for the Pakistanis, and one is in process of creation for West Indians 'so that they have somewhere to take cricket teams after the match instead of just going to the pub'. The idea for the Pakistani centre arose one cold winter when the health inspectors noticed that men were sitting shivering in cold bedrooms; 'but now they've got it they don't really use it much, or only to stand round talking'. Mr. Avison says he is aware that his own belief that different races and nationalities should be encouraged to remain as far as possible within their own community groups is open to criticism; it is also perhaps rather inconsistent with the encouragement to the immigrants to adopt English domestic standards.

The separatist attitude finds expression in the Council's housing policy. Council estates have not been made easily accessible to immigrants although they have formed the majority of the population living in crowded and shared dwellings. Instead, there has been a tendency in common with the other authorities studied to retain such foreign immigrants as have been rehoused by the Council in modernized versions of the old terraced houses in which they have been living as private tenants, and mainly in the same district to which they first came—this is said to be 'what the foreigners prefer'. The extreme version of this policy has taken the form of converting two houses for specific ethnic groups: six West Indian families live in one of these houses as council tenants, and six Italian families in the other.

Some fifty units of converted property have become available through the Council's programme of acquisition of large houses in the 'Saints' district of the town which is the focus of most immigrant multiple occupation. In carrying out what it terms 'Operation Rescue' on these decaying old properties, Bedford Council is in fact doing what local authorities nowadays are frequently urged to do, and what is in itself commendable policy; nevertheless its effect as a reinforcer of any tendency towards neighbourhood segregation must be recognized. The effect might in theory be counteracted to a certain extent if the houses acquired contained existing immigrant tenants who were then dispersed to council estates; but in fact the policy is to buy only with vacant possession.

The rules governing the council house waiting list are devised (as in Wolverhampton) to prevent overseas immigrants gaining the priority which their crowded cricumstances might secure for them. Preference in allocating tenancies is always given to 'Bedfordians'—natives of the town —who frequently get rehoused within a year of application. Other 'British-born' applicants must have lived a year in the town before they can be considered for a tenancy, and applicants in this category usually spend about a year on the list before being rehoused. A third category of applicants are the 'foreign-born' residents, which includes Commonwealth as well as alien immigrants, who must have lived in the town for at least four years before they can be accepted on to the live list. Once on it they compete on equal terms with the British-born immigrants to Bedford, and usually get rehoused fairly quickly. This practice has been adopted in the belief that but for this barrier there would be 'an influx' of overseas immigrants to Bedford attracted there by the desire to occupy one of the Council's houses. This view hardly holds up in the light of the fact that of 1,373 names on the 'live' waiting list in September 1966, only 211 were overseas immigrants. Of these, 175 lived in furnished rooms, compared with a total overseas population of houses in multiple occupation of over 5,000.

Most of Bedford's increase in population in the past decade has been absorbed either through multiple occupation or through private housebuilding. The Council's own building programme is mainly in small flats, plus a small amount of building of family houses for sale. In general, the Council is readier to give a mortgage to an applicant who wants to buy his own house in the private market than it is to expand the public sector. Overseas immigrants have certainly benefited from the Council's mortgage scheme far more than they have from the council waiting-list, although the precise number who have obtained loans is not revealed. It is clear that an immigrant buying a house of his own with a council mortgage is thought preferable to one occupying a council tenancy over the head of the native 'Bedfordian'. In the Council's favour, it must be said that mortgage conditions are fairly generous: for instance second mortgages are allowed and so are lodgers, or part-owners, subject to council approval.

Many immigrants are very happy with this arrangement, and anxious to become house-owners. Local estate agents welcome the high deposits produced by the many immigrants who obtain private mortgages. A fifty-year-old terrace house in Bedford could in 1966 be bought for under £3,500; new houses cost anything from £4,000 to £8,500. When wives work (as many Italians and West Indians do) the cheaper properties are within many people's means. But the fact remains that many overseas immigrants, possibly the majority, cannot afford to buy or to keep up with the burgeoning prices of an expaning area. The local vice-consul estimated in 1966 that perhaps 40 per cent of Italians were owners or part-owners of houses; but that still left a majority who might have been better off as council tenants. The coloured immigrants, who do encounter more prejudice than the Italians in the matter of house-purchase, probably could benefit from this help still more. As far as local authority practice goes, there appears to be equal discrimination against white and coloured 'foreigners'.

In future, if Bedford's population swells still faster with planned population intake, there will presumably have to be some sort of expanded council building programme to provide for those British-born newcomers to the town who cannot afford to buy their own houses. If this occurs, it will be still harder to retain any justification for the differential treatment afforded in this respect to Italians, West Indians, and Asians, whose presence is just as essential to the growth and prosperity of the town. In almost every other way that a visitor can see (without delving deep into things like employment patterns and promotion opportunities) the overseas immigrants are accepted and content in Bedford. There is little obvious basis for the official belief that everyone will be happier if, in residential and recreational matters, each nationality continues to keep itself as far as possible to itself. On the whole, immigration in Bedford has been a success, and this holds much hope for the future provided official attitudes do not stand in the way of assimilation.

X The Action Needed

This chapter is written at a time (April 1967) when the campaign for government action against racial discrimination in housing, employment and services is gathering force. Simultaneously the Government is pondering advice from many angles on how to deal more effectively with the twilight areas and the social problems which go with them. By the time this is in print, new legislative proposals may be too; certainly arguments on all these subjects will have become more crystallized, and means as well as ends will be the subject of debate. Some of the proposals being made in this book may be already on the way to acceptance by the time it is published; if so, that will be all to the good.

The previous chapters have shown up the main shortcomings of the British housing system as revealed by the presence of immigrants. It should now be apparent, too, which are the situations in which discrimination, deliberate or involuntary, is most likely to occur. The problems can be broken down into three groups: those which concern immigrants alone; those which are shared with other categories of people—such as tenants of furnished rooms, or large families; and those where the real problem lies within basic policies or assumptions of government—such as the system of housing subsidies, or the attitude to private landlords. Therefore the solutions, too, range from the very personal level where the immigrant is at particular disadvantage, to the broadest spheres of policy not directly connected with him at all. It is beyond the scope of this book to do more than outline the essential changes which would steer housing policy as a whole towards certain desirable goals which

it seems to be missing at present. On more specific matters
of direct concern to immigrants and to the other people in
comparable situations, rather more specific suggestions can
be made.

The most personal level of all is that of the immigrant
himself. How can he be better informed, and less suspicious
of the public machinery which is supposed to be there to
help him? Where it is in somebody's interest—for instance
an estate agent's—that immigrants should know about
things like council mortgage schemes, the news spreads
quickly and good use is made of the service. But it is in
nobody's interest to inform immigrants about council housing estates. It is neither in the interest of the local authority
which wants to avoid 'trouble' on its estates—and which by
granting mortgages instead, neatly transfers any unpleas-
antness into the private sector, out of its way; nor is it in the
interest or capacity of so-called 'immigrant leaders' who
often represent the landlord class, to give an informed and
unbiassed picture of the public housing sector. It is up to
the local authorities themselves, preferably through a liaison
officer appointed for just this sort of function, as well as
through the Citizen's Advice Bureaux and the immigrants'
own organizations, to make quite sure that immigrants,
particularly the poorest and least educated, realize what
could be available to them, either through the waiting-list
or through slum clearance. This includes drilling them in
the necessary procedures: tell the Town Hall when you
move house, re-apply every year, and so on.

Next, the people who deal directly with immigrants in
the housing selection process—in both the public and the
private sector. This weakest link in the chain is also the
most important of all, for it often determines the *type* of
house occupied by immigrants, and therefore the type of
background with which they become linked. Housing visitors—as indeed health visitors, sanitary inspectors, and
others who in the course of duty visit immigrant homes—
should wherever possible be given crash courses in the background and culture of the ethnic groups with which they
have to deal. In the long term, there should be a fresh look

at the training and calibre required for the job of housing
visitor (if indeed it should be done by the housing department at all). But meanwhile these officials can be made to
recognize realities which may—who knows—cause them to
widen their stereotyped ideas of 'class' and 'standards' to a
degree which might benefit other people besides immigrants.

Still more essential candidates for brain-washing are the
estate agents and building society managers who condemn
coloured people's 'standards' without, perhaps, ever having
set foot inside a coloured family's house. More will be said
later about the use of anti-discriminatory legislation in the
private housing context. But no amount of legislation will
really work as long as so many people in key positions in the
field are so patently biassed in their attitudes. At a national
level, responsible bodies should do what they can to see that
the formulators of building society policy, for example,
really appreciate the nature and aspirations of the different
types of immigrants. At a local level, the liaison officers who
work for the voluntary committees set up by the National
Committee for Commonwealth Immigrants should do all
they can to persuade estate agents, building society managers, and others, to visit immigrant homes and learn to
stop regarding them as something outlandish and dangerous. (The formation of fair housing groups is one way of
doing this.) The same tactics should be applied to public
health inspectors, for only by this means will they cease to
apply methods to immigrants (midnight raids and so on) to
which they would not dream of subjecting the native population.

At the same time as conventional notions about who is
suitable for what kind of house are relaxed, the local
authorities should stiffen their own spines when it comes to
placing immigrants in houses where they can be seen to
have been housed by the council; and not just on the
roughest, shabbiest corner of the least desirable estate,
either. If the public sector can take a lead in this way, the
chances of the effective defeat of discrimination in the
private sector should be immensely improved. As in other

contexts, until coloured people are seen to be in an equal position, public opinion will continue to regard them as less than equal.

In local authority practice this means a change of heart not only in housing committees and in housing managers' offices, but also in the routine performance of middle management. Nearly always the decision of where to place a coloured tenant is an administrative, not a political one—and so it should be. But administrative bias can only be guarded against by keeping an open and conscious watch on the way coloured tenants are dealt with. The authorities who keep records of race are in a position to use this knowledge constructively; the practice should not be shirked because it looks discriminatory. Without it there can be no constructive discrimination.

Here the Ministry of Housing could perform a most useful service, simply by demanding annual returns from local authorities of the numbers of immigrants housed, which could be published along with census-based estimates of total immigrant populations in each area. The same service should be obligatory for other categories of people likely to need special housing help: old people, large families, families living in mutiple occupation. The local authorities are often exhorted by the Government to gear their selection processes in favour of people in genuine housing need; a few statistics would concentrate their minds more wonderfully than pages of exhortation.

Any effective system for providing for people in housing need requires a far more efficient system for locating them. It is clear that housing lists are no guide whatsoever, to judge from the high proportion of needy families in slum clearance areas who are found to be not on the list. It is doubtful if housing lists in their present form serve any useful social purpose whatsoever; administratively some sort of index system is essential, but not the present mess. Another vital task for the Ministry of Housing and Local Government: to devise standard measures of housing need codified into a simple punched card system (a technique which has barely penetrated housing management). Then all local authorities should be obliged to adopt the standard measures, and apply them to everybody.

Traditionally, the central Government has relied on subsidies to obtain the desired results from local housing authorities. But lately, in terms of building methods and standards, it has begun to take a much more detailed interest in how the subsidies are spent. There is not in principle all that much difference between cost-yardsticks for house-building, and socio-economic yardsticks for assessing housing need. Only by such means can the Government be sure that the public housing service really does serve the right people. And unless the authorities can prove that it does, the Government should reserve the right to step in still more directly. In the last resort, central government participation in the allocation of houses would be more effective than merely paying more subsidies aimed at specific groups. It has for instance been suggested that extra housing subsidies should be paid to areas with large immigrant populations. This would be a tactical mistake. It would be an invitation to the construction of segregated housing; and a temptation to continue treating Commonwealth immigrants as though they were some special form of natural disaster.

A better alternative (although one which would require a new approach on the part of the Ministry) is as follows. If, and only if, a local authority had shown itself incapable of acting fairly, the Government or some specially appointed agency should reserve the right to allocate a certain proportion of dwellings itself. This should be for the purpose of the whole range of social needs, not just immigrants as such. In the Netherlands the Ministry of Social Work has a claim on 10 per cent of all subsidized dwellings built each year, known as 'priority dwellings'; they are then allocated to socially needy cases, backed up by loans for the purchase of furniture and so forth. Since the mid-1950s one-half of all these dwellings have been going to 'repatriates'—Dutch subjects of European, Asian, and mixed race from the East Indies. The parallel with Britain's Commonwealth immigrants is not exact. The Dutch repatriates are more like refugees, whereas Commonwealth immigrants have arrived voluntarily for the purpose of work—but the degree of responsibility shown by the Dutch Government as compared with the British is fairly striking, none the less. In a country as small as Holland the system is easier to administer: and it is not suggested that it or anything like it be used in Britain except as a last resort, a big stick to wave at the authorities who do not mend their ways.

One reason why the authorities have baulked at their duty so far is that people in housing need often require a lot of attention in other ways. Immigrants and their neighbours may need help in settling in together. Large families who get into arrears frequently do so as a symptom of some other trouble. These difficulties may be appreciated by officials, but there are just not enough of the right sort of social workers in the right departments to deal with them. Housing management has steered almost completely clear of trained social workers. If the result of the Seebohm Committee recommendations,[1] and the reorganization of local government being examined by the Royal Commission,[2] is to produce unified social work departments, they should be directly involved in housing.

A more realistic approach to the question of housing need should involve an effort on the part of the local authority to seek it out, instead of relying on the very inadequate guide of the housing list. Ideally, the aim should be to establish an index system which would identify everybody likely to need help; which means that it should be actively promoted, and used to identify not only the people who should get first choice of a council tenancy, but also those who might profit from a council mortgage. In such a system there would be no room for irrelevant criteria; for instance in clearance areas no one should be ruled out on grounds of his particular tenure. Rehousing should (within reason-

[1] The committee on local authority and allied personal social services, appointed by the Government in December 1965, Chairman Mr. F. Seebohm.
[2] The Royal Commission on Local Government in England, outside Greater London, appointed February 1966, Chairman Sir John Maud. Another Commission sits for Scotland.

able time limits) involve literally everybody, with the alternative of a mortgage. If local authorities could be made to realize what bad housing costs in terms of other services—why in Lambeth are one-fifth of the children in care coloured?[3] Why do one quarter of maternity beds in Wolverhampton go to coloured mothers?—they might be less unwilling to provide for the worst-off people. Unfortunately, these social costs do not always fall on the authority which is responsible for the housing; but at least in the big boroughs where most immigrants live there is sufficient overlap of housing with health and welfare services to bring the point home.

Recognition of the mutual sources of social stress is one thing; action is another. At the time of writing, the clearest call to action in the socially deprived areas of big cities has recently come from the Plowden Report,[4] with its demand for 'educational priority areas' to counteract the downward spiral involved in the combination of a poor environment and poor educational opportunities. The importance of the Plowden Report is its insistence on the principle of positive discrimination: that the crowded, old-fashioned under-staffed schools of the twilight areas should be made not merely as good as, but superbly better than, those in the more favoured suburbs. This important principle has not yet been spelled out with equal clarity in terms of housing and other environmental factors: partly because a much more complex set of responsibilities is involved; partly because of the very awkward investment decisions which have to be made in balancing social need against the re-development or rehabilitation of houses which are not yet slums.

The tools are gradually being assembled. At the time of

[3] In *West Indian Children in London* (Occasional Papers on Social Administration, Number 19, London, Bell, 1967), Mrs. Katrin Fitzherbert shows how the abnormally high proportion of West Indian children in care is due to different social customs as well as to material circumstances. But housing does play an important part.

[4] *Children and their Primary Schools*, A Report of the Central Advisory Council for Education (England), London, H.M.S.O., 1966.

writing, new powers are being discussed which would enable local authorities (possibly with the help of some outside agency) to control the occupation and rehabilitation of housing in whole areas, identified as those of 'housing stress'. Stress is defined by the indices of overcrowding, shared dwellings, lack of facilities, and general decay—the familiar twilight zone syndrome to be seen in places like central Lambeth. Although it is often associated with the presence of Commonwealth immigrants, it would be a mistake to define 'stress' in terms of their presence, for the same reason as it would be a mistake to give subsidies on this basis. Unfortunately those who have the welfare of immigrants at heart often make this mistake.

There are two main reasons why local authorities feel they need these new powers. The existing legislation which controls multiple occupation and secures improvement of dwellings is on a house-by-house basis (although an 'improvement area' procedure exists in the 1964 Housing Act, it is generally regarded as ineffective). Secondly, although town-planning powers give wide discretion to local authorities to declare 'comprehensive development areas', these are granted for the prime purpose of rebuilding, rather than the rehabilitation which is mainly needed in the areas of stress. Somehow the two must be combined. There must also be a guarantee that the loss which is almost always involved in acquiring densely occupied houses, which are not slums, at market price in order to convert or redevelop them, will be met either by direct subsidy or by some body other than the local authority.

There are a variety of ways in which the last point might be met; one frequently mooted is the formation of agencies for twilight area renewal similar to the New Town Corporations. When it comes to the large-scale clearance of such areas for redevelopment purposes, the Land Commission is expected to take a hand; its contribution could prove a major one. The final combination of responsibility may vary from place to place. The local authorities are likely to be as anxious to retain the initiative as they are to pass on the cost.

Should areas of housing stress be automatically taken into public ownership, or will it sometimes be possible to relieve the stress by less drastic means—for instance by giving the local authorities the power to control lettings, whilst leaving the existing landlords in charge? All these things may have been spelled out further by the time this is in print. A main aim should surely be flexibility; whilst taking areas as a whole, within them different degrees of public intervention should be applied according to the state of the property and whether owner-occupiers, good landlords, or bad landlords are involved. Sometimes the right agency will be a housing association rather than a local authority. Very little has been said in this book of the associations, chiefly because the efficient ones are so few, and their contribution to the total housing situation so slight.

But the impact of an effective association in a particular area can be very great, and is increasingly seen as a help to the local authority in meeting particular needs. A well-known example is the Mulberry Housing Trust, which works very closely with Westminster Borough Council in North Paddington. Half the occupants of its houses are coloured immigrants. A word of warning should, however, be given: housing associations could easily find themselves being used by the authorities to house coloured people who were unwelcome on housing estates, thereby reinforcing segregation. This is one reason why the idea of associations to deal specifically with coloured people should be treated with caution.

This is perhaps linked to another argument often put forward by local authorities, especially in London, that the reason why they cannot at present alleviate 'stress' is that the intensity of occupation would involve so much rehousing that other priorities would be swamped. This argument would lose a good deal of its force if the 'index of housing need' proposed above were in operation, instead of the conventional waiting list, which does not cover the majority of people in the stress areas. If the index genuinely included all people in need, and indicated the degree of urgency, it would soon be obvious that relief of 'stress' was itself a high priority. The difficulties involved would not of course be solved, but they would be put in perspective. There is no social justification, even if there is an administrative one, for the argument heard all too often from officials that there is no point in rehousing one particular family from crowded lodgings if another one immediately takes its place. This may be an argument for municipal control of private lettings in the stress areas; but that is a different matter. By the same token, if a broader view were taken of housing need, there would no longer be the danger that a local authority taking charge of a stress area would try and solve the problem entirely within the area itself, or only in terms of other old housing. The experience of Lambeth Borough Council in Geneva and Somerleyton Roads (described in Chapter V) needs watching very closely in this context.

New procedures for dealing with whole areas of bad housing clearly have to be combined with all the other reforms needed to extend the life of the old housing stock: better improvement grants, better tax treatment of landlords, an improvement of the poor tenants' capacity to pay either through family allowances or a direct housing allowance. These points have immense importance to the whole background to this book, but they can only be mentioned in passing. Given a sounder economic basis, it should be easier to secure the very necessary personal co-operation of tenants, landlords, and owner-occupiers in the rescue of the twilight areas. It has been pointed out in earlier chapters how immigrant owner-occupiers might have a valuable contribution to make.

Increasingly (see Plowden) urban renewal is seen as community renewal, although there are very few places in have even begun to take root. The roots are slow to strike, but at least there is more chance of success where the slow improvement of a neighbourhood, rather than its dispersal under the bulldozer, is the declared public policy. The main problem is the holding together of a disintegrating society while gradual process of change takes place. This is why the notion of 'positive discrimination' is such an important one, applied not only to schools, but to other services (nurseries,

R

playgrounds, clubs, swimming baths, etc.) in the depressed areas. The normal pattern is for the redevelopment of housing to come first, and other services to lag behind. But large-scale redevelopment (or rehabilitation) takes time, and many people have to go on living in poor conditions meanwhile. Far better to insert the services *first*—if grouped in neighbourhood centres this would make planning sense— so that everybody has something better while their housing conditions are improved. More people are needed to go with the services, too—sometimes just to teach others how they should be used. The 1966 Local Government Act contains provision for extra subsidies towards the salaries of staff in immigrant areas (a rather paltry £1,500,000 is being spread round the whole country). This should be expanded to match the growth of community services in appropriate areas. Grants should be used also to promote private enterprise in the form of community associations, advice bureaux, playgroups, etc., without which the renewal process would become dangerously bureaucratic.

Most of the discussion so far has been in the context of the twilight areas and the immigrants who live in them. What of those who move out of these areas? What positive steps should be taken by central and local government to assist dispersal of coloured people (over and above the fact that programmes directed towards improving the twilight areas will themselves promote mobility as well as removing many of the disadvantages of the areas to the people who remain)?

Dispersal will be encouraged by a fairer allocation of council housing to immigrants. Yet it must be remembered that physical distance from existing areas of immigrant settlement is not the be-all and end-all in rehousing immigrants. There are places where this could merely indicate the site of the least desirable overspill estate. Quality, rather than location, is the essential factor: to repeat, this is the way in which local authorities must be seen to take the lead in overcoming discrimination.

Where the idea of quality combines most completely with the dispersal theme is in the New Towns, where at present looking for a coloured man is like the proverbial needle in a haystack. This is primarily because of the industrial selection process on which New Town (and expanded town) recruitment is based. The intake is notoriously middle-to-upper working class. Semi-skilled and unskilled workers, the categories to which most coloured people belong, are in tiny proportions. If more of the coloured population had their fair share of the better jobs, then dispersal from the inner cities would be facilitated; not only in terms of New Town selection, but also in terms of the generally greater mobility conveyed by better economic opportunities. Little is known of how far their present occupations tie Commonwealth immigrants to their present homes; but common sense suggests that the connection is strong.

Mobile, suburban-bound immigrants are most frequently frustrated by prejudice in the sale of private houses, as described in Chapter II. The private housing market is an essential and, particularly in the sale of owner-occupied houses, a controversial field for anti-discrimination legislation. The arguments for extending the law in this direction are well known, and scarcely refutable. As has often been pointed out, only if the law takes the lead will people cease to operate a colour bar which is largely based on (or rationalized by) the fear of a bad reaction from neighbours, tenants, clients, or whoever it may be. There seems every likelihood that, by the end of 1967, a new Race Relations Bill will have been published. It is to be hoped, with regard to housing, it will contain the provisions listed below:

(1) It should be illegal to publish or display any accommodation advertisement stipulating race, nationality or religion (except in the case of lodgings with a family, or in a hostel run, say, for orthodox Jews).

(2) No landlord should be permitted to refuse an applicant on grounds of race, nationality or religion except where he shares the dwelling himself (this could be defined to exempt small boarding houses: what in America is called the 'Widow Murphy' clause).

(3) Any covenants restricting the sale or disposal of any

interest in land on grounds of race, religion, or nationality should be void.

(4) No builder should discriminate in the sale of new houses.

(5) No estate agent, building society, or accommodation bureau should discriminate in their services, or accept discriminatory instructions from vendors.

The above five items should come within the existing conciliation principle of the Race Relations Act 1965. It might also be desirable to include blatant attempts to keep districts 'white' in the criminal 'incitement' clause.

It has been argued that the private individual cannot be forced to sell to someone he dislikes; that in the last resort there should be 'freedom to discriminate' in the disposal of property. Assuming this very dubious proposition to be true, it should be a matter for the individual alone. He should not be in any way encouraged or abetted by others. This is why it is undesirable for an estate agent even to pass on the information that such-and-such an owner is known to be unfavourably disposed towards certain classes of people. At least there is some hope of overcoming prejudice as long as there is nothing to stop a vendor coming face to face with a coloured buyer.

A sea-change in public opinion has to take time. Racial discrimination in housing, or any other field, will not disappear without a long, conscious effort to eradicate it. At present, the public authorities who should be making this effort are nearly always afraid to reveal whether they even stand on the right side of the fence. Sometimes, so it seems from this study, they do not even know themselves. Self-knowledge and courage are easier to preach than to practise. But if this book has said anything that will make either a little easier to achieve for local politicians and administrators, in all humility the author wishes them good luck.

Appendix

Overcrowding, Multiple Occupation, and Slum Clearance: Local Authority Powers

The best summary of the housing powers and duties of local authorities is in *Housing and Local Government* by J. B. Cullingworth (London, Allen and Unwin, 1966). There is also a useful summary of legislation up to 1965 in the Milner Holland Report (*Housing in Greater London*, H.M.S.O., 1965, Appendix 1). More detailed explanation of various Acts of Parliament is best obtained from the relevant Ministry of Housing and Local Government circulars. The following pages summarize the powers relating to overcrowding, multiple occupation, and slum clearance. Other powers of local authorities which affect the private landlord, tenant, or owner-occupier, such as improvement grants, and the granting of mortgages, have been dealt with in sufficient detail in the early chapters of the book.

(1) *Overcrowding*

It is illegal, under the Public Health Act of 1935, to oblige two people of opposite sexes over the age of ten, not living together as husband and wife, to sleep in the same room. For example, one-room households may not legally contain a child over ten as well as a parent of the opposite sex. There is also a code relating to the number of people who may legally occupy a given number of rooms, according to the size of the rooms and the total number of rooms in the house. For this purpose children under one year do not count at all; children under 10 count as half a person. For example rooms of 90 to 110 square feet may house only one-and-a-half persons; over 110 square feet, only two persons. This means that a room measuring 10 feet by 12 feet could legally contain a mother, two children under 10, and a baby of six months, while one twice the size could not legally be a bed-sitter for three adults. Landlords or occupants may be prosecuted for causing overcrowding on this basis. (Natural increase through birth or age does not count.)

This 'statutory overcrowding' is not to be confused with the standard of overcrowding adopted by the Census of 1961—the measure of over one-and-a-half persons per room. (The fact that formerly the Census standard was that of over two persons per room is some indication of how conditions have improved for a large part of the population.) There are still higher standards of overcrowding adopted by many local authorities when allo-cating priorities on the council house waiting-list. These vary widely from place to place.

(2) *Multiple Occupation*

The Housing Act, 1961, defines multiple occupation as a 'house' which, or any part of which, is let in lodgings or occupied by members of more than one family'. This Act gave local authori-ties their first comprehensive powers to control conditions in multi-occupied houses, although up to 1954 they could make their own by-laws (and in fact 'houses let in lodgings' had been subject to regulation since mid-Victorian times). Section 12 of the Act empowers a local authority to apply a 'code of good management' on mismanaged houses, thereby obliging the per-son responsible (not necessarily the landlord) to repair, cleanse, and light the communal parts of the house, to see that services are in working order, to provide refuse bins, etc. Notice of in-tention to serve a management order must be made by the Health Committee, and the manager of the house can prevent or forestall further action by raising objections or undertaking to remedy the situation. Appeal to the county court can be made against this and other orders under the Act. Section 14 em-powers the authorities to require certain specified works to be carried out to remedy the effects of mismanagement (such as mending a broken stair-rail or re-wiring). Under Section 15 a notice can be served requiring the installation of amenities; Section 16 concerns the installation of fire-safety devices. Section 15 can be used in conjunction with Section 19, which fixes the number of people who may occupy the house (known as a direction order). The landlord may not take on new tenants in excess of this number without risk of punishment, but it is not an offence if existing tenants remain. This rule was introduced because the 1957 Housing Act (Section 90), merely gave power to fix the number of people who could sleep in any room, a ruling which encouraged evictions. Nevertheless Section 90 is still used by local authorities who want to reduce overcrowding of single and childless people who will not become their welfare responsibility if rendered homeless through eviction.

If a landlord fails to carry out works under Sections 14, 15, or 16 of the 1961 Act, the local authority may carry out the work in default. The 1964 Housing Act strengthened this by making the cost of work done in default a charge on the property, instead of merely recoverable from the landlord. It also made wilful non-compliance with notices under these sections punishable by fines or imprisonment.

A new power was introduced by the 1964 Housing Act, inspired by the abuses revealed by the Rachman scandal in 1963. In the case of grossly mismanaged houses, where the health, safety, or welfare of the inhabitants is held to be in danger, the local authority may itself take charge of running the house and collecting the rent, for anything up to five years. This is done by the issue of a 'control order' which becomes immediately effective. A sum equivalent to half the gross rateable value is payable to the dispossessed proprietor. Another power aimed at very bad landlord–tenant relations, which applies to all rented property, is incorporated in the 1965 Rent Act (Schedule 6, cl. 3). This enables the local authority to prosecute a landlord for 'harrassment' of a tenant.

The 1961 Housing Act also gave local authorities the power to set up their own registration schemes for houses in multiple occupation, authorizing fines of up to £10 for non-compliance with a scheme. This power did not become effective until three years after the Act came into operation.

In addition to powers specifically applying to multi-occupied housing, the local authority can take action over any house where conditions constitute a serious threat to health or a 'public nuisance'. These powers exist under the Public Health Acts, mainly those of 1936 and 1961. The latter Act speeded up the procedure whereby health departments can step in to abate a nuisance (such as leaking sewage). The authority may do the work in default but without the same powers of recovering the cost as under the 1964 Housing Act. Appeal is to the magistrate's court.

(3) Slum Clearance

Slums are dwellings declared by the local authority's Medical Officer of Health to be unfit for human habitation. The criteria used are health criteria—a concept currently under attack for being too narrow and old-fashioned. The 1957 Housing Act lists the things to be taken into account in assessing unfitness of individual houses. They are: repair; stability; freedom from damp; natural lighting, ventilation; water supply; drainage and sanitary conveniences; facilities for the storage, preparation, and cooking of food and for the disposal of waste water. Section 42 of the Act also refers to *areas* which are unfit owing to the bad arrangement of the housing, the narrowness of streets, etc.; but this has to be very severe in order to be counted a health hazard, and by itself would be most unlikely to condemn the houses. Houses in multiple occupation, which are often comparatively well built, spacious, and well laid out, and usually possess at least some sanitary conveniences, rarely come within the definition of a slum, unless they are suffering from gross structural decay.

The local authority can choose between various courses of action in dealing with unfit houses. The owner can be required to make good the defects, if this is possible 'at reasonable cost'—a provision which makes it very easy for the owner to demur. Or the local authority can require the owner to demolish the house at his own expense; it can acquire the house at site value and demolish it itself; it can order the house (or part of it, such as a basement) to be closed without being demolished. Legally there is no obligation to rehouse the occupants of slum houses dealt with individually in this way, but normally authorities accept the responsibility. Another alternative, since 1954, has been for the authority to acquire unfit houses and make them fit for temporary use until it demolishes them; this is the technique known as 'deferred demolition' or 'patching'.

Most slums are dealt with in areas rather than individually. Under the procedure outlined in the 1957 Housing Act, the local authority may declare any group of two or more unfit houses to be a 'clearance area', in which it can acquire the unfit houses by agreement or compulsory purchase, together with any adjacent property which is not unfit but which is needed for the satisfactory development of the area. Before obtaining ministerial approval of a clearance area it has to show that it can rehouse the people displaced 'in so far as suitable accommodation . . . does not already exist'.

Objections can be raised, as with other sorts of compulsory purchase orders, against clearance areas or parts of them. These must be heard at a public inquiry held by an inspector from the Ministry of Housing and Local Government. A similar procedure takes place in 'redevelopment areas' dealt with under the town-planning Acts. Sometimes a local authority which wants to redevelop on comprehensive lines a large area which contains some slums, some fit houses, and some mixed commercial or industrial development, may combine different types of procedure in different sections of the 'Comprehensive Redevelopment Area'. One complication is that the subsidy received varies according to the different powers used. But the main stages described in the next paragraph but one are more or less identical for any form of compulsory purchase.

Slum houses are acquired at site value unless they belong to owner-occupiers who bought them between 1939 and 1955, who receive market value. This privilege was due to expire in 1965 but, in the Housing (Slum Clearance Compensation) Act that year, was renewed until 1970 for owner-occupiers who have had less than fifteen years' possession of their house when the order is made. More important as far as immigrants are concerned is the provision of the 1965 Act that *all* owner-occupiers shall receive one benefit formerly limited to the 1939-55 group. This is that if the price paid for an unfit house when acquired by the local authority is less than outstanding mortgage commitments, a court may reduce these commitments, taking into account whether the original purchase price was 'excessive'. Owners and tenants of houses acquired at site value may in addition receive a 'well-maintained payment' which takes some account of expenditure on a good standard of maintenance and interior decoration.

Although all local authorities are required to make regular assessments of the number of unfit houses in their territory, no house is officially recognized as unfit until the process of clearance has been set in train. The stages of the clearance-area procedure are as follows:

(1) An inspection by the public health inspector results in the Medical Officer of Health 'representing' to his committee certain houses as unfit. 'Representation' is often the basis on which slum clearance progress is measured, although in fact the

actual clearance is at this point several stages and often several years ahead.

(2) The Health Committee gets the council to pass a resolution declaring a certain area to be a clearance area.

(3) Within six months application must be made to the Ministry of Housing for permission to acquire any unfit houses in the area on which a Compulsory Purchase Order is to be made (as opposed to purchase by agreement). A year may lapse before submitting to the Ministry a Compulsory Purchase Order on the fit houses contained in the area.

(4) Ministerial approval must be obtained, and if there are any objections from the public these must first be heard at a public inquiry held by the ministerial inspector.

(5) Subject to the findings of the inspector, the Minister approves (or modifies) the clearance area proposals. This may sometimes mean that certain houses are excluded from the list of slums, but may still be acquired by the local authority at market price.

(6) Once the Compulsory Purchase Order has been confirmed, notices to treat are served on the owners and notices of entry served on the occupants of the houses. Once this has been done, but not before, the Housing Department may move in and start rehousing the inhabitants. A house has been 'cleared' when all its inhabitants have been moved out; actual demolition may take place some time after. A house may be demolished while arguments are still going on with the owner about price, provided that records are made from which to continue the argument.

Index

S